The General Who Marched to Hell

Earl Schenck Miers

THE
GENERAL
WHO
MARCHED
TO
HELL

William Tecumseh Sherman
AND HIS MARCH TO FAME AND INFAMY

BARNES
&NOBLE
BOOKS
NEW YORK

This edition published by Barnes & Noble, Inc.,
by arrangement with Curtis Brown.
1992 Barnes & Noble Books

ISBN 0-88029-483-3

Printed and bound in the United States of America

M 9 8 7 6

FOR

Edith and *Curley Wilhelm*

INTRODUCTION

A REDHEADED young army lieutenant, traveling from Augusta, Georgia, through the sultry heat of a summer's day in 1844, approached the bustling town of Marthasville. The year before, this trading and railroad settlement had been incorporated and named in honor of Martha Lumpkin, daughter of the governor; a year later the community would grow so rapidly that a more suitable name would be sought, and Marthasville would become Atlanta, in tribute to the commerce coming into its marts over the rails of the Western & Atlantic. The young lieutenant's dark eyes flashed with interest at the stories he heard of the town's drive and hustle. A sawmill, a group of stores, a railroad terminus were part of the emerging pattern by which Marthasville, linked to the sea, promised to dominate one of the most fertile areas of the South. In nearby Marietta rose the wooded slopes of Kenesaw Mountain. On horseback the young lieutenant climbed to its summit and gazed across fifteen miles of rolling country to Allatoona. If in the hour of sunset the sky grew streaked with red, as though a bloody hand moved behind the clouds, who then could have understood that terrible prophecy? The youth wheeled around on his horse and retraced his way down the rocky road. The name on his saddlebag read William Tecumseh Sherman.

Twenty years later, again facing toward Atlanta, Sherman remembered the images that had formed in his mind looking down from the summit of Kenesaw that summer's day in 1844. A ragged red beard intensified the brilliance of the snapping black eyes turned south; a tight, thin-lipped mouth, barking out orders in a quick, nervous voice, revealed the impatience that shaped his personality. The War Between the States, which was to have ended in three months, had dragged through three weary years. The North, with a population of about twenty-two million, had seen almost a miilion men drawn into the conflict; the South, with one third of its population of nine million comprising Negroes, had called approximately eight hundred and fifty thousand men to the colors. The struggle, scarring hearts as well as minds, had grown intensely bitter; still for many, both North and South, the hope of a swift, negotiated peace remained.

But for three men, each drawn from the same young, raw section of the country, the determination that no compromise must be accepted had become a passion. For each of these three men the emancipation of the slaves had been an afterthought of the war. If a religion governed the lives of these men it was the religion of Federalism, bred into the marrow of their bones by the basic tenets of the Ordinance of 1787 that had created the Northwest Territory. Each was committed to preserve the Union or die in its defense. Two of the men were friends; all three would meet together but once. But by emissary, by letter, by hunch, Lincoln, Grant, and Sherman would mold the future of the nation. Each would need the strength of the other two, but the faith of each in the others often would waver. Lincoln, more than Grant, would distrust Sherman; but a day would come when the President would tender "the national thanks" to his redheaded general.

Sherman himself had planted strong elements of doubt in Lincoln's mind. In the President's presence, as in the presence of so many whom he considered political, Sherman rarely put his best foot forward. In moments of crisis he frequently was hesitant, confused, stubbornly inarticulate, and sometimes, at the slightest friction, his temper would flare like a Lucifer match. No one would admit more readily than he that he lacked confidence. The dark shadows that at times clouded his mind, the succession of failures that trailed him from St. Louis to California to New York to St. Louis to Leavenworth to Louisiana to Washington to St. Louis to Manassas Junction to Kentucky reflected his essential insecurity. He was, as one newspaperman said, a creature of "crotchets and prejudices."

The first violent dislike Sherman manifested as a boy was for his red hair; and he tried to dye it, only to have his head turn a hideous shade of green. His attention to detail was again a lifelong characteristic, and once led him to hang a cat nine times to make certain it was dead. When Sherman was nine years old his father died of typhoid fever, and his mother faced the bleak prospect of providing for the eight children who, as though running on schedule like stagecoaches, had arrived every eighteen months. Up the street from the Shermans in Lancaster, Ohio, lived old Tom Ewing, two hundred and fifty pounds of wealth, Whig influence, and kindness, who offered to help the young widow if she would permit him to adopt "the brightest of the lot." So the boy, whom his Dartmouth-educated father had named Tecumseh out of admiration for the Shawnee leader, moved in with the Ewings. His foster mother, a devout Catholic, promptly added the William to his name, since even in the rough-and-ready Ohio of the early 1830's no conscientious priest would administer the baptismal rites of the church in the name of a heathen redskin! Through Tom Ewing's Whig connections, William Tecumseh Sherman, whom everyone called Cump, received an appointment to West Point and impressed relatives in the East as "an untamed animal just caught in the Far West."

In 1836, now sixteen years of age, young Sherman graduated from West Point, standing highest in engineering, geology, rhetoric, mental philosophy, and demerits. His first military assignment was in Florida, but he never encountered a hostile Indian, and was struck only by the ladies in St. Augustine who could "waltz all evening, because it is done slowly, with grace." Luck played into Sherman's hands, and in 1842 he was transferred to Fort Moultrie, South Carolina, on Sullivan's Island and within quick reach of Charleston. Here he remained for four years, soon liking a social life that was "very various," from parties that were "highly aristocratic and fashionable, with sword and epaulettes," to "horse-racing, picnicing, boating, fishing, swimming, and God knows what not." A year later he journeyed to Ohio to become engaged to his foster sister Ellen, and on his return to Moultrie traveled over the heart of the country that joined central Georgia to the sea. When the Mexican War began, Sherman hoped to do "all I can to better my future," but instead of seeing action in Mexico he landed in '48 in California, where the Mexicans in the mountains proved as elusive as the mists through which they disappeared. Sherman found nothing to fight but boredom; gold, discovered at Sutter's Fort, did not improve the situation; now it was not bad enough that "a tailor won't work a day, nor a shoemaker, nor any other tradesman," but daily soldiers were quitting the post to seek fortunes in the gold mines. Nothing could have pleased him more than to be called back to Washington, where Tom Ewing filled the newly created Cabinet position as Secretary of the Interior. Sherman at once married Ellen, received the blessings of "Daniel the Divine" Webster, and rushed off to Niagara Falls for a honeymoon.

The married couple settled in St. Louis, but whenever Ellen became pregnant she returned to her old Ohio home, and so seemed to be there almost constantly, first to await the arrival of Minnie, then of Lizzie. Sherman, saddled with commissary duties, sent to Missouri and Kansas to buy cattle, wrote Ellen that he suffered a "dull, tame life." Next he went to Louisiana to clean up corruption in the commissary there, but was no happier and soon decided to leave the army to represent the St. Louis banking firm of Lucas, Turner & Co. in San Francisco, for an annual salary of $5,000 and a one-eighth interest in the business of the branch. So anxious was Sherman to get back to California and to earn his fortune that he traveled the shorter Nicaraguan land route. On the way he befriended two ladies and discovered, on arriving in California, that one of them enjoyed a respectable reputation for unrespectable activities.

The incident proved strangely prophetic. In California everything went wrong. Ellen joined him for a time, stayed long enough to bear young Willy and nurse him through the first ten months, then returned home while Sherman imagined a weakness in "my bronchial tubes." Disaster rode through the gold fields, and the crash of 1854–5 spelled the beginning of civil unsettlement and the collapse of the San Francisco branch of Lucas, Turner & Co. Sherman came back to St. Louis calling himself "the Jonah of banking." Old army friends like Braxton Bragg from North Carolina had given him $130,000 to invest in the West, and when through normal business risks these investments lost about $13,000 he felt morally obligated to pay back the entire amount. In torment, he finally faced Ellen and Tom Ewing with the truth; they tried to be sympathetic, but the genes of Charles and Mary Sherman had not joined to form their temperaments. No job, no hope, no future. Sherman tried to get back in the army and found he wasn't needed. Tom Ewing wanted him to go to Kansas to manage family properties there; Cump, despising charity, rolling in bed at night and struggling to find another way out, finally had to capitulate; he went to Kansas with dark shadows across his mind, writing Ellen that he had become "a dead cock in a pit."

Typical of Sherman in Leavenworth would be his experience with the law. At the moment when he was quarreling with Ellen over Catholicism and disposing of their property in St. Louis to discharge his debts, and managing between arguments for Ellen once more to become pregnant, he found that he need not take an examination to join the bar but could be admitted "on the grounds of general intelligence." The personal insinuations that the opposing counsel leveled at Sherman when his first case came to trial were more than the temper behind the red beard could take. No jury could have been sympathetic with his impassioned outburst, and his career as a trial lawyer can be called meteoric only in the sense that it was burned out in this one flash of fire. At low ebb, Sherman, the soldier who never had fought a battle, the failure at banking indebted to Southern friends, the one-case lawyer, found that he still could kindle fires of rebellion. Applying to Washington for vacancies among army pay-masters, he learned that Louisiana planned to establish a state military college and would need a superintendent. Old army friends like Braxton Bragg and P. G. T. Beauregard backed Sherman's application; for the first time in many years he found himself in a situation he thoroughly enjoyed, for he was a good schoolmaster, who ranted against teachers indulging in such high-flown imageries that "every damned shot" they delivered went "clear over [the students'] heads." For once Sherman felt completely happy, but in Louisiana, running his military college, the War Between the States overtook him.

At this point in Sherman's life the narrative of *The General Who Marched to Hell* begins. Where Cump Sherman for the first time heard cannonballs crashing overhead, how the dark shadows on his mind after California grew into the darker shadows of Kentucky, and how finally Sherman emerged so that on a May evening in 1864 the redheaded, redbearded general, then in Chattanooga, faced south toward Atlanta, form the prologue of the story about to unfold.

But war is fought on many levels, and Sherman could play but a selected part in its retelling. *The General Who Marched to Hell* actually is an attempt to capture from contemporary records, or from as near-to-the-moment records as exist, the moods and the motivations of one of the unique episodes in American history. This book tries not only to see into the minds, and to evaluate the emotions, of the generals both North and South who threw their troops into battle, but also to present the experiences and the attitudes of the man on the battlefield, of the civilian who heard the roar of cannon and fled to his cellar, and of the politician who already had begun to live history by hindsight. This is a book that, in attempting to recapture the immediacy of feeling at a precise moment, is more concerned with the impression of facts than with the facts themselves. Only historical research can afford to deal with the whole truth; history, as it is lived, must contend with the partial truth by which men fight and bleed and die.

Three factors have governed the selections of the witnesses represented in the pages that follow. First, I have chosen those accounts which give the feeling at the moment of an event and which provide a continuity of action. Second, I have tried to reconstruct the attitudes that must have existed in the minds of those charged with the direction of events, allowing for the bias that is a natural part of any general's reminiscences when years later he is haunted by the dreams of what should have been. Third, I have given preference wherever possible to hitherto unpublished sources. Nowhere in this book is there quoted a conversation for which documentation does not exist. Following the bibliography there are notes on the sources, giving more detailed information on the origins of the materials from which this story has been reconstructed.

Now the author must face the difficult responsibility of acknowledging the many persons who assisted in the creation of the present work. First mention must go to Richard A. Brown, my associate in research, who over two years has tracked down innumerable sources and evaluated their comparative importance. Mention also must go to the following persons for supplying valuable materials and suggestions: Paul M. Angle, director of the Chicago Historical Society; the late Lloyd Lewis, biographer of both Sherman and Grant; Jay Monaghan, director of the Illinois State Historical Society; Thomas Robson Hay, whose *Hood's Tennessee Campaign* remains an exemplary work of scholarship; Roy F. Nichols of the University of Pennsylvania; Wilbur Kurtz of

Atlanta, who for forty years has studied the field operations of Sherman's Atlanta campaign; Beverly M. DuBose, president of the Atlanta Historical Society; Richard A. Harwell, curator of the Confederate Collection of the Emory University Library; E. Merton Coulter of the University of Georgia; and the Rev. Clayton Torrence, secretary of the Virginia Historical Society. For permission to quote from manuscript materials grateful acknowledgment must be made to the Southern Collection of the University of North Carolina, the Duke University Library, the Emory University Library, and the Missouri Historical Society; and for assistance in research the author must certainly mention the courteous services rendered by the staffs of the Rutgers University Library, the New York Public Library, the Columbia University Library, the Georgia Historical Society, and the Library of the New York University Club. The Honorable Clifford P. Case, Representative to Congress from New Jersey, made repeated efforts to pry loose from the Adjutant General's Office in the War Department amnesty papers filed after the fall of Atlanta, but it was decided in Washington that these papers still were so confidential that even an opportunity to explore their contents for the purpose of historical documentation was denied. The author wishes also to acknowledge his indebtedness to Alfred A. Knopf, who was among the first to believe in this book and who has demonstrated his faith in the most realistic manner imaginable—by investing his money in it. For one editor to thank another is always an awkward problem—pigs is pigs and editors is editors—but this *is* a better book for the shrewd and intelligent suggestions of Harold Strauss. But above all others the author must speak for his wife and three children, who have waited patiently through long months for the end of the interruption in their lives that the writing of this book has been. Now—or at least until another book is started—we can be a normal family once more.

EARL SCHENCK MIERS

Stelton, New Jersey—December 1, 1950

Contents

CONTENTS

Maps

(BY CHARLES E. SKAGGS)

ONE
In 1864, as spring crept northward, Grant and Sherman met in Cincinnati to study the areas where, by concerted effort, they could conquer and divide the Confederacy.

MAP FOLLOWING PAGE 21

TWO
For more than a hundred miles, from Chattanooga to Atlanta, Sherman stalked a weaker foe with the relentless tenacity of a frontier hunter.

MAP FACING PAGE 80

THREE
For six weeks the Nation wondered where Sherman's army had gone, while 60,000 Yankees marched through Georgia on the promise that they could feast on oysters when they reached Savannah.

MAP FACING PAGE 226

List of Commanding Military Personnel by Rank and Army

[Rank given is that held at close of war.]

ADAMS, WIRT. Brigadier General, C.S.A.

ANDERSON, ROBERT. Brevet Major General, U.S.A. *Sherman's commander in Kentucky.*

ARMSTRONG, FRANCIS C. Brigadier General, C.S.A.

BANKS, NATHANIEL P. Major General Volunteers, U.S.A. *Commander of the Red River Expedition.*

BARRY, WILLIAM F. Brevet Major General, U.S.A.

BEAUREGARD, P. G. T. General, C.S.A.

BECKWITH, AMOS. Brevet Major General, U.S.A.

BLAIR, FRANCIS P. Major General Volunteers, U.S.A.

BRAGG, BRAXTON. General, C.S.A. *Resigned command of Army of Tennessee following Missionary Ridge.*

BRECKENRIDGE, JOHN C. Major General, C.S.A.

BUCKNER, SIMON BOLIVAR. Major General, C.S.A.

BUELL, DON CARLOS. Brevet Major General Volunteers, U.S.A.

BURNSIDE, AMBROSE E. Major General Volunteers, U.S.A.

BUTLER, BENJAMIN F. Major General Volunteers, U.S.A.

BUTLER, MATTHEW C. Major General, C.S.A. *His cavalry in Columbia, S.C. as Sherman approached.*

BUTTERFIELD, DANIEL. Major General Volunteers, U.S.A.

CANBY, EDWARD R. S. Brevet Major General Volunteers, U.S.A.

CHEATHAM, BENJAMIN F. Major General, C.S.A. *Distinguished in action at Kenesaw.*

CLEBURNE, PATRICK R. Major General, C.S.A.

COBB, HOWELL. Major General, C.S.A. *Secretary of the Treasury under Buchanan.*

COCKRELL, FRANCIS M. Brigadier General, C.S.A.

CORSE, JOHN M. Brevet Major General Volunteers, U.S.A. *Commanded defense at Allatoona.*

COX, JAMES D. Major General Volunteers, U.S.A.

CRUFT, CHARLES. Brevet Major General Volunteers, U.S.A.

LIST OF COMMANDING MILITARY PERSONNEL

DAVIS, JEFFERSON C. Brevet Major General, U.S.A.

DODGE, GRENVILLE M. Major General Volunteers, U.S.A.

ECTOR, MATTHEW D. Brigadier General, C.S.A.

EWING, CHARLES. Brigadier General Volunteers, U.S.A. *Inspector General on Sherman's staff.*

FEATHERSTON, WINFIELD S. Brigadier General, C.S.A.

FLOYD, JOHN B. Major General, C.S.A.

FORREST, NATHAN B. Lieutenant General, C.S.A.

FRANKLIN, WILLIAM B. Major General Volunteers, U.S.A.

FRÉMONT, JOHN C. Major General, U.S.A. *Nominated for the Presidency by the Radical Democracy, 1864.*

FRENCH, SAMUEL G. Major General, C.S.A. *Distinguished in action at Little Kenesaw; led attack at Allatoona.*

FROST, DANIEL M. Brigadier General, C.S.A.

GARRARD, KENNER. Brevet Major General, U.S.A.

GEARY, JOHN W. Brevet Major General Volunteers, U.S.A.

GOVAN, DANIEL C. Brigadier General, C.S.A.

GRANT, ULYSSES S. Lieutenant General, U.S.A.

HALLECK, HENRY W. Major General, U.S.A.

HAMPTON, WADE. Lieutenant General, C.S.A. *In command of defense of Columbia, S.C.*

HARDEE, WILLIAM J. Lieutenant General, C.S.A. *Corps commander, Army of Tennessee.*

HARROW, WILLIAM. Brigadier General Volunteers, U.S.A.

HAZEN, WILLIAM B. Major General Volunteers, U.S.A. *Led attack on Fort McAllister.*

HEINTZELMAN, SAMUEL P. Major General Volunteers, U.S.A.

HINDMAN, THOMAS C. Major General, C.S.A.

HOOD, JOHN BELL. General, C.S.A. *Succeeded J. E. Johnston in command of Army of Tennessee.*

HOOKER, JOSEPH. Brevet Major General, U.S.A.

HOWARD, OLIVER OTIS. Major General, U.S.A. *Succeeded McPherson in command of Army of the Tennessee.*

LIST OF COMMANDING MILITARY PERSONNEL

JACKSON, THOMAS J. Lieutenant General, C.S.A.

JOHNSTON, ALBERT S. General, C.S.A.

JOHNSTON, JOSEPH E. General, C.S.A. *Succeeded Bragg in command of Army of Tennessee.*

KILPATRICK, JUDSON. Brevet Major General, U.S.A. *Commanded Sherman's cavalry division.*

LEE, ROBERT E. General, C.S.A.

LEE, STEPHEN D. Lieutenant General, C.S.A.

LEGGETT, MORTIMER D. Major General Volunteers, U.S.A.

LIGHTBURN, JOSEPH A. J. Brigadier General Volunteers, U.S.A.

LOGAN, JOHN A. Major General Volunteers, U.S.A.

LONGSTREET, JAMES. Lieutenant General, C.S.A.

LORING, WILLIAM W. Major General, C.S.A. *Temporarily succeeded Leonidas Polk as Corps Commander, Army of Tennessee*

LOVELL, MANSFIELD. Major General, C.S.A.

McCOOK, DANIEL. Brigadier General Volunteers, U.S.A.

McCLELLAN, GEORGE B. Major General, U.S.A. *Nominated for the Presidency by the Democratic Party, 1864.*

McCLERNAND, JOHN A. Major General Volunteers, U.S.A.

McDOWELL, IRVIN. Major General Volunteers, U.S.A.

McLAWS, LAFAYETTE. Major General, C.S.A.

McPHERSON, JAMES B. Major General Volunteers, U.S.A. *In command of the Army of the Tennessee.*

MORGAN, JAMES D. Brevet Major General Volunteers, U.S.A.

MORGAN, JOHN H. Brigadier General, C.S.A.

MOWER, JOSEPH A. Major General Volunteers, U.S.A.

NEWTON, JOHN. Brevet Major General, U.S.A.

PALMER, JOHN M. Major General Volunteers, U.S.A.

PEMBERTON, JOHN C. Lieutenant General, C.S.A. *Defender of Vicksburg.*

PENDLETON, WILLIAM N. Major General, C.S.A.

PILLOW, GIDEON J. Brigadier General, C.S.A.

POE, ORLANDO M. Brevet Brigadier General, U.S.A.

LIST OF COMMANDING MILITARY PERSONNEL

POLK, LEONIDAS. Lieutenant General, C.S.A. *Protestant Episcopal Bishop of Arkansas; Corps Commander, Army of Tennessee.*

POLK, LUCIUS E. Brigadier General, C.S.A.

PORTER, FITZ JOHN. Major General Volunteers, U.S.A.

PORTER, Horace. Brevet Brigadier General, U.S.A.

RAWLINS, JOHN A. Brevet Major General, U.S.A.

ROSECRANS, WILLIAM S. Brevet Major General, U.S.A.

SCHOFIELD, JOHN M. Major General Volunteers, U.S.A. *In command of the Army of the Ohio.*

SCOTT, WINFIELD. Brevet Lieutenant General, U.S.A.

SEARS, CLAUDIUS W. Brigadier General, C.S.A.

SEDGWICK, JOHN. Major General Volunteers, U.S.A.

SHERIDAN, PHILIP H. General, U.S.A.

SHERMAN, WILLIAM T. General, U.S.A.

SICKLES, DANIEL E. Major General, U.S.A.

SLOCUM, HENRY W. Major General Volunteers, U.S.A. *In command of the Army of Georgia.*

SMITH, GILES A. Major General Volunteers, U.S.A.

SMITH, GUSTAVUS W. Major General, C.S.A. *In command of the Georgia militia.*

SMITH, MORGAN L. Brigadier General Volunteers, U.S.A.

STANLEY, TIMOTHY R. Brevet Brigadier General Volunteers, U.S.A.

STEWART, ALEXANDER P. Lieutenant General, C.S.A. *Permanently succeeded Leonidas Polk as Corps Commander, Army of Tennessee.*

STONEMAN, GEORGE. Brevet Major General, U.S.A.

TAYLOR, RICHARD. Lieutenant General, C.S.A.

TERRY, ALFRED H. Brevet Major General, U.S.A.

THOMAS, GEORGE H. Major General, U.S.A. *In command of the Army of the Cumberland.*

THOMAS, LORENZO. Brevet Major General, U.S.A.

WALCUTT, CHARLES C. Brevet Major General Volunteers, U.S.A.

WALKER, WILLIAM H. T. Major General, C.S.A.

WALLACE, LEWIS. Major General Volunteers, U.S.A.

LIST OF COMMANDING MILITARY PERSONNEL

WHEELER, JOSEPH. Lieutenant General, C.S.A.
WILLICH, AUGUST. Brevet Major General Volunteers, U.S.A.
WILSON, JAMES H. Brevet Major General, U.S.A.
WOODS, CHARLES R. Brevet Major General, U.S.A.

YOUNG, WILLIAM H. Brigadier General, C.S.A.

ZOLLICOFFER, FELIX K. Brigadier General, C.S.A.

PART ONE

✗✗✗✗✗✗✗✗✗✗✗✗✗✗✗✗✗✗✗✗✗✗✗✗✗✗✗✗✗✗✗✗✗✗✗✗✗

"Men are Blind and Crazy"

—the years before the Georgian campaign

1. "THE UNION ESTO PERPETUA" [1860]

THE heart of William Tecumseh Sherman burned with bitterness and resentment. Nothing but pig-headed blundering had precipitated this war, and the fool politicians, listening to "the prejudices of the people and running with the tide," had succeeded in destroying the Government! He had favored Seward over Lincoln for the Presidency because he had feared this moment; now, for all his intense love of the South, he must leave it. The Louisiana sunlight, stealing through the half-drawn blinds and revealing flecks of gold in the reddish beard, the reddish hair, cast shadows across the sheet of paper on which Sherman's deep-set, introspective eyes focused. He addressed his letter of resignation to Governor Moore at Baton Rouge. Dipping his pen into the old inkstand, he wrote with sad, hesitant strokes:

> Sir: As I occupy a quasi military position under the laws of the State, I deem it proper to acquaint you that I accepted such position when Louisiana was a State in the Union and when the motto of this seminary was inscribed in marble over the main door: "By the liberality of the General Government. The Union Esto perpetua." . . .

Did these lines sound stiff and pompous? If they did, let them stand! In those nervous days of January, 1861, the Governor of Louisiana had ordered the forcible seizure of Forts Jackson and St. Philip near the mouth of the Mississippi, and of Forts Pike and Wood at the outlets of Lakes Borgne and Pontchartrain, cutting off any approach by sea to New Orleans. Sherman's temper had shortened almost hourly, and a feeling of impending disaster had closed down upon him like a winter fog. His pen scratched on: ". . . If Louisiana withdraw from the Federal Union, I prefer to maintain my allegiance to the old Constitution as long as a fragment of it survives. . . ." These were not calculating words inspired by a sense of history; the man writing them was virtually a nobody, who saw his life following a blind, discouraging pattern. Everything he ever had endeavored, all he ever had planned, had ended in disaster. These words merely expressed a stubborn choice, wrung from a heart that felt no faith in the war, no belief in either its justice or its necessity. Armed conflict between North and South had become inevitable simply because, as he would write his daughter Minnie, "Men are blind and crazy." Almost weeping, he had cautioned a Southern friend: "You are bound to fail" because "the North can make a steam-engine, locomotive or railway car" whereas the South hardly could manufacture "a yard of cloth or a pair of shoes."

Now past forty, William Tecumseh Sherman had learned to view the world through the disillusioned eyes of a realist. Perhaps his passions often grew violent, perhaps his emotions frequently swept him into risks that were ill-advised and calamitous, perhaps his tenacious convictions made of his red beard and his red hair the symbols of a fiery personality that sometimes possessed no alternative but to burn itself out; but throughout his lifetime his gift of prophecy proved unfailing. No one had foreseen more keenly than Sherman the gathering dangers that had threatened the security of the country; no one had spoken out more violently against the rash acts and the hot words that had vibrated with the sinister portents of impending calamity. The non-appeasers in Congress had elicited his scorn, the abolitionists his contempt. The deep roots of four youthful years spent in the South following graduation from West Point had nourished his understanding of problems peculiarly regional; and old Southern friendships, especially for men like P. G. T. Beauregard and Braxton Bragg —men who had stood by him in dark hours and had secured for him his present position—had placed natural claims upon the loyalty of his heart.

Still, the loyalty of Sherman's mind must hold even more unflinchingly to the cause of the Union, and so, a sad and tormented man, he had been buffeted by the storm that had brewed over the nation through all of 1860. The sovereign state of Virginia had hanged John Brown for the raid on Harper's Ferry and Henry Thoreau had compared the doughty, hard-faced old abolitionist to Christ. At the Wigwam in Chicago, according to a popular campaign song, "Old Abe Lincoln came out of the wilderness" to win the Republican nomination for President, and when the Democratic Party split helplessly between Northern and Southern factions Lincoln's election was assured. Violently the storm of 1860 broke around Sherman on every side. On the 10th of December the Louisiana legislature met at Baton Rouge and called for a convention in early January, but the schoolmaster knew that "all attempts at reconciliation will fail." From Washington, Sherman's younger brother John, Congressman from Ohio, wrote: "Don't for God's sake subject yourself to any slur, reproach, or indignity!" The smile that touched the older brother's lips must have seemed pinched and cynical. Then, on the 10th of January, 1861, the Governor of Louisiana seized the arsenal at Baton Rouge. Sherman dipped his pen in the old inkstand and wrote his letter of resignation.

2. "IN A HELL OF A FIX" [1861]

IN MARCH 1861 Sherman came to Washington, ostensibly to see his brother John, but actually to seek a connection with the War Department. The behavior of the city scandalized the ex-schoolmaster. Every day Southern legislators hurled sneers and threats at their Northern colleagues in House and Senate, then stomped off to join the Confederate Congress at Montgomery. The "open, unconcealed talk" that he heard "even in the War Department, and about the public offices" deserved no better name than "high-treason"! John found occasion to call on Lincoln in reference to a number of minor appointments in Ohio, and took his brother with him.

"Mr. President," John said, "this is my brother, Colonel Sherman, who is just up from Louisiana. He may give you some information you want."

Lincoln looked up prefunctorily; his days were spent receiving advice—most of it bad. But he inquired: "How are they getting along down there?"

Sherman answered promptly: "They think they are getting along swimmingly—they are preparing for war."

"Oh, well," the President said, "I guess we'll manage to keep house!"

Sherman lapsed into silence, sensing that the interview had ended on this silly note; and once beyond the President's ear-shot his anger exploded. Damn the politicians! "You have got things in a hell of a fix," he snarled at John, "and you may get out of them as best you can!" John begged him to be patient, but the older brother had lost all patience with Washington, Lincoln, and Congress. He was going back to St. Louis to accept the presidency of the Fifth Street Railroad, a position that an old friend had secured for him. The salary of $2,500 a year wasn't handsome, but it would do.

St. Louis seethed with unrest. Southern sympathizers had established headquarters in a house on the northwest corner of Fifth and Pine, and here the Rebel flag was boldly hung. Any stroll through the lobby of Planters' House filled one's ears with brittle Rebel talk. At Camp Jackson, near the city limits, General D. M. Frost, despite his Northern origin and West Point training, was flagrantly pro-Confederate. Five or six companies of United States troops guarded the city's arsenal, and among the loyal German population regiments of

Home Guards organized and drilled. Thus St. Louis divided as the nation was dividing—one side flinging threats that it was coming to take the arsenal, the other that it would put an end to the mobs of damned traitors. "I tried my best to keep out of the current," Sherman recalled, "and only talked openly with a few men." When Sherman did speak out, however, he was tart if not actually abusive. To an old army friend living near Alexandria, Virginia, Sherman described himself as a man of peace, thoroughly domesticated, who enjoyed going to market and seeing "the vast abundance of cheap food." Bitterly he deplored "this foolish war, got up by a set of reckless politicians."

On April 6—less than a week before Sherman's old friend Beauregard would order the bombardment of Sumter, and Sherman's old commander at Fort Moultrie, Major Robert Anderson, would rally his small garrison to the defense of the fort—a telegram from Washington offered Sherman the chief clerkship of the War Department and the title of Assistant Secretary of War. Sherman wired back: "I cannot accept." Clearly he remained miffed at the treatment he had received when he had gone to Washington in March; he had proffered his services and been refused; with a large family he had required immediate employment, and now that he had settled in St. Louis and rented a house he was no longer "at liberty to change." This fuller explanation, reaching Washington by letter, impressed many as offensive; "some of Mr. Lincoln's cabinet," Sherman learned later, "concluded that I too would prove false to the country." But John continued talking up his brother to anyone who would listen, and on April 12— Fort Sumter Day—he wrote, greatly encouraged:

> . . . Civil war is actually upon us, and, strange to say, it brings a feeling of relief: the suspense is over. . . . There is an earnest desire that you go into the War Department . . . you would be virtually Secretary of War, and could easily step into any military position that offers.

7

John also suggested an alternative:

> . . . If troops are called for, as they surely will be in a few days, organize a regiment or brigade, either in St. Louis or Ohio, and you will then get into the army in such a way as to secure promotion. . . . You are a great favorite in the army and have great strength in political circles. I urge you to avail yourself of these favorable circumstances to secure your position for life. . . .

Sherman replied that "volunteers and militia never were and never will be fit for invasion, and when tried, it will be defeated, and dropt by Lincoln like a hot potato." The time would come, he predicted, when professional knowledge would be appreciated, "when men that can be trusted will be wanted, and I will bide my time." Meanwhile: "The first movements of the government will fail and the leaders will be cast aside. A second or third set will rise, and among them I may be, but at present I will not volunteer as a soldier or anything else."

Filled with the sad news of the fall of Sumter, John declared: "Neutrality and indifference are impossible. . . . Can't you come to Ohio and at once raise a regiment?" It was true, Sherman conceded somewhat stiffly, that the country must expect every man to do his duty, "but every man is not at liberty to do as he pleases."

To Secretary of War Cameron, Sherman explained why he would not volunteer. "Rightfully or wrongly," he said, "I feel myself unwilling to take a mere private's place." He had lived so long in California and Louisiana that the men would not be "well enough acquainted with me to elect me to my appropriate place." No direct reply came from Cameron.

On the 9th of May, Sherman and his children rode the streetcars to visit the arsenal. Inside they found four regiments of the Home Guards drawn up in parallel lines. Faces looked grim, nerves taut, and the guardsmen, he saw, were "distributing cartridges to the boxes." Sherman knew that this meant business, but whether the Home Guards were preparing for a defense or an offense he could not be sure. He hustled the children home.

Next morning rumors were thicker than Mississippi green flies. St. Louis residents barricaded their homes and wondered if the German Home Guards really were moving on the pro-Confederate Frost and his boys at Camp Jackson. Feet pounded down the street; everyone appeared to be running toward the camp to watch the fun. Sherman hurried through his office chores and sped for the house he occupied on Locust Street. Eliza Dean, a neighbor, intercepted him; her brother-in-law was at the camp and she knew that he'd be killed. Young men from the first and best families of St. Louis filled the camp, she said; they were proud and sure to fight. Sherman told the woman that "young men of the best families did not like to be killed better than ordinary people," and when later St. Louis streets reverberated with the shout that the boys at Jackson had surrendered, Sherman thought he would relay this news and allay the woman's fear.

In a burst of anger Miss Dean slammed the door in his face.

The prisoners from the camp had been herded into Lindell's Grove at the head of Olive Street, and with seven-year-old Willy in tow, Sherman set off to watch the activities. Almost at once he found himself in "a promiscuous crowd, men, women, and children." Bands played. But the crowd's mood was surly. Someone shrieked, "Hurrah for Jeff Davis!" Another took up the shout. The crowd edged toward the regulars, bayonets flashed. The crowd quieted, the music resumed; then (as he would later write John):

I heard a couple of shots, then half a dozen, and observed the militia were firing at the crowd . . . but the fire kept creeping to the rear along the flank of the column, and, hearing the balls cutting the leaves of the trees over my head, I fell down on the ground and crept up to where Charley Ewing had my boy Willy. I also covered his person. Probably a hundred shots passed over the ground, but none near us. As soon as the fire slackened, I picked Willy up, and ran with him till behind the rising ground. . . .

Now Sherman and his son were safe. But the war no longer remained something at Washington or Baltimore, at Sumter and Harper's Ferry. There was no remoteness in the fact that at Lindell's Grove two or three men, a woman, and a child had been killed, and several other persons wounded.

When a few days later word came that Sherman had been appointed a colonel of the Thirteenth Regular Infantry, and was wanted at once in Washington, he no longer hesitated.

W. T. Sherman began his journey—to fame and infamy.

3. A "NERVOUS-SANGUINE TEMPERAMENT" [1861–1862]

THE temper of Washington had changed. Through the hot days of June 1861, troops crowded into the city wearing uniforms "as various as the States and cities from which they came." Sherman watched them and shook his head; these citizen-soldiers were so loaded down "with overcoats, haversacks, knapsacks, tents, and baggage" that anywhere from twenty-five to fifty wagons were necessary to move a single regiment; and the cooking establishments and bakeries at many of the camps "would have done credit to Delmonico." General Winfield Scott, now about seventy-five and excessively overweight, stomped around the War Department in a constant rage against the President, Congress, and the Secretary of War. All the fools were calling for quick action, but Scott had set his mind on organizing "a grand army of invasion" with the regulars as his "iron column." And who would lead the army in the field? Why, he would, Scott thundered, drawing himself erect with as much dignity as his unwieldy frame would permit. But while Scott hesitated, deaf to the rising clamor of "On to Richmond!" Sherman's old friend Beauregard quietly moved a Confederate army into Manassas Junction, anchored his advance guard at Fairfax Court-House, and almost looked down into the streets of Washington. The Battle of Bull Run was hours away.

Sherman started for Manassas Junction, by way of Centreville, on a hot day in July, commanding five regiments of ragtag, undisciplined troops. A colonel of the Second Wisconsin knew "no more of military art than a child"; the men straggled at almost every sight of "water, blackberries, or anything on the way they fancied." But the morale of the troops was high, for these were the days when everyone in the North was supremely confident that the Union needed only "to make a bold appearance, and the Rebels would run." Sherman felt uneasy. Scarcely a man under him—farm boys and city lads turned soldiers for ninety days, as though it were a lark—ever had heard a cannon or musket; years later, writing his *Memoirs*, Sherman must have wiped a hand across his face in that quick, nervous gesture that grew so characteristic, trying to forget those moments:

> . . . when for the first time in my life I saw cannonballs strike men and crash through the trees above and around us, and realized the always sickening confusion as one approaches a fight from the rear; then the night-march from Centreville, on the Warrentown road, standing for hours wondering what was meant; . . . the terrible scare of a poor Negro who was caught between our lines; . . . the scenes of a field strewed with dead men and horses. . . .

Along the road to Manassas Junction, Sherman led his five regiments to a hill where the battle crashed down like a thunderclap. A woods on the left front swarmed with Rebels;

Sherman threw in his regiments, one at a time, and saw each driven back, battered and bleeding; but after two hours Sherman still fought on, with "no idea that we were beaten." To learn the lesson of when to stop fighting, Bull Run cost Sherman, among his five regiments, 111 killed, 205 wounded, 293 missing. When finally the Union forces fled in full retreat, Sherman's men didn't wait for him to give the order. They simply ran. But after Bull Run five colonels who had fought at Manassas Junction were raised to brigadier general, Sherman among them. No decision reached by the War Department during the war would cause greater surprise; Heintzelman, one of the promoted colonels, cried feelingly: "By —— ——, it's all a lie! Every mother's son of you will be cashiered." All five felt that they deserved to be.

Then Sherman was summoned to Willard's Hotel, where he was greeted by his old commander from Fort Moultrie, General Robert Anderson. The Department of the Cumberland was being formed to support the Kentucky Legislature with its two pro-Union votes to every slave vote, and Anderson, as the Department's commander, wanted Sherman as one of his two brigadiers. For the other, Anderson would take George Thomas, Don Carlos Buell, or Ambrose Burnside. Sherman had known both Thomas and Buell at the Academy, and his choice, resting between these two, obviously favored the good-natured Thomas even though the high-strung Buell was a fellow Ohioan. Later Lincoln came to Willard's. The President raised his brows doubtfully at the suggestion of Thomas; look at that Virginia background, the President argued; too many Southern officers already had "played false." Sherman spoke up, defending his old West Point roommate with a vehemence that led Lincoln to capitulate, and Anderson moved west with Sherman and Thomas.

In the east McClellan would replace Scott but the military situation still would border on chaos as "Little Mac" rode through the streets of Washington with a puffed-out chest, insulted the President, and nourished wild political dreams.

The situation in the west, as Sherman would soon discover, was little better. Here Frémont, recently returned from California, had established himself in St. Louis at Planters' House as commander of the newly organized Department of Missouri and nourished dreams even wilder than Little Mac's. Recruits were badly needed in Kentucky, but as soon as Indiana or Illinois raised a regiment Frémont grabbed it. Sherman's dander rose and with Anderson's permission he set off for St. Louis to thrash out the issue with Frémont. He got nowhere. Frémont, he would report to Anderson, had become "the scandal of the day," surrounding himself with sentries and guards as though he were "a great potentate," running "a more showy court than any king," and keeping everybody "dancing attendance for days and weeks before granting an audience." Sherman took one look at the type of hangers-on who had followed Frémont from California, and pinched his nose; an old maxim sprang to his mind: "Where the vultures are, there is a carcass close by." As though Frémont hadn't harmed Kentucky sufficiently by robbing it of recruits, he now issued a remarkable proclamation—all slaves of owners who rebelled against the Government henceforth were free! No blow could have hurt Kentucky more, struggling as it was to hold its slave-owning elements in the Union! Sherman writhed and Anderson with him. Lincoln quickly annulled Frémont's proclamation and sent Halleck to take over his command. Henry Halleck could translate *The Political and Military Life of Napoleon*, but he couldn't undo the damage Frémont had achieved in arousing tempers. And the recruits still were lacking!

Throughout September, fires of war nibbled at the bluegrass fringes of Kentucky. Up from Tennessee marched the Confederacy's fighting Episcopal bishop, Leonidas Polk, scanning the heights above Paducah and reckoning—with God's help—that batteries placed there would control both the Tennessee and Ohio rivers. Polk prayed a little too long; out of Cairo rode the slouching figure of U. S. Grant, seizing

Paducah, then asking headquarters in St. Louis if he might do what had already been accomplished! Meanwhile through Cumberland Gap the Confederacy's Zollicoffer brought a second Rebel army into Kentucky, announcing that he would take Louisville.

Muldraugh's Hill, lying across Zollicoffer's threatened advance, claimed its own strange place in history. Tradition insisted that a scrawny-kneed youngster named Abe Lincoln used to sit on its slope, sucking his lip and brooding over the years ahead. Now on that same slope Sherman waited, surrounded by troops little better than those he had taken down to Bull Run. He smoked incessantly, lighting a cigar as though it were the worst sort of "penny grab," puffing on it furiously, using up matches by the box before he finally snatched the half-smoked, still unlighted stump from his mouth. Sherman seemed nervous, absent-minded, irritable. "He's a bitter pill to take," the men said, "a gruff old cock." They called him "Old Pills" till they knew him better; then he became "Old Sugar-Coated." But though Sherman fussed and worried, the Confederates were not ready to carry out Zollicoffer's boast. Simon Bolivar Buckner burned a bridge over Salt Creek, but refused to cross the Green River; at Bowling Green one of the most feared generals in the South, Albert Sidney Johnston, gathered forces for a more systematic advance.

In October, Sherman stepped into a hornet's nest by succeeding Anderson as commander in Kentucky. He plainly feared the responsibility of a command, and before leaving for the west had tried to impress on Lincoln "my extreme desire to serve in a subordinate capacity, and in no event to be left in a superior command." Now he was right where he had not wanted to be, and he looked tired, fretful, obsessed with the "crotchets and prejudices" of the old Leavenworth days. He left cigar stumps everywhere—"Sherman's old soldiers," growled the porters cleaning up after him—and Henry Villard, visiting Louisville as correspondent for the *New York*

Herald, heard from Sherman's neighbors in Galt House that if he wasn't insane he was acting damned queer.

The need for recruits preyed on Sherman's mind. His estimates of the forces Buckner and Johnston could throw against him were wildly exaggerated. He hammered at Washington for reinforcements, and when they didn't arrive went on hammering until Secretary of War Cameron quietly appeared in Louisville. Sherman's high-strung way of talking, pacing the floor as he spoke and as often throwing his questions toward the windows or door as toward his listeners, could be maddening. To the methodical Cameron, Sherman's quick-trigger thought processes, jumping from point to point by intuition rather than by logic, could only become a test of patience. The interview started badly; over Sherman's objection, Cameron insisted that Adjutant General Lorenzo Thomas attend the conference; irked, Sherman blasted away at Cameron, saying in substance: "My forces are too small for an advance, too small to hold the important positions in the state against an advance of the enemy, and altogether too large to be sacrificed in detail." How many troops did he need, asked Cameron. Sherman's mind flew over the task of cleaning the Rebels out of the entire Mississippi Valley and answered promptly: "Two hundred thousand!" But Cameron and Lorenzo Thomas had come to talk only about Kentucky; they laughed scornfully. My God, two hundred thousand men—the suggestion was preposterous!

Sherman's dark eyes flashed; all right, he snapped in another intuitive jump, then abandon Kentucky! Cameron shook his head; the Secretary, supported by Lorenzo Thomas, proposed to divide Sherman's army in two, with one column operating from Cincinnati against Knoxville and the other from Louisville against Nashville. Sherman threw up his hands. This *was* preposterous! Let somebody else take command and he would return to duty in the field. Cameron's shrewd, glittering eyes must have revealed that at last Sherman had begun

15

to make sense; as soon as the Secretary could execute the orders he would send Buell to take over the command.

Sherman seethed as he came out of Galt House and his unlighted cigar rode at a dangerous tilt. With dark shadows haunting his mind, he clomped down to the offices of the Associated Press, where he went almost every night to read the dispatches. According to one witness, Samuel Wilkerson of the *New York Tribune* cornered him there, seeking permission to pass south through Sherman's lines. Sherman refused. Sam Wilkerson's bridling temper must have been fine-edged, or at least he could not perceive when a man's ruffled nerves were at the breaking point. If Sherman wouldn't let him through, he said, then Cameron would! Sherman almost bit through his cigar. Wilkerson had two hours to clear out of Louisville, or, by God, he, Sherman, "would hang him as a spy."

Almost without exception, the newspaper fraternity lined up against Sherman, and his idiosyncrasies suddenly grew numerous enough to feed the smoldering scorn. Everybody knew that Sherman hated female nurses. Everybody knew that he "mothered" his troops. Everybody knew that he smoked too many cigars—a habit, one correspondent declared, "peculiarly injurious" to his "nervous-sanguine temperament." Everybody knew too that he was hipped on his old Southern connections—could his loyalty be completely trusted?

Some wrote about these rumors, others merely whispered them, and the shadows deepened in Sherman's mind. A confused and angry man, he waited in Louisville for Buell to relieve him. He saw bogies in the night darkness—one especially said that the enemy was about to crush him. Although the Union forces then moved steadily toward the Cumberland Gap, he ordered the advance stopped. No fear could have been more groundless, no action more unfortunate. Halleck sent him to Sedalia, Missouri, to inspect troops, a mission that seemed safe enough; but the bogies traveled to Sedalia with Sherman, telling him that the Confederates were massing for an attack, that he must prepare to meet it. Everyone but Sherman seemed to know he moved in a world of hallucinations. How sick Sherman had become can only be conjectured, but Halleck, hauling him back to St. Louis from Sedalia, would think that he presented a "broken down appearance," that his remarks were "rather imprudent." The final blow came on December 11, when a headline in Murat Halstead's *Cincinnati Commercial* proclaimed:

GENERAL WILLIAM T. SHERMAN INSANE

Phrases leaped out from the page: ". . . he was at the time while commanding in Kentucky, stark mad . . . he has of course been relieved of command. . . . It seems providential that the country has not to mourn the loss of an army through the loss of the mind of a general. . . ." The request to evacuate Kentucky, the retreat from Cumberland Gap, the assertion that Louisville could not be defended were among the evidences cited of Sherman's "mad freaks." At home his wife Ellen's heart was wrung when her son burst into the house with the exciting news that "Papa was crazy." Sherman wrote old Tom Ewing, his foster father, "You will be mortified beyond measure at the disgrace which has befallen me." Ewing was too hopping mad to be mortified; he and John Sherman both urged Sherman to sue "the scoundrels who have libeled you." Then, in the more temperate, objective mood of the elder· statesman, Ewing counseled his foster son:

You estimate the comparative power of the South higher than most men, and I think too high, but right or wrong, it does no good to express an opinion until you can in some way control and change the matter. . . . You have kindly feelings toward many engaged in the contest on the other side arising from old friendships. You ought not to give it voice. . . . You are engaged in the war and can say nothing with propriety against its justice or policy.

Murat Halstead admitted that Henry Villard had come from Louisville declaring Sherman insane and had pleaded with Halstead to publish the story in the *Commercial* before Sherman wrecked the army. Halstead, confronted by the refutation one of Ewing's sons had prepared in consultation with Sherman, promised to print a full retraction, and did so two days after the original story had appeared. Meanwhile the "insanity story" was printed in the *St. Louis Democrat* and other papers; Ellen believed that a definite plot existed to destroy her husband. But Sherman blamed only himself. Sent to Benton Barracks to attend to the routine drilling of recruits, he wrote John:

> I am so sensible now of my disgrace from having exaggerated the force of our enemy in Kentucky that I do think I should have committed suicide were it not for my children. I do not think I can again be trusted with a command. . . .

But there was yet Shiloh.

4. "SHERMAN, YOU KNOW THAT I AM IN THE WAY" [1862]

GENERAL HENRY W. HALLECK was known to the army as "Old Brains." Halleck had been shrewd at law and he was shrewd at war, and his personal ambition ran deeper than the mud in the Mississippi over which his canny military eyes watched. That ambition saved Sherman. Halleck was far from satisfied with command of the Department of Missouri; he wanted control over all the armies of the west; and to win it, he knew, he must do two things—beat Buell to a smashing victory and mend his political fences. With John Sherman and Tom Ewing among Lincoln's intimates and with both pressing for Sherman to be given another chance,

Halleck could not see where he had much to lose by calling
Sherman back to his staff. The maneuver worked well from
the start. "Old Brains" probably knew more military lore
than the combined bigwigs of the War Department, and in
Sherman he discovered another alert, intelligent military
mind. So in St. Louis the pair took to studying the maps and
to wondering if Albert Sidney Johnston might not be something of a stuffed shirt. Even Sherman, who had feared "Awesome Albert" at Bowling Green almost to the point of his own
mental breakdown, now conceded that Johnston looked vul-
nerable. Considering all the time Johnston had been given,
what had he done to protect the Tennessee and the Cumberland rivers save hastily to construct Forts Henry and Donelson? Halleck wanted control of those rivers. "Old Brains"
rubbed his chin and thought. Grant was the man—Grant,
who had outwitted Polk even it he hadn't outprayed him. And
Paducah was the spot to place Sherman to keep supplies
moving while Grant operated against Henry and Donelson.
Before Sherman reached Paducah, Grant already had captured Henry and was hell-bent to marshal his gunboats and
forces on the Cumberland to blast Buckner out of Donelson.
In many ways, Grant didn't appear to have much sense. Since
time immemorial, military strategists had known you couldn't
attack fortifications without the odds overwhelmingly in your
favor. Hell, Buckner would have as many men inside Donelson
as Grant had outside—old slouching Sam seemed touched in
the head. But at Paducah, Sherman didn't think so. Grant
would remember how Sherman kept the supplies coming down
the river, sending notes "of encouragement," offering to
"waive rank" if as Grant's senior officer "he could be of service at the front." In temperament, mannerism, habit, method,
these two men appeared to have little in common; you needed
only to watch them smoking cigars, W. F. G. Shanks told the
readers of *Harper's New Monthly Magazine*, to realize the difference, Grant smoking "his tobacco as the Chinese do opium"
and Sherman smoking "as if it were a duty to be finished in

19

the shortest imaginable time"; but somehow they worked well together, quietly understanding that they could never be alike except in originality of mind, in depth of affection.

When Grant struck at Donelson, ignoring all the military textbooks, Buckner's jig was up; Buckner couldn't even bargain sensibly with Grant, receiving the curt answer that nothing but unconditional surrender would do; so Buckner watched from twelve to fifteen thousand prisoners fall into Grant's hands and doubtless thanked God that Confederate ex-Secretary of War General Floyd and General Pillow slipped across the Cumberland in time to escape capture. The North rocked with joy, but Halleck's eyes narrowed. True, he had bested Buell—the Confederate line in the west so tottered that even Albert Sidney Johnston must withdraw from Bowling Green—but he had gained a new and thoroughly dangerous rival for the western command in the nation's new idol, Unconditional Surrender Grant! When Grant hurried after the Confederates toward Nashville, losing touch with Halleck, Washington heard that Halleck had confined Grant to his tent without a command as punishment for another of his roistering drunks. Lincoln put down his foot. Grant had given the North its first major victory at Donelson and his reward would be the stars of a major general.

Cheerlessly, the South accepted the loss of Donelson. Suddenly in the west many of the finest fighting generals of the South appeared—Beauregard, Bragg, Breckinridge, Pillow, Floyd, Polk, Cheatham, Hardee, Cleburne, Hindman—aching for a fight, a counterbalancing victory. Halleck, at last winning command in the west, raising Sherman to the favorite on his staff and sensing shrewdly that the dark shadows were ebbing from Sherman's mind, eyed the Memphis & Charleston Railroad. That was the plum he would pick next! Sherman steamed down the Tennessee, sucked in his breath at the sight of the old warehouses along Pittsburg Landing. Here was the spot, twenty miles from Corinth, astride a main travel line, to concentrate troops! Sherman walked up from the river two miles and pitched his tent by a log church, the Shiloh Meeting-house. In the evening, when he walked down for a look at Snake, Owl, and Lick Creeks, the peach blossoms smelled fine.

The newspaper correspondents asked Sherman, in effect: "Aren't you afraid of a Confederate attack?"

Sherman nodded.

"Why don't you tell Grant?"

Sherman grinned. "They'd call me crazy again."

If there were bogies in Sherman's mind now, they were distant cousins to the bogies of Louisville and Sedalia. When Grant arrived for inspection Sherman estimated the enemy concentration around Corinth at twenty thousand—actually it was forty thousand. Sherman couldn't believe that Beauregard would be "such a fool as to leave his base of operation to attack us in ours." Nor did Grant. Soon thirty-three thousand Union troops strolled the yellow heights at Shiloh. All felt safe. But on April 3 forty thousand Rebels did the unexpected, picking up their muskets and starting the twenty-mile march toward the log meeting-house. As they started they were told: "The eyes and hopes of eight millions of people rest on you."

Bloody Shiloh lasted two days.

On Sunday morning, the 6th of April, the picket firing was heavy before breakfast and Sherman rode out to see what was wrong. What he saw was "the Rebel lines of battle in front coming down as far as the eye could reach." That was how the fighting started.

At this moment, nine miles away, Grant was eating breakfast at his headquarters in the beautiful Cherry home. At the sound of the firing he was soon off, but by the time he reached the field the battle was hours old. By then Southern boys with flintlocks and shotguns were fighting Northern boys who knew no more than thirty days' drilling in the art of war. It was Southern dash against Northern pluck, Grant would think; sometimes it was brigade against brigade, regiment against regiment, but more often one confused mob would simply fight

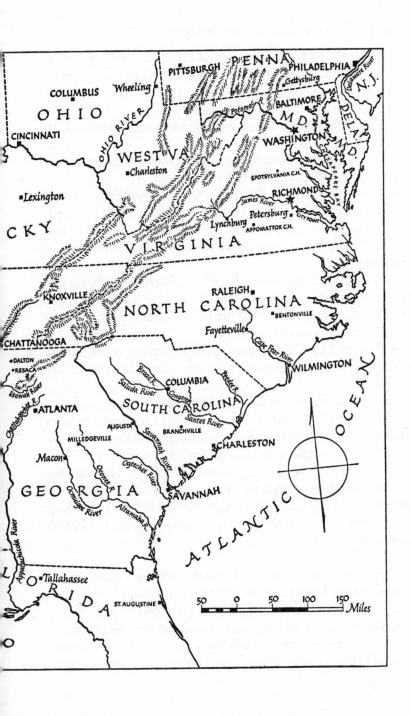

another confused mob. The story of Shiloh in terms of tactics, in terms of what happened and what should have happened, is involved, tedious, rarely clear or convincing. Shiloh as it was lived became pictures such as these:

—One lean tree trunk with ninety bullets in it, another with sixty.

—The Kentucky brother who told another, firing at a man near a tree: "Hold on, Bill—that's Father!"

—Governor Harris of Tennessee seeing Albert Sidney Johnston swaying in his saddle. "General, are you hurt?" he asked. "I am afraid so, and seriously," Johnston answered. He was dead within minutes, a stray bullet having severed an artery in his leg.

—Daniel McCook remembered for *Harper's:* "Thousands of soldiers, panic-stricken, were hiding under the bank [of the river], and, not satisfied with their own infamy, were discouraging our troops newly arrived."

—But Ed Russell, shot through the stomach, shook hands with every man in his battery in the twenty minutes of life left to him.

Four horses were shot from under Sherman that day, fighting off the brunt of the first attack; there were not enough matches at Shiloh to keep Sherman's cigar smoking. McCook would recall the enemy repulsed "within twenty feet of Sherman's semicircle of blazing batteries"; Albert Richardson remembered that Sherman's "face was besmeared with powder and blood." Perhaps no single passage in Sherman's long official report on the battle better reveals the spirit of Shiloh than this:

> Several times during the battle, cartridges gave out; but General Grant had thoughtfully kept a supply coming from the rear. When I appealed to regiments to stand fast, although out of cartridges, I did so because to retire a regiment for any cause has a bad effect on others. I commend the Fortieth Illinois and Thirteenth Missouri for

thus holding their ground under heavy fire, although their cartridge-boxes were empty.

Darkness and torrents of rain closed down on what looked like a Confederate victory, but with the dawn of another day Buell arrived with twenty thousand reinforcements, Lew Wallace with another six thousand. The Confederates retreated, leaving behind 10,694 in killed, wounded, and missing. Union losses were 13,047.

The North, at first joyful, suddenly felt repelled when the losses at Shiloh became known. Grant's unpreparedness, his placing of Lew Wallace's troops so far from Pittsburg Landing, his ignoring of Halleck's orders to dig entrenchments with an army backed against the Tennessee River, were only a few of the charges leveled against the commander. Halleck, quite unjustly, accused the hero of Donelson of being too drunk to mount a horse. The nation was distressed, and in the White House friends of the President urged him to dismiss Grant. Grant hadn't known an attack was coming; God, on the fifth of April, with forty thousand Rebels only two miles away from Shiloh, hadn't he wired Halleck: "I have scarcely the faintest idea of an attack . . ."? Lincoln, who had put his foot down after Donelson, could do so again. He said: "I can't spare this man—he fights!"

Grant chafed under the criticism, under the anomalous position to which Halleck reduced him. One day Sherman learned that Grant had asked for a thirty-day leave and might quit. Seeking Grant out in his tent, Sherman asked if the rumors were true.

Grant said: "Yes."

But why, Sherman asked.

The slouching little man shifted unhappily. "Sherman," he said, "You know that I am in the way here. I have stood it as long as I can, and can endure it no longer."

But where would he go?

"St. Louis," Grant answered vaguely.

Had he any business there?

"Not a bit."

Sherman drew a deep breath. Perhaps he remembered when he had returned to St. Louis from California, the "Jonah of banking," in debt to his friends. He had walked the streets, distracted and on edge. A veteran of the Mexican War who then lived outside St. Louis and made a scant living delivering wood had watched Sherman prowling the streets, and had stopped to speak to him. Thus, on the edge of obscure failure, Sherman and Grant met for the first time. California, St. Louis, Kansas, Kentucky—no one could know more acutely than Sherman how it felt to stand at low ebb! Now, looking across at Grant, Sherman also must have remembered Paducah, Fort Donelson, his own agreement that an attack at Shiloh seemed unreasonable. Sherman wrote in his *Memoirs:*

> Before the battle of Shiloh, I had been cast down by a mere newspaper assertion of "crazy"; but that single battle had given me new life, and now I was in high feather; and I argued with him that, if he went away, events would go right along, and he would be left out; whereas, if he remained, some happy accident might restore him to favor and his true place. . . .

Once again Sherman's prophetic nose had scented correctly. The name of the "happy accident" was Vicksburg.

5. "VOX POPULI, VOX HUMBUG!" [1863]

IN BOSTON, in New York, in Philadelphia, in Washington, the man in the street found Yazoo, Yalobusha, and Tallahatchie strange-sounding words. The fall of '62 dragged into the blustery winter months of '63 and Northerners read of the rivers that bore these names, understanding in a remote, disquieting way that among the swamps and live-oak tangles bordering these streams Union soldiers fought malaria, mumps, measles, and smallpox, mud and incessant rains, bullets and boredom. Other names—Eagle Bend, Muddy Bayou, Moon Lake, Five Mile Creek, the Big Sunflower—also possessed a vague, unreal character; men read that these works designated the inlets and curves formed by the Mississippi as the river twined in a serpentine course past the bluffs of Vicksburg; but unless one penetrated inch by inch a stream too narrow for a gunboat to turn about in, unless one waded hip-deep through swamps steaming with fever or saw the cypress and cottonwoods a foot in diameter clogging the bayous, how could one know the backaches and the heartbreaks that were piling up day after day, week after week, month after month as North and South locked in a death-struggle for control of the Mississippi? Newspaper correspondents visited these scenes and departed, unmoved, uninformed. Carl Sandburg would sense the paradox succinctly: "Under their noses was an epic of mud, struggle, and blood; not one of them saw it and wrote it."

Both Jefferson Davis and Abraham Lincoln faced a common problem. In the South critics of the government cried that General John C. Pemberton would wreck the Confederacy and sell out Vicksburg to the Union for a traitor's pittance; and in the North other critics, no less abusive, scorned Lincoln's choice of Grant as commander of the Vicksburg campaign, foreseeing another disaster that would outstrip even the shame of bloody Shiloh. But both Davis and Lincoln could be stubborn men, whether in the cause of states' rights or the Union. The Chief Executive in Richmond conceded that Pemberton had been Pennsylvania-born; what of it? Pemberton's West Point training, his record in the Mexican War, were distinguished; Davis permitted Pemberton to speak for himself:

> You have heard that I am incompetent and a traitor; and that it was my intention to sell Vicksburg. Follow me

and you will see the cost at which I will sell Vicksburg. When the last pound of beef, bacon and flour, the last grain of corn, the last cow and hog and horse and dog shall have been consumed, and the last man shall have perished in the trenches, then, and only then, will I sell Vicksburg.

Against Grant, Lincoln heard many charges, including the opinion of a Congressman that any general whose "entire baggage consists of a tooth brush" lacked dash. Other critics, puzzling over names like Tallahatchie and the Big Sunflower, Yalobusha and Moon Lake, declared that Grant simply was wandering around, baffled and outwitted, wasting men, time, and patience. Grant was a hopeless drunkard, charged another coterie; and there were even those who said bluntly that Grant's choice of Sherman as next in command merely demonstrated how in time "crazy" birds of a feather flocked together. But Lincoln listened more attentively to Charles A. Dana, who had been sent to travel with Grant's army and to report confidentially to the President and to the Secretary of War. Dana understood at once the epic being fashioned in the swamps and bayous of Mississippi; both Grant and Sherman, he wrote Washington, were remarkable men. Lincoln admitted that he never had met Grant, that he knew nothing of how much or how often he drank, but at Donelson he had liked the stamp of the man. Of a distinguished divine the President inquired whether anyone had learned the source whence Grant obtained his liquor, because, he said, he wished "to furnish a supply to some of my other generals who have never yet won a victory."

Through January and February, Sherman supervised the building of a system of canals opposite Vicksburg whereby Grant hoped to turn the Mississippi at this point or at least make a passage deep enough for Yankee gunboats to cross the peninsula west of the city. The men dug and swore, fighting the war with pick and shovel; their greatest enemy was the Mississippi, rising from day to day, threatening to sweep away the levees and drown the sweating workmen. Later, when the canals were dug, the river fell and there were no channels for the gunboats.

In March Grant sent Sherman with the XVth Corps into Black Bayou to search for a route into the Yazoo through which the army might be thrown against Vicksburg from the east. The channel of the bayou was as crooked as the limbs of the oaks overhanging its banks; at one time Sherman watched the gunboat *Silver Wave* crashing through the trees until everything above deck was carried away—pilot house, smokestacks. The guerrilla operations of the Confederates added to the harassments of nature. Across the swamps on foot Sherman led his men, wading through water up to the waist, seeing "the smaller drummerboys . . . carry their drums on their heads," while "most of the men slung their cartridge-boxes around their necks." Trees, stumps, levees gave perfect cover to enemy sharpshooters. Men died in the dismal swamps; the weeks dragged on; the toil, the misery, the problems of Vicksburg could be comprehensible only to those who were there.

Meanwhile Sherman's spirits were sorely bruised when General McClernand, once a Congressman from the President's home district, appeared with orders from Lincoln that placed McClernand over Sherman. Sherman wrote John that "Mr. Lincoln intended to insult me . . . and I would have quietly folded up my things and gone to St. Louis only I know in times like these all must submit to insult and infamy if necessary." Clearly the President couldn't forget Sherman's failure in Kentucky and distrusted the officer Grant had selected for his principal lieutenant. Still, for many Lincoln's action defied understanding; from the Vicksburg front Dana would report that McClernand offered little promise as a field officer; but even Dana's report could not assuage Sherman's ruffled pride. "I never dreamed of so severe a test of my

27

patriotism as being superseded by McClernand," he told John, "and if I can keep down my tamed (?) spirit and live I will claim a virtue higher than Brutus."

With the press, with whose representatives Sherman constantly seemed in trouble, his spirit proved anything but tamed. "Newspapers can now turn armies against their leaders," he growled to John in January, and in another letter elaborated this view:

> The press has now killed McClellan, Buell, Fitz-John Porter, Sumner, Franklin, and Burnside. Add my name and I am not ashamed of the association. If the press can govern the country, let them fight the battles.

To Sherman "these newspaper correspondents hanging about the skirts of our army reveal all plans, and are worth a hundred thousand men to the enemy." Who had revealed McDowell's movement on Manassas and "enabled Johnston so to reinforce Beauregard that our army was defeated"? Who had revealed the Union movement on Vicksburg? Who had "prevented all secret combinations and movements against the enemy"? To each of these questions, Sherman shouted scornfully: "The press!"

Thomas W. Knox of the *New York Herald* wrote letters for publication which had not passed under the scrutiny of the commanding general. Sherman arrested Knox, tried him by court-martial, and prohibited the correspondent from entering army lines. The Knox case reverberated in Washington, where a committee of newspapermen called on Lincoln; again Sherman's fat appeared in the journalistic fire, but Lincoln had his wily moments: he told a few stories and referred the matter to Grant. Sherman wrote John: "Grant is honest and does his best. I will do as ordered."

The Vicksburg campaign seemed hopelessly bogged down as April brought flaming blooms along the Mississippi. The clamor increased against Grant, inspired, Sherman insisted, by the "notorious . . . intriguing" of McClernand; Lincoln refused to budge in his faith in his commander, remembering the man who had told Buckner at Donelson: "No terms but unconditional surrender!" Grant's quiet mind, contemplating Vicksburg, seeing it as Sherman saw it, "an impregnable Gilbraltar" controlling the Mississippi, placed details in order. On the 19th of May Grant opened his assault and failed, renewed the assault next day and failed again. Pemberton's thirty thousand men inside Vicksburg waited patiently, willing to see as much Union blood spattered over their parapets as Grant wished to spill. Down in the Black River country Joe Johnston collected another Rebel army to attack Grant from the rear. Grant came to see Sherman. Joe Johnston stood in his own class among Confederate generals, in Grant's judgment—the only Rebel general Grant feared. Could Sherman hold Johnston in check while the rest of the army laid siege to Vicksburg? Sherman nodded. On the 20th of June he was headquartered on the Big Black daring Johnston to cross. The Confederate demurred.

Vicksburg lay under siege. Inside the city, civilian Edward S. Gregory would remember how "hardly any part of the city was outside the range of the enemy's artillery." From across the river the Union's eleven-inch and thirteen-inch mortars tore up the streets and pounded iron on rooftops. For forty days and nights the terror continued, growing almost commonplace until, Gregory would recall, "ladies walk quietly along the streets while the shells burst around them, their heads protected only by a parasol held between them and the sun." Hunger became a bigger enemy than the falling shells; toward the end of the siege Sergeant Osborn Oldroyd would report: "I once made a hearty breakfast on fried rats and found the flesh very good." Watching the men of the garrison subsisting on rats, bark, and cane shoots, even the stubborn Pemberton could no longer hold out. On July 4, 1863, Vicksburg surrendered, the day after Lee had retreated from Gettysburg.

Overnight Grant grew into a national idol. To the man in the street Grant's taciturnity, his slouching unpretentiousness, his diffidence in public places gave him a plainness that seemed thoroughly trustworthy, and even the Congressman who once had told Lincoln that Grant lacked dash now thought of him as a "man of deeds, and not of words." Sherman felt that the adulation being showered on Grant was entirely deserved. "The campaign of Vicksburg, in its conception and execution," he said, "belonged exclusively to Grant, not only in the great whole, but in the thousands of its details." But Sherman would remember the storm that had been raised against Grant after Shiloh and during the early stages of the Vicksburg campaign; he would remember too the discouraged Grant who had believed he was no longer wanted and might as well return to St. Louis; cynically Sherman wrote home:

> [Grant] is now belabored with praise by those who a month ago accused him of all the sins in the calendar, and who next week will turn against him if so blows the popular breeze. Vox populi, vox humbug.

But the popular breeze kissed Grant's grizzled cheeks with increasing persistency. The Confederate defeat at Vicksburg was followed by another at Chattanooga. In the White House on the first day of January 1864, those who attended Lincoln's reception crowded noisily into the East Room to watch the awkward hero and the President meet for the first time. Grant blushed and looked scared; cheers rocked the crystal chandeliers; Secretary Seward presented Grant to Mrs. Lincoln and people climbed onto chairs and sofas to catch a glimpse of the unhappy little general. Now that Grant had won control of the Mississippi for the Union, he wanted to march to Atlanta and smash the resistance of the Western Confederacy! But Lincoln had another mission for the man he soon would ask Congress to make lieutenant general—the taking of Richmond! Almost reluctantly Grant assumed command of the Army of the Potomac and studied the task of defeating the wily Lee. He placed Halleck in Washington to attend to the headquarters details there. Then for the military prize Grant himself had wished to win—Atlanta—he chose a general in whom he had implicit faith, William Tecumseh Sherman.

Lincoln, Grant, Sherman each understood that 1864 must be the year of decision. The Confederacy had reeled under the blows on successive days of defeat at Gettysburg and Vicksburg, and then had righted itself and fought on. But wars never were won on battlefields unless what happened there permanently affected the political situation. In 1864 Lincoln would stand for re-election, opposed by the "peace platform" of the Democratic Party. The issue at last had been clearly drawn so that bullets and ballots might both decide. Writing to General J. A. Rawlins, after Vicksburg, Sherman admitted: "I know that in Washington I am incomprehensible, because at the outset of the war I would not go it blind and rush headlong into a war unprepared and with an utter ignorance of its extent and purpose. I was then construed *unsound;* and now that I insist on war pure and simple, with no admixture of civil compromises, I am supposed vindictive." Sherman reminded Rawlins of the advice Polonius gave to his son Laertes: "Beware of entrance to a quarrel; but, being in, bear it, that the opposed may beware of thee." Sherman continued:

> . . . What is true of the single man, is equally true of a nation. Our leaders seemed at first to thirst for a quarrel, willing, even anxious, to array us against all possible elements of opposition; and now, being in, they would hasten to quit long before the "opposed" has received that lesson which he needs. I would make this war as severe as possible, and show no symptoms of tiring till the South begs for mercy. . . . I don't want our Government to be bothered by patching up local governments, or by trying to reconcile any class of men. The South has done her worst, and now is the time for us to pile on our blows thick and fast.

Lincoln, sitting in the state dining-room of the White House while Francis B. Carpenter spent days sketching the room and the President in preparation for a painting of Lincoln reading the Emancipation Proclamation to his cabinet, must have known the temper and mood of the two men in whom the military destiny of the nation had been entrusted. Grant and Sherman worked in the utmost secrecy: no news was permitted to leak out of the plans that were being formed for the joint exploit beside which even the epic written in the mud of Vicksburg would pale. A woman asked Secretary of State Seward what was in the wind. Mr. Seward bowed courteously and replied: "Madame, if I did not know, I would tell you."

PART TWO

✳✳✳✳✳✳✳✳✳✳✳✳✳✳✳✳✳✳✳✳✳✳✳✳✳✳✳✳✳✳✳✳✳✳✳✳

A Night in May 1864

—and kindred matters

1. "A GHASTLY, GHOSTLY SIGHT"

Foot Soldier Theodore Upson of the 100th Indiana Volunteers left the little theater in Chattanooga delighted with the play he had seen. The night was warm, a pleasant contrast to the cold rain that had fallen over northern Georgia during the first week of May 1864, and a full moon shed silver light upon the road Upson traveled to rejoin his regiment. For a few hours he had forgotten the dirt and short rations and weary miles of marching that were so much a part of war; now, with Sherman's armies on the move, he wondered how many weeks must pass before he could enjoy another evening in a world where, as Poe would say, "The play is the tragedy, 'Man,' and its Hero the Conqueror Worm."

To Upson, jogging along in an army wagon, war seemed the one pattern dominating the first eighteen years of his life. He had grown into war naturally, as he had grown into his first pair of long pants, cutting down the passions and the prejudices of his parents to fit his size. He could remember the night in 1858 when he attended a meeting at the Baptist Church in Lima, Indiana, to hear a black man tell "awful stories about how the slaves were treated and how he ran away and was chased by great dogs called bloodhounds." Upson's reasonable boy's mind thought: "If they use the slaves that way they ought to be set free."

He remembered also the Fourth of July celebration in 1860. Phrases like "Territorial Rights" and "Bleeding Kansas" and "downtrodden slaves" rolled from everyone's lips as easily as beads of foam from a mug of beer. Ted's father, a Whig turned Free Soiler, hurrahed with the crowd for "Old Abe the Rail Splitter"; and the boy wished he could vote, for he'd "be for Lincoln sure." But nobody could stop him from tagging along behind the members of the Republican marching club, who called themselves "the Wide Awakes" and wore caps and capes of black oilcloth. The boy would see their torches flickering through the Indiana night like elephant-sized fire-flies, and his throat would grow husky and choked-up when he heard their voices booming: "John Brown's body lies molder-ing in the grave, but his soul goes marching on."

An April day in 1861 remained indelibly etched in his memory. Father and he were husking corn. A neighbor hopped across the field, as excited as a dog with a flea bite. Sumter had been fired on! In his diary the boy would write: "Father got white and couldn't say a word."

But sooner or later Ted Upson and his father must face the bitter decision. When commencement night came that year the entire audience sang "We'll hang Jeff Davis to a sour apple tree" until everyone was so hoarse that Ted could have sworn it was the sore-throat part of winter. With war meetings going on, with able-bodied boys enlisting and hurrying off to Michigan or Fort Wayne, with school out, a self-respecting lad, even if he wasn't sixteen, couldn't dodge the question forever. Why *didn't* he enlist? Under a tree where he and his father sat down to eat their dinner, the man placed his hand on his son's "and looked at me sort of queer."

"My son," the father asked, "won't you please tell me why you want to go? Surely not for the little money they will pay you as a bounty."

"Why no," Ted answered, "that never came into my mind."

"Have we not given you a good home and been kind to you?"

Ted felt "like crying." The struggle between them was as old as time; as old as a father's love for his son; as old as all the fathers who had watched their boys go off to war in ancient Carthage or Troy or Megiddo. Ted said: "You have given me a good home; you have been kinder to me than I deserve; it is not that."

His father's voice, "soft and low like," persisted: "Won't you tell me why you want to go?"

The boy could not understand why he felt scared. He rose to his feet and paced the grass beneath the tree. "Father," he would remember saying, "we must have more soldiers. This Union your ancestors and mine helped to make must be saved from destruction. I can go better than some others. I don't feel right to stay at home any longer."

The struggle was old, and so was the inevitable surrender. The father said: "If that is the way you feel about it you may go and God bless and keep you, my boy."

All the props fell from under Ted's world, he felt so "broke up." There remained nothing more to say, and they went home.

Ted Upson enlisted in the Union Army in April 1862, and in September was mustered into the 100th Indiana Regiment, joining Company C with the other boys from Lagrange County. In northern Mississippi and southwestern Tennessee and later at Collierville, Tennessee, where Union eyes watched the vital Memphis and Charleston Railroad, Ted's first recollections of the war would consist of rain, sleepless nights in the mud, and sparse meals on black "Nigger beans." Then the call came for the One Hundredth to pile into steamboats at Memphis and join Grant's army in front of Vicksburg. Here during the last torturing weeks of the siege Upson and the boys from Lagrange County prowled the countryside, looking for Confederate reinforcements under Joe Johnston. Neither Johnston nor the reinforcements crossed the Big Black where Sherman had entrenched; Vicksburg capitulated; and Upson waited four months for his first real battle. Then forty-three per cent of Upson's regiment would fall at Missionary Ridge; and he would remember going "back after some ambulances" and seeing "a pile of legs and arms as big as a haycock where they were amputating." In war, a boy grew up overnight.

Now another spring had come. As Upson rode out of Chattanooga through the full moonlight, he put the past behind him. Just what Sherman planned no one appeared to know, except that all hell apparently was fixing to break loose. Ted had stolen his evening's respite in Chattanooga, and if he knew what was good for him, he'd rejoin his regiment on the double-quick. A shortcut took him over the ground where the Battle of Chickamauga had been fought eight months before, in the first of a succession of struggles between North and South for the control of Tennessee. He reached the old battlefield, and:

> . . . I could see the broken Artillery wheels, fallen limbs of trees, scattered remnants of arms and cassions. . . . Thousands of dead hastily buried were around me. The winter rains had in many places washed off part of the thin covering, and arms and legs protruded from the ground. It was a ghastly, ghostly sight, and I should not have been surprised if I had seen ghostly forms around me, but nothing disturbed the stillness of the night but the hoot of an owl or the distant firing at Dalton miles away where our men are engaged with the enemy.

Foot Soldier Theodore Upson drove on, viewing the scene with the stoical eyes of an eighteen-year-old veteran.

2. THE LITTLE TRAGEDIES OF WAR

A LONG vigil had ended for Major James Austin Connolly. In late February Connolly had accompanied the advance forces that the Federals had pushed out as far as Ringgold, Georgia, to hold the Confederates out of Tennessee. Now, at long last, Sherman had made up his mind, and on the evening of the 6th of May Connolly could write his wife:

> Half an hour since the General said to me, "Major, be ready to march at daybreak tomorrow." I never saw

so large an army before as we have gathered here now. Last night, from the mountain top, I looked down on the camp fires of 80,000 men in the valley below me.

I went with General Sherman this morning to guide him to General Howard's headquarters. Hooker and Sickles rode by a few minutes ago. Thomas, Butterfield, Barry, Palmer, Willich, Cruft, Davis, Johnson, in fact *everybody* is here, and within three days we will be in Dalton, or badly whipped. . . .

I think Howard moves first because Sherman went to his headquarters this morning, and because most of the army correspondents are with him. . . . General Sherman looks very much like his brother John at Mansfield, but more seamed and weather-beaten. . . . I don't know when I can write you again, but hope it may be very soon, probably from Dalton. Address me as before and I'll get your letters *somewhere, sometime.*

Major Connolly's marriage fell under the classification of a war casualty. In February 1863, he had secured a short leave, rushed to Mt. Gilead, Ohio, to be married, and those few days and his letters to his wife from the battlefield constituted the sum of his wedded life. "Didn't I leave you suddenly though?" Connolly would write his bride from Nashville, virtually within hours of their briefly stolen honeymoon. But it was better, he thought, to leave "on the run" and to spare the pain of parting. "I hope you are cheerful and happy for I am," he added. "I begin to feel like a soldier again." Still, his wife had come "very near stealing me away from my allegiance and duty."

Connolly's regiment was the 123rd Illinois Infantry, and within three weeks of breaking camp the bite of enemy fire caught the 123rd Illinois at Perryville, Kentucky. Eighteen thousand Union troops fought the Rebels there, and Connolly saw every general in his division killed—Jackson by a musket ball, Terrell by a shell that tore away his chest. Both officers

fell within arm's length of Connolly; the bullets, singing over
the major's head, "sounded like a swarm of bees running away
in the hot summer air"; but Connolly had been too green at
Perryville to feel either shock or surprise, or even a sensation of
danger. The sickening sight of bodies splattered with blood, of
a face shot half away, of a dismembered hand flung against
a stone wall would impress him later; then he would want
never to fight another battle; but for the 123rd Illinois,
Perryville proved simply the prelude to Chickamauga, to
Missionary Ridge.

Major Connolly arrived in Ringgold on the 26th of February, knowing "the purple testament of bleeding war." Two
days previously he had ridden through Tunnel Hill, Georgia,
where the Western and Atlantic Railroad skirted a ridge to
join the East Tennessee and Georgia Railroad at Dalton.
There had been brisk skirmishing at Tunnel Hill, and Connolly, traveling on toward Ringgold, reached a house occupied by a widow and three little children. The woman
wept bitterly, for Union skirmishers from Tunnel Hill had
carried away everything in the house that could be eaten.
"Her children," Connolly wrote his young wife, "were hanging to her and crying as though their little hearts would break."
Connolly carried no food, but he gave the woman ten dollars,
then rode on, hating the greed, the inhumanity, the sheer
beastliness that a war produced. Then:

> . . . after dark, while we were yet lying on the field
> of the fight, a little lamb came up to me bleating most
> piteously; I took it up in my arms, petted it until it fell
> asleep like an infant, and lay sleeping on my lap an hour.
> I couldn't think of leaving it there to starve, and I
> couldn't take it with me, so I carried it to a house, about
> a half mile distant, and gave it to a little girl who promised
> to take good care of it. . . .

What war revealed of a man's character depended on the
man who went to war. Again, early in April, Connolly rode

near Tunnel Hill when he discovered a Reb "off to the left of the road, about a quarter of a mile distant, dodging along behind a fence, and running toward the mountain." The major spurred his horse over the low fence; the Reb soon gave up the chase; he surrendered, stretching out his arm as if to shake hands, and "the color was gone from his face, he shook as with an ague, but he couldn't utter a word." When at last the Confederate could speak he told a story any married man could understand, of how he had slipped away from his regiment to spend the night with his family. Touched, Connolly drove the captive past his home so that his wife might see he was unharmed. The Rebel's wife and four children rushed out; let Papa stay another night, they begged, and they would come with him in the morning and deliver him to the Yankees. Connolly looked down at the unhappy family; duty gave him no choice other than refusal; and he rode away

. . . leaving that little family alone among the frowning mountains, for grim Despair to assume the husband's place by that wife's side, and gaunt hunger to pinch the cheeks and chill the blood of those innocent children . . . are the prayers of that lonely wife for her captive husband, stealing out from that lowly dwelling, creeping up that ragged mountain side and winging their way to heaven, or are the cries of the helpless famishing children rising from that broken home and reaching to the Throne above, there to be recorded against me? . . .

The little tragedies of war, Connolly told his wife, were far more dreadful than the larger ones. But the cruelties of war recognized no national boundaries; both North and South men would call on God to support the work to which the devil drove their hands. In mid-April, Connolly would write home that he had just read the dispatch of the capture by Confederate General Forrest of Fort Pillow on the Mississippi. The garrison of some three hundred Negro soldiers had been massacred. Thus the pendulum of hatred and violence swung to and fro. Meanwhile a man went on living. The war even produced its own humor, and probably with the rest of the Union forces Connolly laughed at the wretched joke that had come out of Vicksburg concerning the major who complained that the men were stealing horses. His general replied: "Major, in war you must contend both with hostilities and horse-stealities!"

War was like the story, popular in 1864, of the little girl who was asked, on returning from a Sunday morning in church, if the minister had told her how to be good. "No," she answered, "he just preached." And war was just fought. War was a farmhouse where you could get a warm bath, an evening reading Cullum's *Art of War* until drowsiness closed your eyes over the explanation of how General Pillow had built his famous fortifications in Mexico, the language an army invented so that you were never "killed in action" but simply "gobbled." Major Connolly would write his wife, while waiting at Ringgold:

> . . . We had another April shower this afternoon; it rained quite hard for a few minutes, then the sun came out hot and in a few minutes the rain was stealing away to the clouds, like a bashful lover, after having kissed all the little flowers and caused them to blush scarlet. . . .

Now on a night in May the word had come—Sherman had reached his decision. "The army is in fine fighting condition . . . the Rebels must be whipped . . . everybody about me is bustling and hurrying. . . ." In phrases such as these Major Connolly revealed that another ingredient of war was the ability to whistle in the dark!

3. "TO KNOCK JOS. JOHNSTON"

ON THAT evening in May, William Tecumseh Sherman felt that he knew the people he had set out to conquer. In a letter to Halleck after Vicksburg he had divided the population of the South into four classes. The large planters he saw as "the ruling class . . . educated, wealthy, and easily approached . . . bitter as gall . . ." with whom "nothing but the logic of events touches their understanding." A second class of "smaller farmers, mechanics, merchants, and laborers" were "essentially tired of war, and would slink back home if they could"; this was the class the Southern politicians understood, using "them as the French do their masses—seemingly consult[ing] their prejudices, while they make their orders and enforce them." For a third class, the Union men of the South, he held little respect; they were "afraid of shadows," and "their sons, horses, arms, and everything useful are in the army against us, and they stay at home, claiming all the exemptions of peaceful citizens." A fourth class—the young bloods of the South, "men who never did work and never will" —were the real problem. Sherman told Halleck:

. . . War suits them, and the rascals are brave, fine riders, bold to rashness, and dangerous subjects in every sense. They care not a [sou] for niggers, land or anything. They hate Yankees *per se*, and don't bother their brains about the past, present, or future. . . . Stewart, John Morgan, Forrest, and Jackson, are the types and leaders of this class. These men must all be killed or employed by us before we can hope for peace. They have no property or future, and therefore cannot be influenced by anything, except personal considerations. . . .

Against this enemy, Sherman held poised for the knife-thrust into Georgia one of the finest fighting forces the Union ever had assembled. His old roommate George H. Thomas, whom Lincoln had permitted to go to Kentucky with Anderson only because of Sherman's devoted plea in his behalf, commanded the Army of the Cumberland. With 54,568 infantrymen, 2,377 men in the artillery, and 3,828 cavalrymen, Thomas's army would carry the brunt of the fighting. W. F. G. Shanks would tell the readers of *Harper's* that whereas Sherman's strength came from "the momentum resulting from the rapidity with which he moves," Thomas, moving more slowly, accomplished his purposes by "sheer strength." Shanks felt that Sherman could be called a nervous man and Thomas a man of nerve; Sherman was naturally "the dashing leader of light, flying columns" and Thomas "the director of heavily-massed columns"; Sherman's plans were "original, embracing new rules of war," and Thomas, while originating nothing, most skillfully directed "his army on well-defined principles of the art." Sherman jumped at conclusions where Thomas deliberated; one was quick and positive, the other slow but equally positive; and to sum up the two personalities, Shanks believed, Sherman could be described as "an innovator on the customs, not only of the army but of every phase of social life," and was "at least one generation ahead of the American people, fast as it imagines itself," whereas Thomas belonged "to a past generation, and his exceedingly regular habits to the 'good old times.'" Alone of the generals who would support Sherman on his drive into Georgia, Thomas refused to accept the new-fangled order to dispense with a headquarters-camp; he traveled in a big wagon converted into an office, ignoring the smart-alecks who referred to his headquarters as "Thomas's circus." But Thomas was accustomed to living comfortably, even elegantly, in camp, and he could not be changed; his habits were his virtue, for had he not made a habit of covering Rosecrans's disastrous retreats and saving the day, first at Stone River and then at Chickamauga? His was the type of ballast that Sherman needed.

To operate on Thomas's flanks, and to attack the railroads

far in the rear of the enemy, Sherman relied on the smaller Army of the Tennessee * under James B. McPherson, and the still smaller Army of the Ohio under John M. Schofield. When Dana had gone to Vicksburg to file his confidential report for the President and the Secretary of War, he had been as much impressed by McPherson as by Grant or Sherman. McPherson, who had been No. 1 in his class at West Point, and a natural engineer, was to Dana "a very handsome and gallant-looking man, with rather a dark complexion, dark eyes, and a most cordial manner." Like Grant and Sherman, McPherson was Ohio-born, another indication to Dana that these three generals "were as alike as three peas." Sherman had fought with McPherson at Vicksburg; to John he had written: "McPherson is a splendid officer."

John Schofield, who would succeed Stanton as Secretary of War under Andrew Johnson, had won Sherman's approval from the day he read newspaper reports that Buell's friends wanted Buell to replace Schofield as leader of the Army of the Ohio. "The damned newspaper mongrels," Sherman had stormed; if Schofield wanted job insurance, he could have found no better with Sherman. Schofield was West Point— in fact, he had taught there a year as professor of natural philosophy before coming to St. Louis as professor of physics at Washington University—and had been fourth in the line of heads of the Military Department of Missouri. After Vicksburg thousands of soldiers from the defeated Confederate armies had overrun Missouri with guerrilla bands; Schofield's job had been to clean them out, and clean them out he did. But Missouri was a hotbed, part pro-slave, part pro-Union, and no head of the Military Department could be popular with both factions. There had been strong agitation to remove Schofield, but Lincoln had supported him; and Sherman, reading that one of the charges against Schofield was "muz-

---

* To avoid confusion, the reader should remember that Northern armies always were named after rivers, as: "Army of *the* Tennessee," and Southern armies after states, as: "Army of Tennessee."

zling the press," must have nodded his red head with vigorous approval. Schofield could fight—that was enough for Sherman. In one month of guerrilla warfare in Missouri, often outnumbered as much as four or five to one, Schofield's cool, blond head had come through a hundred engagements.

Sherman loved columns of figures, and now to the strength of Thomas's Army of the Cumberland he added from McPherson's Army of the Tennessee 22,437 infantry, 1,404 artillery, and 624 cavalry, and from Schofield's Army of the Ohio 11,183 infantry, 679 artillery, and 1,697 cavalry. The aggregate of the three armies, as of the 1st of May, came to a fighting strength of 98,797 men, the total of heavy guns to 254. These were armies filled largely with men like Foot Soldier Theodore Upson of the 100th Indiana and Major James Austin Connolly of the 123rd Illinois. These were men Sherman understood, with whom he felt at ease; to Ellen he would write: "The soldiers think I know everything and that they can do anything."

Throughout late March and early April, as Washington buzzed with rumors of what was afoot, Grant and Sherman had agreed on a simple plan of "enlightened war" designed to squeeze the last breath of life from the Confederacy. At Grant's invitation the two warrior friends met in the Burnet House in Cincinnati. In another room Ellen and Mrs. Grant discussed babies, rising prices, and spring cleaning. The two generals waved aside the cigar smoke and studied a map of the country. With the victories at Gettysburg, Vicksburg, and Missionary Ridge, the military triumph of the North should have been assured, but instead of consolidating Yankee forces for a last smashing succession of blows, what had the idiots in Washington achieved? Looking down at the map, Grant and Sherman must have wondered if Lincoln's general staff had mistaken the war for a circus carnival! Where was the logical, concentrated effort? Nowhere! Below the Rapidan in Virginia or across the Valley of the Chickamauga dividing

Tennessee from Georgia, what did one find but a series of silly military side shows? The fighting had been permitted to go on everywhere—in Florida, in Kentucky, in the Carolinas, across the prairies of eastern Mississippi, along the coasts of Texas and deep into the Red River country of Louisiana— but what at best had any of it produced? Waste. Diversion. Breathing space for some set of tricky politicians to maneuver a negotiated peace. Look at that fool Nathaniel Banks along the Red River. Troops from one of Sherman's armies already had been withdrawn to help Banks, but suppose the Red River expedition did seize Shreveport and overrun Texas, would that end the war? The time had come to stop these scattered sallies all over the lower South as though enough of Lincoln's generals, dashing around like chickens with their heads chopped off, could conquer the Confederacy with their combined squawking!

Grant chewed his cigar and probably Sherman, as usual, consumed a box of matches trying to keep his lighted. Then two sweeps of Grant's hand cut the map in halves as though between them the two generals were dividing an apple pie. Sherman nodded. Winning the war must be reduced to two sensible, carefully integrated objectives. Whip Lee in Virginia. Smash through Johnston's Army of Tennessee to Atlanta and deprive the Richmond government of its military, agricultural, industrial, and economic reserves. Here was a kind of war that Sherman liked, a war of "blows thick and fast." Later, after Grant had reached City Point, Virginia, and Sherman had gone to Nashville, a series of letters between the two friends directed all other military operations, in Sherman's words, "to act on a common plan, converging on a common centre." For his own part, Sherman promised, he would not "let side issues" interfere with the main plan "to knock Jos. Johnston, and to do as much damage to the resources of the enemy as possible." The month of April, he thought, would be required to call in furloughed veterans, bring back two divisions of the Army of the Tennessee now operating with Banks on the Red River, and collect "provisions and cattle." From the outset Sherman planned to utilize his army as today a coach would operate a football team. Thomas would be his weight in the center of the line, hitting the enemy straight on, "fighting him cautiously, persistently, and to the best advantage." Schofield and McPherson, lighter and faster, would be his ends, breaking constantly around Johnston's flanks, bedeviling his rear, and forcing him to fall back to either the Coosa or the Chattahoochee. Sherman wrote Grant:

> Should Johnston fall behind the Chattahoochee, I will feign to the right, but pass to the left and act against Atlanta or its eastern communications, according to the developed facts.
>
> This is about as far ahead as I feel disposed to look. . . .
>
> If Banks can at the same time carry Mobile and open up the Alabama River, he will in a measure solve the most difficult part of my problem, viz., "provisions." Georgia has a million of inhabitants. If they can live, we should not starve. If the enemy interrupt our communications, I will be absolved from all obligations to subsist on our own resources, and will feel perfectly justified in taking whatever and wherever we can find.
>
> I will inspire my command, if successful, with the feeling that beef and salt are all that is absolutely necessary to life, and that parched corn once fed General Jackson's army on that very ground.

Grant, now at Culpeper Court House, Virginia, warned Sherman on the 19th of April that when the squeeze tightened from the two directions, the Confederates conceivably might withdraw from one front or the other and concentrate on smashing a single drive, "believing a single defeat without any victory to sustain them better than a defeat all along the line." Sherman had "too much experience in traveling light, and subsisting upon the country," Grant believed, "to be caught by any such *ruse*." Replying from Nashville on the 24th, Sherman felt certain that "Johnston will be compelled to hang to his railroad, the only possible avenue of supply to his army."

The question of supplies hung heavily on Sherman's mind, for on his ability to solve this problem the success of the Georgia campaign hinged. The railroads from Nashville to Decatur and Chattanooga, short of both locomotives and cars, barely supplied the daily requirements of the armies dependent on them. An invasion, however, called for the accumulation of a surplus. Sherman acted with characteristic singleness of purpose. Thomas had been using the railroads to bring in provisions for the distressed civilian population between Chattanooga and Knoxville. Sherman forbade the use of the railroads for this function, and the order, as he had anticipated, "raised a howl." Lincoln, who throughout the war felt a special affection toward the pro-Union people in Tennessee, appealed to Sherman to repeal or at least modify the order, but the only response the President elicited was a polite, firm refusal. A great campaign was impending, "on which the fate of the nation hung," Sherman argued; he could supply the armies or the civilian populations, but not both, and until he had discharged his responsibility for provisioning his armies, the people would have to haul their supplies by wagon from Kentucky.

"Mr. Lincoln seemed to acquiesce," Sherman recalled; at any rate, the order stood. To be reasonably certain of feeding his men, and after allowing "for occasional wrecks . . . and for the interruption of the road . . . by guerrillas and regular raids," Sherman estimated that he needed one hundred and thirty cars, of ten tons each, rolling into Chattanooga every day. The quartermaster wrung his hands. Between Nashville and Chattanooga there weren't enough locomotives and cars to do the job. He would require one hundred locomotives and had sixty, and the six hundred cars he now possessed should be one thousand. Sherman's jaw tilted; even with one hundred and thirty cars reaching Chattanooga daily, beef-cattle would have to be driven on the hoof and all troops except the train-guards would be forced to march. But the solution to the quartermaster's quandary was simple, Sherman thought; let him grab every locomotive and car that rolled into Nashville from Louisville. When the president of the Louisville and Nashville Railroad protested these seizures, declaring that without locomotives and cars he couldn't very well bring supplies into Nashville for shipment to Chattanooga, Sherman suggested that they both play the same game. Grab the locomotives and cars you need at Jeffersonville, Indiana, Sherman directed, and ferry them across the Ohio River. The scheme worked beautifully. "Months afterward," Sherman wrote, "I was amused to see, away down in Georgia, cars marked 'Pittsburgh & Fort Wayne,' ' Delaware & Lackawanna,' 'Baltimore & Ohio,' and . . . the names of almost every railroad north of the Ohio River."

On the 28th of April, Sherman moved his headquarters to Chattanooga, prepared "for taking the field in person." At first Grant had set April 30 as the date of the simultaneous Union movements against Virginia and Georgia, then had changed the date to May 5. By then McPherson's Army of the Tennessee was moving rapidly, on rail and foot, into Chattanooga and out toward Gordon's Mill; Thomas's Army of the Cumberland rested at Ringgold, eighteen miles from Chattanooga, with its left at Catoosa and its right at Leet's tan-yard; and Schofield's Army of the Ohio, closing upon Thomas's left, held Red Clay. Grant could not have asked for more.

In Dalton, Georgia, at that moment a worried, unhappy general paced the floor. His name was Joseph E. Johnston, and his men called him "Old Joe." The trouble in which "Old Joe" had been wallowing for the past six months certainly was not of his own making. Actually the calamity that stalked Johnston had started at Missionary Ridge, where for the second time the frail roots of Tennessee had been shaken by the hostile winds of North and South. At Missionary Ridge George H. Thomas had boxed the ears of Braxton Bragg so soundly that Bragg forgot he recently had joined the church, and his soldiers heard him "cursing like a sailor."

4. "UNFIT FOR ACTIVE SERVICE"

BRAXTON BRAGG, flushed with his new religion, felt that he fought on God's side when on the morning of November 25, 1863, he surveyed the situation at Missionary Ridge. After three days the fighting that had seared the slopes of Lookout Mountain and flamed through Orchard Knob was now centered on Missionary Ridge, where Bragg's men crouched in three rows of rifle pits. Bragg considered his position impregnable, the victory of the sometimes euphemistically misnamed Battle above the Clouds within grasp. The name, Grant would say, was "all poetry," and so, too, was Bragg's growing confidence. His position was extremely perilous, for he stood separated from his supply depot by the deep-flowing Chickamauga Creek, and both flanks were dangerously exposed.

From daylight to three in the afternoon, Sherman hammered at the Confederate flank with six divisions, charging the rugged slopes, fighting bayonet to bayonet, hand to hand. With only one grayback division, spunky Pat Cleburne held Sherman off, raining down shell and canister; when the guns no longer could be swung into position, heavy boulders bounced down the slopes to crack open Union heads. Sherman kept on, grim and puzzled, wondering why the support of a simultaneous assault by Thomas didn't materialize; then, by mid-afternoon, Cleburne's withering fire began to tell and Sherman reeled backward to nurse the bruises of flesh and spirit.

Grant gnawed his lip. He saw Sherman thrown back. Hooker, who had been ordered to come out of the valley and strike the ridge, needed simply to bleat to complete his role of a lost sheep meandering aimlessly among the crooks and hollows of Chattanooga Creek. If Grant wasn't swearing, he should have been. Acting with the desperation of the moment, he ordered Thomas to take his twenty thousand men up the center of the two-hundred-foot ridge as far as the first row of rifle pits and wait for instructions. Thomas swept forward, routed the Rebels in a quick skirmish, halted. From above, the other two rows of riflemen popped away briskly. Yankees started dropping with bullets through an arm or leg, throat or chest. A growl among Thomas's men rolled into a roar. To hell with this. Orders or no orders, they weren't standing there to be picked off like flies on a cow's rump. If those bastards on that ridgeside wanted a fight they could damn well have it. Raging mad, Thomas's boys started after the next row of rifle pits.

Bragg couldn't believe his eyes. Nothing could stop Thomas. Straight up the center of the ridge, slipping past ravines and swales, the angry Union men stormed through, taking the second row of pits, overrunning the third, while Bragg would report that "A panic which I had never before witnessed seemed to have seized upon officers and men, and each appeared to be struggling for his personal safety, regardless of his duty and his character." Bragg might have lumped himself with those willing to run for any cover, for he would write Jefferson Davis, as though to place the blame elsewhere: "Breckinridge was totally unfit for any duty from the 23rd to the 27th—during all our trials—from drunkenness." The South, listening to Bragg, remembered Lee after Pickett's charge had failed at Gettysburg. Lee had stood at the front, rallying his bleeding boys as they fell back: "Don't be discouraged. It was my fault this time. All good men must hold together now." Lee, the soldier and gentleman! The South's tight-lipped refusal to believe that everyone but the commander at Missionary Ridge had failed staggered and stung Bragg. In his miserable humiliation he resigned his command of the Army of Tennessee.

For Jefferson Davis each hour seemed to create a new bedevilment. Seated at the rosewood table where the President often liked to work, it was no great problem to scrawl an acceptance to Bragg's resignation; but Davis was fond of Braxton, could overlook the comment of one Richmond observer that Bragg was "like a good dog howling on his hind legs," and had no wish to lose the general's services permanently. So Davis avoided this dilemma by appointing Bragg to his staff as a special military adviser. The anti-Davis faction, increasing steadily as one weary war year piled upon another, stirred with excitement. Wrote Edward A. Pollard in the *Richmond Examiner:* "This happy announcement should enliven the confidence and enthusiasm reviving among the people like a bucket of water on a newly kindled fire." Even a friend in the War Department felt a need to admit that the President's handling of the Bragg case had been "a little oppugnant."

Davis ignored Pollard's sneering. When troubles were multiplying faster than guinea pigs, he certainly couldn't waste time with the runts and sports. His immediate concern now was finding a new commander for the Army of Tennessee. The logical choice would have been General William J. Hardee, who had ranked next to Bragg, but Hardee had been through enough at Chickamauga and Missionary Ridge not to wish the appointment "if designed to be permanent," and James A. Seddon, fifth in the line of Secretaries that had whisked in and out of the War Department, would report that Davis, irked by Hardee's "distrust of himself," dismissed the thought of his selection as "hazardous and unwise." Under Grant's steady pressure, affairs in Tennessee and Georgia had reached a state where they preyed on the President's mind until this theater of war now impressed him as requiring "the best commander." Would Lee consider it? Lee would not, reminding the President that he was then commanding the Army of Northern

Virginia. Lee proposed Beauregard, but Davis's nerves were frayed to the point where he found it difficult to accept both a rebuff and a suggestion. The time had come when the ministerial conscience of Leonidas Polk directed that he must speak. The command obviously belonged to Joseph E. Johnston, and though Polk knew that Davis, Seddon, and other members of the Cabinet disliked "Old Joe" because of what ex-Secretary of War Judah Benjamin had described as "tendencies to defensive strategy," Polk literally wagged his Bishop's finger at Davis as he warned that

> When there is so general a desire on the part of the army and country as there is to have General Johnston placed in that command, a part of your duty seems to your friend to be to yield to this general desire, that those whose all is staked upon the issue may have something to say as to the hand in which it shall be saved or lost.

Neither Davis nor Seddon were happy with the thought of Johnston as commander of the Army of Tennessee, and likely both wished that Polk would tend to his business in Mississippi. Even Seddon's Virginia-bred tactfulness—surely of superior dimensions, since it kept him in office as Secretary of War longer than the combined services of his four predecessors—had grown ruffled with Johnston during the Vicksburg campaign. "Old Joe's" attitude then clearly had been that Pemberton was something of a fool for not abandoning Vicksburg and saving his army, and, in the same spirit, he stoically had refused to lead his inferior forces across the Big Black for Sherman to slaughter. What could his twenty-three thousand men hope to achieve against total Federal forces of sixty thousand? Goaded by Davis, Seddon's wire to attack had said tartly: ". . . it is better to fail nobly daring than, through prudence even, to be inactive." Johnston, equally tart, had replied that there had been "no voluntary inaction"; only a damned simpleton wasted lives that could be spared. The failures of Vicksburg lingered like a wound in Richmond memories, but Polk had salved the outward sting, and the command of the Army of Tennessee went to Johnston even though Seddon confessed that Davis held "doubt and misgiving to the end." In an atmosphere ostensibly pleasant, but bristling underneath with mistrust, Johnston set off for Dalton in December of '63.

No matter what misgivings the President, the Secretary of War, and the Richmond cabinet secretly held, the South believed in "Old Joe." With the first verified news of secession Johnston, then stationed in Washington as Quartermaster General of the United States Army, had resigned. "Free government," he would declare, "is founded on the consent of the governed, and . . . every community strong enough to establish and maintain its independence has the right to assert it." As a brigadier general Johnston would claim prominence as the officer in the Army relinquishing the highest rank to join the Confederacy, and he felt keenly the sting of Northern editors and politicians who accused him of perjury in breaking his oath of allegiance. "The acceptance of an officer's resignation absolves him from the obligation of his military oath as completely as it releases the government from that of giving him the pay of the grade he held," he retorted stiffly. But to his friends he confessed that he had been "determined to return to the State of which I was a native, join the people among whom I was born, and live with my kindred, and, if necessary, fight in their defense."

Johnston came down to Dalton, feeling that he had demonstrated his fitness to command. At Manassas he had slipped through the Shenandoah Valley with eleven thousand men to join Beauregard and supply the crushing power to the Confederate punch. At the Battle of Seven Pines, where McClellan's dreams on the Peninsula ended, Johnston had opposed a numerically superior Union army that almost had glimpsed the church spires of Richmond. Recovering from wounds at Seven Pines, Johnston next appeared in Chattanooga to command military operations between the mountains and the Mississippi River. With Grant on the prowl, with Bragg at Murfreesboro watching what move Rosecrans would make southward from Nashville, with Pemberton holding Vicksburg, Johnston looked over a vast territory and saw his armies so threatened both in Tennessee and in Mississippi that neither could reinforce the other. The solution obviously must rest with the inactive Army of Arkansas; but General T. C. Hindman disliked the order that would send him with ten thousand men to assist Pemberton. He decided first to have one more fling against the Yankees at Prairie Grove, and was defeated with such staggering losses that no troops remained to travel east of the Mississippi. Thus Johnston became stymied; either Bragg must reinforce Pemberton's army or Pemberton must reinforce Bragg's, and in either case Peter would be robbed to pay Paul; Johnston bickered with Davis over transferring eight thousand men from Bragg to Pemberton and the President ignored his objections. There followed the hard, bitter campaign to defend Vicksburg.

The basis of the emotional rift between Davis and Johnston belonged to the earliest days of the war. As a brigadier general upon resigning from the United States Army, Johnston's rank among Southern generals could be considered either first or fourth, depending on whether he was ranked by detail or according to his permanent lineal rank. The President decided to place him fourth. So wounds had accumulated between Davis and the new commander of the Army of Tennessee— wounds that would itch and burn with almost every change of temperature. Two days after Johnston's arrival at Dalton a letter from the Secretary of War did not ease the festering tension.

"It is apprehended," wrote Seddon, in part, "the army may have been, by recent events, somewhat disheartened, and deprived of ordinance and material. . . . It is desired that your early and vigorous efforts be directed toward restoring the discipline, prestige, and confidence of the army . . .

and, as soon as the condition of your forces will allow, it is hoped you will be able to resume the offensive."

Johnston felt irritated; the letter supplied nothing in the way of military instruction; but still it must be answered. He decided to reply "gravely," informing Seddon that after forty-eight hours in Dalton he estimated the enemy strength at eighty thousand, and that because of the heavy rains he had found "the country unfit for military operations." After a routine discussion of the problems of supply, Johnston penned two sentences that must have chilled Seddon's heart, stimulated as it so clearly was by an aggressive ardor:

> This army is now far from being in condition to "resume the offensive." It is deficient in numbers, arms, subsistence stores, and field transportation.

Now Davis posted a letter that irked Johnston even more than Seddon's meaningless epistle. If the President's communication possessed a military object, the general at Dalton obviously felt that he must possess a crystal ball to divine it. Davis quoted the report of his aide-de-camp, Colonel Ives, who recently had been to Dalton; Ives had told him the army was in good spirit, that he might take "a not unfavorable view of the material of the command." Johnston's mouth tightened; did the President think he "was to be taught the moral and military condition of the army" by someone like Ives "who had never seen military service"? With a burst of pleasant optimism, Davis continued: "I assure you that nothing shall be wanting on the part of the Government to aid you in your efforts to regain the territory from which we have been driven." In God's name, what did the President expect? What "forward movement" had the army been able to make two months earlier, *before* Sherman had reinforced the Federals with twenty thousand veterans from Mississippi, *before* Longstreet had withdrawn his corps of about fourteen thousand of the best Confederate troops, *before* the losses at Missionary

Ridge? Apparently neither the President nor the Secretary of War bothered to compare notes; Seddon admitted that the army had suffered depletions of men, morale, and material, while Davis chattered blandly of "the effective condition" of the army as "a matter of much congratulation"! But of all the statements in the President's letter which could lead Johnston to speculate as to whether Davis now lived in a world of fantasy, none equaled this astonishing claim:

> . . . the morning reports exhibited an effective total, that, added to the two brigades last sent from Mississippi, and the cavalry sent back by Longstreet, would furnish a force exceeding in number that actually engaged in any battle on the Confederate side during the present war. . . .

Johnston writhed. The Army of Tennessee was "the remnant of that which fought at Chickamauga and Missionary Ridge." A schoolboy with a slate and a knowledge of simple ciphering could have estimated the difference. Eighteen thousand men had been lost at Chickamauga, at least seventeen thousand at Missionary Ridge, and more than fifteen thousand had been sent to other corps (to Ector's and McNair's, in addition to Longstreet's). "The two brigades last sent from Mississippi" totaled three thousand; and at best, Johnston reckoned, "four thousand of the fugitives at Missionary Ridge had rejoined their regiments at Dalton." Thus losses and withdrawals aggregated forty thousand, against seven thousand replacements, so that the army's "effective total" scarcely exceeded half the number at Chickamauga. "Old Joe" fumed to himself, then wrote the President an exceedingly courteous reply:

> Your Excellency well impresses upon me the importance of recovering the territory we have lost. I feel it deeply, but difficulties appear to me in the way.
> . . . I can see no other mode of taking the offensive

here, than to beat the enemy when he advances, and then move forward. But, to make victory probable, the army must be strengthened. A ready mode of doing this would be by substituting Negroes for all the soldiers on detached or daily duty, as well as company cooks, pioneers, and laborers for engineer service. This would give us at once ten or twelve thousand men. . . .

Johnston saw the army's base at Dalton as containing "neither intrinsic strength nor strategic advantage." The position represented no plan, but merely the point where the retreat from Missionary Ridge had ceased and huts for the winter had been constructed. "Old Joe's" trained military eyes looked dubiously at the spot three and a half miles beyond Dalton where the railroad from Atlanta to Chattanooga passed through Rocky Faced Ridge by Mill Creek Gap. The course of the road he calculated at about thirty degrees west of north, that of the ridge at about five degrees east of north. At once danger signals flew up in his mind. The ridge, terminating but three miles north of the gap, offered little obstacle to the advance of a superior force from Ringgold to Dalton. Between Mill Creek and Snake Creek Gaps the ridge might protect the road to Atlanta on the west, but the ridge also covered any direct approach from Chattanooga to Resaca or Calhoun, vital points on the route from Dalton to Atlanta. And what of flank movements in that direction by an army in front of Mill Creek Gap? All of Johnston's military instincts warned him to get out of Dalton, to withdraw his troops to Calhoun and free that exposed left flank, but he was thwarted by "the earnestness with which the President and the Secretary of War . . . wrote of early assumption of offensive operations and apprehension of the bad effect of a retrograde movement upon the spirit of the Southern people."

Peeved at Seddon and Davis, held at Dalton in a position not to be trusted, Johnston sweated out the winter months of '64. Every inspection he made of the Army of Tennessee depressed him more. The horses of the cavalry and artillery, the mules for the wagon trains, were largely "unfit for active service," and the only forage the commissary could provide consisted of "weevil-eaten" corn. Not only were blankets scarce, but, he would recall, "it was painful to see the number of bare feet in every regiment." The infantry lacked six thousand small arms; the artillery horses, in early February, still were too feeble to draw the Napoleon guns "up a trifling hill."

But Johnston refused to be defeated by these internal problems. Shoes were secured when the blockade runner *Giraffe* arrived from Nassau. Johnston appealed to Governor Brown of Georgia, and soon more food moved over the tracks of the Western and Atlantic Railroad. Brown sent Johnston two regiments of state militia, a nice complement to the five thousand absentees who, by the end of winter, had been brought back to the army by the establishment of a reasonable system of furloughs. The troops of the Army of Tennessee, now better fed and better clothed, openly admired their new commander. Certainly some cheering note was needed; northern Georgia struggled through a cold winter with the temperature falling to three degrees below zero. Snow fell heavily in March.

Trouble of a serious politico-military nature soon threatened Johnston from two directions. In early February, Polk notified Johnston that Sherman was moving eastward from Vicksburg with thirty-five thousand infantry and artillery. In Richmond, in Dalton, at Polk's headquarters in Mississippi, the lights burned at night as tired eyes studied the military maps. Sherman, crossing the Pearl River at Jackson, moved along the railroad toward Meridian with Mobile as his apparent objective. Davis and Johnston quarreled by telegraph for a week as to whether the Army of Tennessee could afford to. reinforce Polk in Mississippi; then, with the greatest reluctance, Johnston sent Hardee to Polk's assistance with the divisions of Cheatham, Cleburne, and Walker.

Grant had sent Thomas to Knoxville with every troop that could be spared from Chattanooga "to cooperate with the Army of the Ohio in driving Longstreet from East Tennessee," but within twenty-four hours Grant countermanded that order and veered Thomas's direction "to gain possession of Dalton, and as far south of that as possible." Meanwhile Sherman passed Meridian, destroyed the town, and then turned back toward Vicksburg, leaving everything up in the air in Mississippi. Hardee's troops swiveled back for Dalton, and Johnston prayed that they marched on the double-quick, for scouts reported the Federals stretched from Chattanooga to Ringgold, with another large force moving from Cleveland to Red Clay. Late in February the inevitable happened—the Union troops struck Johnston's weak left flank at Mill Creek Gap—and only Hardee's divisions, reaching the scene at the high tide of battle, saved the Confederates and forced Thomas back to Chattanooga.

Thus Johnston eased out of his first threat of trouble. The second, the arrival of John Bell Hood to command a corps under Johnston, possessed a different stripe. In this conflict a very delicate balance was involved—the emotions of Hood, Davis, and Johnston.

5. "THE PALADIN OF THE FIGHT"

OFFICIAL Richmond adored Hood, who had lost the use of his left arm at Gettysburg and suffered the amputation of his right leg after Chickamauga. Since West Point, Hood had been called Sam, a nickname of affection, and the sentimental streak of this Texan-by-adoption grew as tall as a Texas story. He would remember when the Minié ball pierced his leg that "I turned from my horse upon the side of the crushed limb and fell—strange to say, since I was commanding five divisions—into the arms of some of the troops of my old brigade." He gave the scene the touching sadness of a steel engraving in *Harper's*, recalling almost at once that "this noble brigade" had fought from "the hour of its first encounter with the enemy at Eltham's Landing, on York River, in 1862" with "signal achievements . . . never . . . surpassed in the history of nations." Who but his brigade had marched as the advance guard when Jackson had moved upon McClellan? What other brigade among Longstreet's Corps more often was foremost in an attack or pursuit of the enemy? Hood rapsodized: "If a ditch was to be leaped, or fortified position to be carried, General Lee knew no better troops on which to rely." To a South that had sung the mournful words of *Lorena* until its heart was almost wrung dry, Hood was a fine symbol of the chivalry it adored and which justified so many sacrifices.

Mary Boykin Chestnut would describe Hood in her witty, candid *A Diary from Dixie* as she first met him in Richmond after Sam had received the two stars of a major general at the request of Saint Stonewall:

> When he came with his sad face—the face of an old crusader who believed in his cause, his cross and his crown—we were not prepared for that type of beau ideal of wild Texans. He is tall, thin, shy, with blue eyes and light hair, a tawny beard and a vast amount of it covering the lower part of his face. He wears an appearance of awkward strength. Someone said that his great reserve of manner he carried only into the society of ladies. Mr. Venable added that he himself had often heard of the light of battle shining in a man's eyes, but he had seen it only once. He carried orders to Hood from General Lee, and found him in the hottest of the fight. The man was transfigured. "The fierce light of his eyes," said Mr. Venable, "I can never forget."

Thus Sam Hood captivated even the wary Mrs. Chestnut. In November 1863 Hood was back in Richmond, waiting

for his surgeon-general to slip through the blockade to Paris
and bring him "three cork legs, and a diamond ring." Romance encircled the hero's head with a halo of purity or the
thorny crown of jealousy, depending on the circumstances.
Rumors long had persisted that Sam liked to court the girls,
almost indiscriminately, although the whispers now were that
the engagement ring he had ordered was intended for beautiful Louly Wigfall. Mrs. Chestnut sent the wounded man a
rice pudding, and Sally Preston, daughter of General John S.
Preston, told her spitefully: "I never cared particularly about
him, but now that he has chosen to go with those people, I
would not marry him if he had a thousand legs, instead of
having just one." Mrs. Chestnut raised her brows. Marry him?
"But I asked no questions," she confided to her diary.

Louly was the daughter of Senator Louis Wigfall, and, in
the judgment of sober Senator Herschel V. Johnson, it was the
"Wigfalls, and Toombs and Brown" who followed a course
"calculated to destroy the confidence of the people in the
government" so that they might lead a "counter-revolution."
Suddenly, around Christmas time, Sam's romance with Louly
floundered, and many saw cupid's bow snapped across Hood's
knee out of loyalty to Davis. Or out of ambition. Still, married
to D. Giraud Wright and publishing *A Southern Girl in '61*
forty years later, Louly would write of Sam: "A braver man, a
purer patriot, a more gallant soldier never breathed." Hood
drew people to him, Mrs. Chestnut would observe, "as if he
were the Prince of Wales's new-born baby."

Sam basked in his Richmond popularity, felt his leg mending, began riding again in mid-January, and often was
accompanied on these gallops by Davis. The President's "wonderful nerve and ability, displayed at a most trying epoch in
our history, commanded my admiration," he would recall.
Perhaps thinking of the Wigfalls, he added: "He was not only
battling with enemies abroad, but with a turbulent Congress
at home." In September, Longstreet had recommended Hood's
promotion to lieutenant general, and in writing Wigfall for an

endorsement Seddon had said: "He is a true hero, and was the Paladin of the fight." Sam Hood held the affection of both the President and the Secretary of War; if Johnston still placed store on that accomplishment, he might have admired Hood for this at least. Hood possessed dash, rash courage, a restless will; but frequently he was headstrong rather than thoughtful, often intuitive without the brilliant originality that saved Sherman.

If Davis and Seddon had been more astute in their judgment of men, they would have recognized instantly that "Old Joe" and Sam never had been intended for military wedlock. When on the 4th of February Hood, raised to a lieutenant general, reported at Dalton, Johnston's sixth sense, if he had one, must have begun vibrating. About the only virtue Johnston and Hood could claim in common was the human trait of rationalization, for each would devote the remainder of his life to judging himself right and the other wrong. Hood thought and lived in purple passages, Johnston in simple prose; Hood fought to win and Johnston to endure until he could calculate the cost of victory.

The dissension between Hood and Johnston quickly ignited. Disliking Dalton as a base, watching Thomas advancing from Chattanooga, Johnston had thought of falling back on Calhoun; Hood had believed in standing pat, in slugging it out. In his ears his tender parting with General Breckinridge in Richmond rang like a golden note from a lost past. "My dear Hood," Breckinridge had said in the saccharine mood of the moment, "here you are beloved by your fellow-soldiers, and, although badly shattered, with the comfort of having done noble service, and without trouble or difficulty with any man." Hood had believed every sentimental word Breckinridge had uttered; "but alas," he would write in later years, "after a journey over the smooth sea for many days—aye three years —a storm suddenly arose." To associate Johnston with a "storm" was the most belligerent quality either Hood or Richmond ever would attribute to him; it was because Hood saw

Johnston as the calm, and not the tempest raging to drive the enemy to the Ohio River as Davis and Seddon yearned, that the bitterness between them deepened.

Into Johnston's not-oversympathetic ear Hood poured arguments to support the Davis and Seddon dream. Polk's forces should be joined with the Army of Tennessee, Johnston should march around Chattanooga, effect a juncture with Longstreet somewhere between Chattanooga and Knoxville, and swarm over the Federals. Johnston heartily approved of the suggestion that Polk and Longstreet should reinforce him—but at Dalton. Davis boiled with the passion for recovering Middle Tennessee and Bragg wrote Johnston on the 4th of March: "It is hoped but little time will be required to prepare the force now under your command, as the season is at hand, and the time seems propitious." Johnston responded that if a "particular plan of operations" had been prepared "it has not been communicated to me." With obvious pique he reminded Bragg that under the regulations of the War Department plans should be prepared in Richmond and not in the field. Was it possible that the enemy's force would increase during the spring or be diminished in May or June by expiration of terms of service? Let Bragg answer that question and a policy could be formulated. For a postscript Johnston saved his most ominous note: "Should Sherman join Thomas, this army would require reenforcements to enable it to hold its ground."

Davis prodded both Seddon and Bragg. Chickamauga and Missionary Ridge were all the failures the Confederacy could afford in the struggle to control Tennessee. Now Bragg wrote Johnston that for a third effort to wrest Tennessee from the Federals by drawing troops from Polk, Beauregard, and Longstreet, Johnston's fighting force could be increased to seventy-five thousand. The more the better, "Old Joe" might have answered, for he was beset with worries of his own. Grant was at Nashville, Sherman by last reports had reached Memphis, and Johnston wired Bragg: "Where Grant is, we must expect the great Federal effort." In a letter, Johnston reminded Bragg that Grant hadn't returned to Tennessee to stand on the defensive; Knoxville, he argued, could never be isolated "because we cannot hope to be able to take with us such supplies as would enable us to remain on the line of communication long enough to *incommode* the forces there"; since Grant would be ready to act first, "our first object should be . . . to bring on a battle on this side of the Tennessee"; and he urged the quick movement of Polk from Mississippi.

Bragg wired back on the 21st of March:

> Recent Northern papers report Grant superseded Halleck, who becomes chief of staff. Sherman takes Grant's command. Your dispatch of the 19th does not indicate an acceptance of the plan proposed [i.e., to join Polk and Longstreet for the attack in Middle Tennessee]. The troops can only be drawn from other points for an advance. Upon your decision on that point further action must depend.

Johnston replied at once, using cipher for the words indicated by italics:

> In my dispatch of the 18th I expressly accept *taking the offensive*. Only differ with you as to details. I assume the enemy will be prepared *to advance before we are*, and will make it to our advantage. Therefore I propose, as necessary both for offensive and defensive, to *assemble our troops here* immediately. Other preparations *for advance* going on.

Bragg paid no heed to "this explanation." Johnston fretted over the silence in Richmond and over scouting reports that the Federals "were assembling in our front a much greater force than that which had driven us from Missionary Ridge a few months before." On the 8th of April Johnston's patience could endure no more and his old friend, Colonel B. S. Ewell, was sent to Richmond to tell Bragg what he had meant and "to endeavor to remove any misapprehension of the subject that might exist in his Excellency's mind." From Richmond a day or two later came General Pendleton, sent by Davis "to explain his Excellency's wishes in relation to the employment of the Army of Tennessee, and to ascertain if I was willing to assume the offensive with an army weaker by six thousand men" than proposed in Bragg's estimate of seventy-five thousand. Pendleton and Ewell returned to their bases having accomplished nothing. Later Johnston would stand accused "of disobeying the orders of the President and the entreaties of General Bragg to assume the offensive." Unknown to "Old Joe," Sam Hood would write the President privately, in March: "I am eager for us to take the initiative."

The scouting jitters of April grew into well-founded suspicions in early May. Bragg felt Johnston was "deceived" by no more than "*mere demonstrations,* made for the purpose," when he reported close enemy reconnaissance at Tunnel Hill, the Federals repairing the railroad from Chattanooga to Ringgold. Johnston calculated his fighting strength: 36,652 infantry, 2,812 artillery, 2,392 cavalry—41,856 against Sherman's 98,000! Johnston drew a deep breath and wired Richmond to send him half of Polk's infantry. On the 5th of May a telegram from Polk announced that he had been ordered to join the Army of Tennessee with *all* his infantry. "Old Joe" needed a fighting man who also knew how to pray. On reaching Georgia, Bishop Polk baptized Hood. The water sprinkled on Hood's head did not lessen his animosity toward Johnston, but the Confederate soldier in the ranks, needing a blanket, sometimes barefooted and hungry, understood nothing of the conflict among his commanders.

6. "A FACE LESS PLUTONIAN"

In their winter huts at Dalton, where, as John Alcée Augustin of New Orleans would versify,

> Our bugles had roused up the camp,
>> The heavens looked dismal and dirty,
> The earth was unpleasant and damp,
>> Like a maid on the wrong side of thirty—,

the Confederate soldiers nursed their wounds and bruised pride after Missionary Ridge and waited for the sudden cold blasts to subside. Augustin scribbled his verses, later to be set to music and published at Augusta under the truthful title of *Short Rations*. Dedicated "To the Corn-fed Army of Tennessee," the song accepted cheerfully the privations well known to the men "in the field near Dalton" during the dreary January days of '64. Under the pseudonym of "Ye Tragic," Augustin's rollicksome lines proclaimed:

> Tell me not of the Lacedemonian,
>> Of his black broth and savage demeanor,
> We carry a face less Plutonian,
>> But I swear our corn coffee is meaner!
> Tell me nothing of ancients and strangers,
>> For on seeing our Southern-bred Catos,
> I have laughed at old Marion's rangers
>> Who feasted on roasted potatoes!

Augustin's lyrics invited "Fair ladies and maids of all ages," home guards, newspaper editors, legislators, staff officers, and "fobs of the nation," to "Come list to my song of starvation." He laughed at the thought that rations had been reduced at all, asking: "We had one meal a day, it was small, are we now, holy Gods, to have none?" "Erewhiles," Augustin wrote, the army had enjoyed "chickens and roasters," which were "sent

68

to long pater nosters," and "the deed was not stamped as atrocious." He pictured how the times had changed:

> But since men have been shot for the same,
>> We parch corn, it is healthier, but tougher;
> The chickens and pigs have got tame,
>> But the horses and mules have to suffer!

Closing on an optimistic note, Augustin maintained that the "Corn-fed" was "proof to all evils"; the "Corn-fed" could oke at hardships and troubles, for

> He is bound to be free, and he knows it,
>> Then what cares he for toil and privation!
> He is brave, and in battle he shows it,
>> And will conquer in spite of starvation.

In a less optimistic mood, Captain Thomas J. Key, who commanded a battery of artillery in Pat Cleburne's division, lived through the winter at Dalton. After twenty months of separation from his family, Key saw the war as a tiring, lonely ordeal that appeared "to have demoralized everyone" when "the girls smoke and chew tobacco and drink whiskey as if they are fond of the article." If rumor could be trusted, Key said, "almost half of the women in the vicinity of the army, married and unmarried, are lost to all virtue." The country around Dalton he found "worth but little," the natives "illiterate and of the poorer class." Key was a deeply religious man; he had read through the New Testament and the Psalms three times during '63 and now studied the writings of Bishop Morris, pondering such Wesleyan precepts as "He who lives not by rule, lives not at all." When the thermometer dropped toward zero, Key wrapped up in a Yankee overcoat purchased from the battlefield of Missionary Ridge. Overcoats sold for from two hundred to three hundred dollars, onions for two dollars a dozen, eggs for three dollars a dozen, supporting the popular Richmond quip that Mrs. Chestnut reported: "You take your money to market in the market basket, and bring home what you buy in your pocketbook."

Captain Key had been educated at LaGrange College, had brought the *Day Book* (more often called the *Franklin County Democrat*) in Tuscumbia, Alabama, and had gone to the Kansas Territory in 1856 to establish the *Kansas Constitutionalist* at Doniphan. His stanch convictions of a Southern Democrat were certain to lead him into trouble in a country where the issue of slavery was bursting into flame. Key attended the Lecompton Convention, bridled when the Lecompton Constitution was rejected, dripped with rage every time the abolitionist-inspired elements tossed both him and his press into the river, and retraced his way south to Helena, Arkansas. As a member of the state legislature he would vote "aye" for secession, but, having a wife and three children, he put off enlisting until the spring of '62. Then the Battle of Shiloh, where he went to claim the body of a cousin killed in action, decided him. Soon he was in the thick of the fighting in northern Mississippi, in Kentucky, at Murfreesboro, Chickamauga, and Missionary Ridge. His promotion to captain came after Missionary Ridge; there, no longer able to swing his guns into position, Key had been one of the sweating soldiers who had rolled down stones on the heads of Sherman's men as they tried to scale the ridgeside and crack Bragg's flank.

Throughout the winter months at Dalton, when Key wasn't studying Bishop Morris or reading a translation from the Italian of Botta's *History of the American Revolution*, he pored over newspapers and tried to gauge the Northern attitude toward the war. In December he would gloat over an article in the *Memphis Appeal* that waded "into the Lincoln despotism ungloved" and denounced "the test oaths required in the recent elections in the State of Delaware"; but the reports in January depressed him. By a vote of 152 to 1 the Northern Congress "had passed a resolution that it is the duty of Congress to furnish all the men and means that their government may require to crush the rebellion," and, over a motion for tabling, Smith of Kentucky also had pushed through a resolution "that no armistice or proposition for peace should be received as long as a Rebel is in arms," by a vote of 93 to 64. Gloomily, Key thought: "Congress is determined to prosecute the war to the bitter end." Even General Lucius Polk felt despondent, telling Key that Southern independence now could only be obtained "by a revolution in the North or by aid from some foreign power." Society seemed to have reached a disgusting level, Key would reflect; look how the girls enjoyed a man's arm around their waists or necks! If Key had not been convinced earlier that the North was "bent on subjugation," he had only to read, later in January, of how Congress had handled a resolution by Dawson of Pennsylvania denying that the war was waged for conquest and "requesting the President to issue a proclamation that when any State in insurrection shall agree to submit to the Federal Government, hostilities against such State shall cease and she shall be protected against all interference with her local laws and institutions." Dawson's resolution had been tabled by a vote of 79 to 58! The doctrine of miscegenation, espoused by the New York correspondent of the *London Times*, so scandalized Key that his heart yearned "to sweep from the face of the earth the base and amorous race of Puritans which has so degraded itself and villified and slandered the Southern ladies." The mere thought of the mixture of races—and miscegenation implied especially the sexual union of whites with Negroes—left Key writhing:

> Is it surprising that the Southron, whose veins throb with the proud blood of the Anglo-Saxons, should fight with double daring, fearless of death, when he remembers that if the Yankee subjugate his country his sister, wife, and mother are to be given up to the embraces of their present "dusky male servitors"?

At the moment, however, a virtual intellectual revolution was sweeping the Army of Tennessee on the Negro question, and its agitator was Key's division commander, General Patrick Cleburne. Born in Ireland, educated at the University

71

of Dublin, Pat Cleburne brought to the South the passionate affection of an adopted son without the inheritance of her inborn prejudices on the slavery question. Cleburne sought out Key in his tent one cold December day to tell him the proposal he had made at Johnston's staff meeting. He would at once bring three hundred thousand Negroes into the service! How? By an Emancipation Act on the part of the Confederacy which would make Lincoln's Emancipation Proclamation worthless and "at once take the wind out of the sails of Northern Abolitionists." General T. C. Hindman, Colonel D. C. Govan, General Lucius Polk, General William Hardee, even General John Breckinridge, Pat Cleburne said, had gone along with his general principles, though Breckinridge had seemed to hedge over whether the time had yet arrived for bringing the Negro into the army. Key himself felt inclined to hedge; Cleburne's proposal would "make or ruin the South" and either "conclude the war speedily or cause blood to flow more freely than heretofore."

Key discussed the plan with Charles Swett, another captain of the artillery. Hell, Swett implied, "he wanted his Negro women to keep his wife from the wash tub"; but later Swett admitted that he did not value his slaves above a "dime each" and would free them "to close the war and give us liberty." Thus Pat Cleburne began to win converts; the general confided to Key that he had been to Mobile in January, had spoken to many of the wealthy men of Alabama on the subject, and had found a number who "advocated the measure and believed that it would redound to the advantage of the South." Actually the assent to Cleburne's proposal among Johnston's top officers wasn't so enthusiastic as the Irishman intimated to Key; Johnston refused to transmit the plan to Davis, but General W. H. T. Walker considered it so "incendiary" that he forwarded a copy to Richmond. Davis and Seddon frothed; Cleburne's idea, Davis believed, invited "discouragement, destruction, and dissension"; Key would report that the President's letter in reply stressed that "the matter should not be agitated." The vindictive streak running through Richmond, with the split for and against Davis, leaped on any new flurry; many believed that Cleburne's contribution to this unrest cost him a promotion from major general to lieutenant general. Too late, Davis would be favoring in 1865 much of what Pat Cleburne had proposed!

The Army of Tennessee stirred as spring slipped over the mountains into Dalton. Humors improved. The standard joke was to swear you had seen vermin with "I. W." stamped on their rears, meaning, of course, that they were "in for the war." In mid-April, surrounded by hundreds of ladies, "Old Joe" reviewed his army amid the "notes of the shrill fife and bass drums." Dams built on the creek between Dalton and Tunnel Hill so retarded the water that the valleys overflowed and promised to mire any Yankee advance from Ringgold. Still, rumors of bigger Federal concentrations persisted and the scent of war was on the warming breezes. Three hundred Tennesseeans joined the church and Key was delighted that "there appears to be a wonderful reform among the soldiery, for they are leaving off card playing, profanity, and other vices, and are humbling themselves before God." Key read *General Orders for 1863* and Ander's *Artillery Drill*. On May 1 the newspapers carried the House speech of Harris of Maryland favoring peace. "The North is divided in sentiment," Key thought, "and cannot prosecute the war much longer." The success at Fort Pillow, the reported capture of two thousand Yankees in a battle at Plymouth, North Carolina, the spanking Banks had received in Louisiana, all betokened a reawakening strength for the Confederacy!

Then Sherman ordered his armies to move. Key cooked one day's rations and stuffed them in his haversack. "May we be prepared and nerved for the conflict," he wrote in his diary for May 7.

PART THREE

✷✷✷✷✷✷✷✷✷✷✷✷✷✷✷✷✷✷✷✷✷✷✷✷✷✷✷✷✷✷✷✷✷✷✷✷✷✷

Sherman Runs the Ends!

Chattanooga to the Chattahoochee

1. "FIGHT ANYTHING THAT COMES"

O<small>N THE</small> 7th of May the city of Washington could no longer conceal its quickening tension. Men and women moved restlessly through the streets, dawdled over their food in restaurants, and gathered in curious, fretful groups on the lawn south of the White House, where the Marine Band played its usual Saturday afternoon concert. A copperish sun blazed down from an almost cloudless sky and Washington panted at the beginning of a hot blast. On every pair of lips the same question formed. Where was Grant? Three days before, the Army of the Potomac had crossed the Rapidan and plunged into the Virginia Wilderness. Was it true, as rumor persisted, that Grant had telegraphed for forage, an unfailing sign of a Union advance pressing forward toward Richmond?

On the lawn south of the White House, where daffodils sparkled in brilliant clusters and the tulip trees rustled their green boughs, the Marine Band ceased playing, for a tall man with tired eyes and a sober, serious face appeared on the portico. The crowd burst into a roar, pushed forward, urged Mr. Lincoln to speak. The president smiled; he understood what was in their hearts and what they wanted to know, but the only response he could make was the suggestion that they all join in three cheers for Grant. Lustily the ovation was given and Mr. Lincoln returned to his official duties.

The eager eyes that scanned the headlines and the dispatches in the Sunday newspapers next morning learned nothing more. The President paced the White House in his old carpet slippers, taut lines pinched the mouths of sweethearts and wives worrying over their long-haired men who had

77

disappeared into the thickets of Virginia, mothers went to church and prayed for their bearded soldier-sons. Then the wounded started coming back. The nation knew. Grant had met Lee at Spotsylvania; a bloody, see-saw battle reddened the soil of the Wilderness; and to friends the quartermaster of the Army of the Potomac declared that "the world never heard of war before." In the quiet night women both North and South cried themselves to sleep, burying their faces in damp pillows so that the children would not hear their sobs.

At that moment the nation almost had forgotten the three armies moving into Georgia under William Tecumseh Sherman. On the 7th of May—practically at the time the Marine Band had been playing on the lawn south of the White House —Thomas's Army of the Tennessee had overrun a picket guard at Tunnel Hill and Sherman, climbing to the summit, had looked down into the gorge through which the railroad passed. A "straight and well-defined range of mountains, presenting sharp palisades" dominated the position. Natives called the range Rocky Face, the gorge the Buzzard Roost. Sherman "could plainly see" the enemy in the Buzzard Roost; not only did Confederate batteries crown the cliffs on either side, but Mill Creek, flowing through the gorge toward Dalton, had been dammed to form "a sort of irregular lake" and make the roads impassable.

Unless Joe Johnston were a fool—and that was the last thing Sherman would have called him—the past six months had been devoted to fortifying this spot by every conceivable means. Only an ass would squander time and men on a frontal attack. Let Johnston sit in his mountain fortress—the longer the better—for Sherman intended to swing McPherson's Army of the Cumberland to the rear, pounce on the railroad, force Johnston to "detach largely against" McPherson and, in all probability, to evacuate Dalton altogether. Meanwhile Thomas's Army of the Tennessee and Schofield's Army of the Ohio would be alerted to "press strongly at all points," to stand ready to "rush in on the first appearance of 'let go,' and, if possible, to catch our enemy in the confusion of retreat."

The movements worked more easily than even Sherman hoped. By the 9th of May the head of McPherson's column passed through Snake Creek and found it "perfectly undefended." The Confederates had been caught napping. McPherson's sole opposition had been one cavalry brigade that had been quickly driven north toward Dalton with "the first serious intimation" to Johnston of the trap forming in the rear. Around the fly tent that Sherman used for his headquarters, eyes sparkled and voices rose excitedly. A short note from McPherson, written at two o'clock in the afternoon, set his advance at within a mile and a half of the railroad, above and near Resaca. Jubilation ran through Sherman's renewed orders to Thomas and Schofield to be poised for an instant pursuit. When the trap was sprung, Sherman reasoned, Johnston would be driven in retreat over the rough, impracticable roads east of Resaca, and Thomas and Schofield would be chasing no better than "a broken and disordered army."

Nightfall brought more sobering news from McPherson. Wishful thinking was all right, but Resaca looked too-strongly held for a surprise, so he had fallen back to the mouth of Snake Creek Gap and begun to dig in. Sherman's heart sank. Couldn't McPherson understand that he had twenty-three thousand men with Hooker in close support? Why, by the saints to whom Ellen was forever praying, McPherson could hold all of Johnston's army in check should "Old Joe" abandon Dalton, and that movement was unlikely in so far as Johnston had "fixed . . . up" Dalton "on purpose to receive us." Sherman prodded McPherson to "strengthen your position; fight anything that comes; and threaten the safety of the railroad all the time." If Johnston would only stay in Dalton two more days he would "find in his rear a larger party than he expects in an open field." Then, Sherman felt, he could choose his own ground and force Johnston "to move out of his works."

When Sherman bedded down on the ground that night more than the ticks threatening to lodge in his red beard accounted for his restlessness. Why didn't McPherson simply walk into Resaca, get astride the railroad, and dare Johnston to come down and attack him? A decade later, as Sherman labored over his *Memoirs*, he still could not understand why McPherson hesitated at an opportunity that "does not occur twice in a single life." Sherman would write:

> . . . I am certain that Johnston would not have ventured to attack him in position, but would have retreated eastward by Spring Place, and we should have captured half his army and all his artillery and wagons at the very beginning of the campaign.

How completely Cump Sherman had forgotten the days of his old Kentucky command, when he had known how easy it was to overestimate the strength of an opposing force (if, indeed, it existed at all)! "At the critical moment," Sherman would argue throughout his lifetime, "McPherson seems to have been a little timid"; but at the same critical moment, though he rolled and tossed in his fly tent, the general must admit that McPherson, entrenched in Sugar Valley on the Resaca side of Snake Creek Gap, held "an unassailable defensive position." By morning Sherman decided to pass the whole army through the Gap and move on Resaca.

The 13th of May found the bulk of Thomas's and Schofield's troops through the Gap, with Thomas taking the center, Schofield the right, and McPherson the left for the three-pronged assault on Resaca. Inside the sleepy little Georgia town Johnston waited with the army he had withdrawn from the prepared defences of Dalton. "Old Joe" had not spared the pick and shovel from the instant he had reached Resaca; his entrenchments rimmed the town. On the 14th and 15th of May—about the time when from Spotsylvania Grant was telling the nation: "I propose to fight it out on this line, if

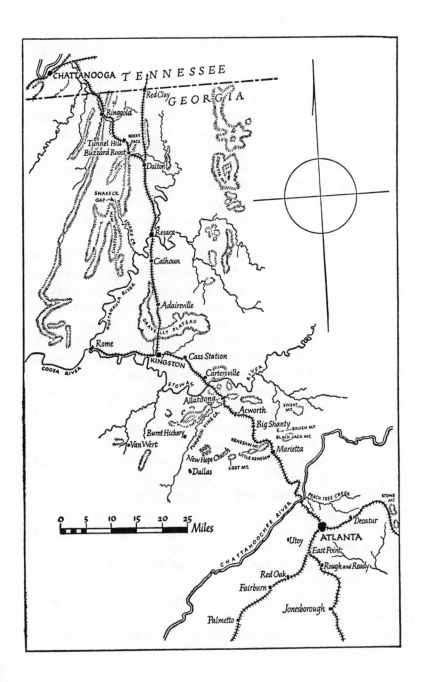

it takes all summer"—the thunder of battle rumbled through the hills around Resaca.

On the 14th the men in the division of Federal General Oliver Otis Howard had spent much of the day "creeping up among the bushes, rocks and ravines" as they moved upon Johnston's position at Resaca shaped so much like the horseshoe line at Gettysburg. They were tired, disgusted, bruised —in no mood, certainly, to find Sherman sitting on a log, his back hunched against a tree, asleep!

"A pretty way we are commanded!" one soldier grumbled.

Sherman awakened. "Stop, my man," he cried. "While you were sleeping last night, I was planning for you."

But while Sherman dozed, Ted Upson of the 100th Indiana found the action at Resaca the kind of battle that makes a man fighting-mad. Four days earlier, marching through Snake Creek Gap, Ted had spent his last thirty-five dollars on a Henry rifle, "a 16 shooter," purchased from a wounded man in the 97th Indiana. A Henry was a good weapon and gave a man a comfortable feeling to think he had "so many shots in reserve." But at Resaca Ted would learn once again that "the Johnnys shoot very careless and would as lief hit us as not." Ted saw Sam Allbright, an old friend, struck by a piece of shell—one of the thirteen men of the 100th that would be wounded that day. Now, that ain't nice, Ted might have said, except at that moment a spent ball hit his belt buckle and knocked him out. Comrades dragged Ted under a tree, deciding that he had been "gobbled," but after a time his eyes blinked open. He was sick at the stomach and "pretty sore." Maybe he wouldn't have been struck if a tree hadn't blown down and he hadn't been so eager to use that Henry. But the roots of the tree had a lot of dirt on them, and by punching holes through the dirt Ted had been able to open up with his new Henry on a Confederate battery across a field. Soon the men of the 100th had those Confederates dancing like a pack of jigaboos and wishing to hell they could be left alone long enough to do their work. Ted and his pals figured they might as well rush across the field and capture those unhappy graybacks. Everything worked out exactly as they reckoned—except that Ted was smacked in the stomach by that spent ball.

James Austin Connolly, writing to his wife "near Resaca," scrawled the date of May 15 across the page and stopped. Near his headquarters an enemy shell exploded. The time, the major guessed, was about nine at night; over the hills and valleys the moon revealed in "misty light" the curtain of battle smoke. The mournful notes of a whippoorwill mingled with the shouts of the Yankees, the answering hoots of the Rebels, the incessant chatter of the "rattling fire" from the skirmish line. Today, like yesterday, had been a hard, back-breaking game of tug and give—driving the Johnnys within their fortifications, taunting them by planting your colors there, then jigging under a hiss of bullets until you were glad to draw back, at least as far as the cover of a woods.

From that cover Major Connolly now wrote to his wife. He supposed that there might be another engagement tonight, but he hoped not, for "I don't want to be disturbed after I get to sleep, and then I don't like fighting in the night, any-how." Sherman had the men to whip Johnston and if "Old Joe" didn't get out of Resaca quickly he never would. The Yankees had the railroad running several miles south of Dalton as far as Tilton and supplies were no longer a problem. With the weather so fine, and the men flushed with success, Connolly prayed that Sherman would "push right on, day and night, though we be ragged, tired and hungry, until we exterminate these battalions of treason."

Inside the Confederate lines at Resaca, Lieutenant L. D. Young would hear "the crack of rifle or roar of a can-non." To Yankee music Young slept, to Yankee thunderings he awoke as Resaca became a "death struggle with Sherman's well-clothed, well-fed and thoroughly rested veterans who moved against us in perfect step, with banners flying and bands playing, as though expecting to charm us." Young remembered:

> When they had come within seventy-five or eighty yards, our lines opened a murderous fire from both infantry and double-shotted artillery. Having retired in disorder to their original position in the woods, they rallied and again moved to the attack to be met in the same manner and with similar results. Three times during the morning and early afternoon [of May 15] were these attacks made upon our lines. It was a veritable picnic for the Confederates, protected as we were by earthworks and with clear and open ground in front. Had Sherman continued this business during the entire day (as we hoped he would) the campaign would have been ended right there.

General Howard saw the fighting at Resaca as unimportant —quite as much, he thought, "might possibly have been accomplished if we had used skirmish lines alone"—but on the Confederate side Lieutenant Young realized that the fighting on the 15th had been no more than "a clever ruse of Sherman's." Again the Federals moved on the rear of Johnston's army, aiming for any point that would threaten the railroad below Calhoun and above Kingston. Garrard's division of Union cavalry had slipped down the Oostenaula by the Rome Road as early as the 14th; the danger signals had not been unnoticed by the wary Johnston, and on the night of the 15th he took his army across the Oostenaula, setting fire to the bridges.

Sherman saw the charred pilings next morning. War was a test of patience. War was a cold, merciless application of pressure. Sherman regretted that he had not "crippled" Johnston more "at that particular stage of the game," but the pattern by which Sherman had determined to fight Johnston was dogged and realistic. War had changed since '62 and '63. A military era had ended at Gettysburg; no longer was there any brotherhood of rival knights in battle; the mud and the slime and the misery of Vicksburg had created a new fashion in war. Ensnarement and strangulation, an equal indifference to the suffering of the enemy's military and civilian populations shaped the new attitudes of war.

So Sherman turned to the task of pursuing Johnston, responding to the instincts of the frontier hunter who would follow the bloody tracks of his wounded adversary, weaken him with further thrusts, stalk him relentlessly, and offer him no respite until a fatal misstep had been achieved. Segment by segment he would trap and destroy Johnston and his weary graybacks until the Army of Tennessee no longer could fight; through the length of Georgia—clear through hell, if necessary—he would pursue and kill and ravish the countryside until both the resources and the spirit of rebellion had been destroyed in the West and Grant in Virginia was free to fall upon the bleeding, reeling enemy for the final blow. The rapid success of the Union armies in forcing the Confederates from Dalton and Resaca "gave us the initiative," Sherman gloated, "and the usual impulse of a conquering army."

But Sherman may have sensed only part of the triumph he already had won. Perhaps his greatest victory at that instant would be found in the questions and indecision that were forming in the mind and heart of John Bell Hood.

2. THE "PRIDE, POMP AND CIRCUMSTANCE OF GLORIOUS WAR"

THE Army of Tennessee had gained a new folklore hero. His name was Oliver and he served with Wheeler's cavalry. Oliver was an Alabamian, earthy in thought and pithy in speech. Somewhere between Dalton and Resaca, standing behind a slim sapling, a Minié ball caught Oliver in the "part of his anatomy that fitted the saddle." The suggestion that Oliver retreat to the rear was more than the Alabamian could endure.

"Go back to the rear, hell!" screamed Oliver. "I would be only too glad to go back if wounded anywhere else, but I'll be damned if I go back, shot where I have been!"

Joe Johnston needed more of Oliver's spirit—and there were those who wished that "Old Joe" might be wounded where Oliver had been if the effect would be the same. "Old Joe" acted scared. Clearly he had been outguessed by Sherman. He had expected Sherman with his "great superiority of numbers" to fight him at Dalton. "Old Joe" had been ready for him there. But Sherman had sent McPherson down to Resaca and it had raised hell, just as the Minié ball had upset Oliver.

Whenever Johnston thought of the opposition he faced, images seemed to haunt his mind—perhaps images not so black as those which had haunted Sherman's mind in the days of '61 at Louisville and Sedalia, but images that still bore a disturbing resemblance. "General Sherman's troops, with whom we were contending, had received a longer training in war than any of those with whom I had served in former times," ran the sobering trend of Johnston's thoughts. To foot soldiers like Sam Watkins of the 1st Tennessee, "Old Joe" might be the kind of general who made a private's tread "light" and his soul "happy," but when Johnston lived candidly with himself he saw deepening uncertainties in the dark shadows of his wall tent.

Out of those uncertainties a pattern emerged. He must stand on the defensive. Increasingly through his thoughts passed the same conviction that he had held before Vicksburg, when Davis and Seddon had urged him to cross the Big Black. Again, he must "*spare the blood* of our soldiers by fighting under cover habitually." He could hold a position only so long as his communications were not seriously threatened, and then he must fall back. The very phrases that filled his reflections revealed the cautious tone of a conservative mind: he fought with "greatly inferior numbers," he must "reduce the odds against us by partial engagements," he must depend on "a material reduction of the Federal army . . . by the expiration of terms of service of the regiments that had not reenlisted." Johnston led the Army of Tennessee as a boxer fights a slugger—weaving and ducking, jumping back, jabbing in the clinches, bouncing off the ropes, hoping that quicker footwork, a greater endurance, a more scientific knowledge of the fisticuffer's art would tell in the late rounds.

Across the Oostenaula, Johnston hoped to find a position near Calhoun where he could cover the several roads leading southward from Snake Creek Gap and Resaca. But Adairsville looked better, for there the Oothcaloga Creek formed a narrow valley where the heights could be held by the flanks. Johnston rested his army almost a day, then sent Hardee's corps along the road out of Snake Creek Gap and the corps of Hood and Polk along the Spring Place Road.

Once more Sam Hood traveled a road in retreat, hating every bounce of the saddle. Sam had fought under Lee, Jackson, and Longstreet, and from these leaders of the Army of Northern Virginia had learned a deep distrust for entrenchments. Put a soldier behind breastworks for a month or two, Sam would tell you, and his "spirit of devil-me-care independence" disappeared. The soldier's imagination would grow "vivid under bullets and bombshells" until "a brush-heap will so magnify itself in dimension as to induce him to believe that he is stopped by a wall ten feet high and a mile in length." True, these were opinions that Sam expressed years later when, like a pair of lamed cocks in an imaginary pit, both he and Johnston were hopelessly involved in fighting over what might have been, but the cast of Sam's prejudices must have been well shaped that warm May day, jogging over the Spring Place Road.

Elements of rationalization creep into every argument formed after the fact, and half truth inevitably is made into whole truth, but Sam Hood in 1864 was still the impulsive general, impatient to lead, as cocksure as when he smiled at any Richmond belle, as strong-willed as a Texas steer under a branding iron, as occasionally unfair in his judgments as only a sentimentalist can be. The very word "retreat" soured in Sam's mouth like a rind of lemon. An army standing its ground and fighting, he would say, counted few stragglers and deserters. But an army "fighting and retreating at the same time, taking up positions, day after day, to be given up only under cover of darkness" grew as grimly silent as the muffled wheels of its wagons. Such an army lost "the pride, pomp and circumstance of glorious war." Even its wounded could not return home "buoyant and hopeful."

Retreat and defeat were synonymous to Sam Hood. In March, writing as one who spoke with a "whole heart," he had told Jefferson Davis that Virginia could be held by Lee while the Army of Tennessee marched "in force from our centre, the vital point of every nation." That confident prediction could only come back to torment him and to make him feel a fool as his horse jostled him over the Spring Place Road toward Adairsville. In April he had written to Braxton Bragg: "When we are to be in better condition to drive the enemy from the country, I am not able to comprehend." And now, scarcely a month later, with both Dalton and Resaca surrendered, Johnston's army fled like a dog with its tail on fire! Rebellion rankled through all the deep emotional intensities that gave an edge to Sam Hood's personality. The army must stand firm and fight! So reasoned Sam Hood then, but within forty-eight hours, when at Cassville the army had the chance to fight precisely as Hood wanted, Johnston would accuse Sam of being the first to run!

Johnston paused in Adairsville only long enough to become convinced that the valley of Oothcaloga Creek was too narrow to give his army the proper advantage of the ground and pressed on for Cassville. Here "Old Joe's" heart lifted. Cassville looked right for a battle. Immediately south of the town spread a ridge "with a broad, open, elevated valley in front" that could be "completely commanded by the troops occupying its crest." The position, Johnston recalled, was "the best that I saw during the war." Hood's and Polk's corps and half of Hardee's were placed along the crest, with the other half of Hardee's troops prolonging the line over "undulating ground."

Private Sam Watkins shared "Old Joe's" elation, agreeing that here was the spot to give the Yankees a drubbing. Watkins had found the march down to Cassville anything but a picnic. At times, Sam would remember, "two hundred cannon were roaring and belching like blue blazes," and Sam would learn that cannonballs soon acquired varying personalities. Some balls, tearing overhead, sounded "mad," others seemed "to be laughing," still others could be described as "mild." And some, Sam would add, could "scream like the ghosts of the dead."

At Kingston, on the road to Cassville, Johnston had issued his first battle order. The line had been formed, the skirmishers engaged. "There were no earthworks on either side," Sam said. "It was to be an open field and a fair fight." But the order to fall back soon followed, for Hood's line was being enfiladed and his position could not be held. Now at Cassville the line of battle had reformed, and looking down from the ridge Sam's heart bounded:

> . . . I never saw our troops happier or more certain of success. A sort of grand halo illumined every soldier's face. You could see self-confidence in the features of every private soldier. We were confident of victory and success. It was like going to a frolic or a wedding. Joy was welling up in every heart. We were going to whip and rout the Yankees. It seemed to be anything else than a fight. The soldiers were jubilant. Gladness was depicted on every countenance. I believe a sort of fanaticism had entered our souls. It seemed that whoever was killed would be carried to the seventh heaven. Then:

"Halt!" "Retreat!"
"What is the matter?"

"Old Joe" would have given Watkins one answer and Sam
Hood another as between them they created one of the great
riddles of the war. Only one fact is known with certainty. On
the night of May 19 Johnston called a conference at Polk's
headquarters and at this meeting Hood and Polk later were
joined by Hardee. Stormy General Samuel G. French and
Captain Walter J. Morris, who was Polk's engineer, also
claimed to have attended. Not too many days before, Bishop
Polk had taken time off from his military responsibilities to
baptize Joseph E. Johnston in the presence of Hood and
Hardee, but tonight the atmosphere among the generals was
strictly martial and brittle.

Who said what? Did Captain Morris declare that a personal
inspection of the lines had convinced him "there was no cover
for the men within a reasonable distance of the crest," and
from the extreme positions of the left batteries of the enemy
"it would be necessary for them to cease firing during the
attack until their infantry had reached a line very close to
the crest of the ridge occupied by General Polk's command"?
Did Morris say that these enemy batteries "necessarily enfiladed a considerable portion of General Hood's line"? Did
Hood tell Johnston that in view of this enfilading he and Polk
must *either attack or abandon* their position? Or, as Johnston
maintained, did Polk and Hood urge him "to abandon the
ground immediately and cross the Etowah"?

French, who should have been able to answer these questions
with the least bias, found his memory shadowy, except that
he didn't believe Hood and Polk were right about anything.
But no matter who wanted to fight or who to retreat, Johnston
decided that the army must cross the Etowah at once. Hardee,
square-jawed, dissented violently. Hood, Polk, Morris were
wrong—the ground at Cassville could be held. Hardee's
military opinions usually carried weight—his *Infantry and Rifle*

Tactics was a standard reference with both the Union and Confederate armies—but Johnston, once deciding to run, couldn't be swayed. He picked Allatoona Pass as the point where he would fall back behind the Etowah.

Private Sam Watkins accepted the decision philosophically. Sam loved "Old Joe," who had saved the morale of the Army of Tennessee when the soldiers were "crushed," when "discipline had gone," and when "a feeling of mistrust" had "pervaded the whole army." Johnston was "the very picture of a general" and there was not "a soldier in his army, but would gladly have died for him," for he had "brought the manhood back to the private's bosom." "Old Joe knows what he is up to," Sam said. "When we went to sleep we felt that Old Joe, the faithful old watch dog, had his eyes on the enemy."

Writing from Kingston next day, James Austin Connolly felt that, no matter how carefully one studied "Loyd's *Map of the Southern States*," one had to march with Sherman and feel the sting of constant skirmishing, as the pressure on Johnston's flanks forced him to pull back his army, to understand how "the fields . . . are being reddened by the blood of our soldiers," and how "hundreds of little mounds . . . are rising by the wayside day after day, as if to mark the footprints of the God of War as he stalks through this beautiful country." Kingston served as the juncture point for the railroads from Chattanooga and Atlanta, and, Connolly told his wife, "such has been the extraordinary rapidity with which the railroad has been repaired, as we have pushed along, that a train from Chattanooga ran into Kingston this morning, while at the same time a Rebel train from Atlanta was whistling on the same road, and only two miles distant." By nine that morning the last bridge had been burned across the Etowah, the last whistle of a Rebel train had sounded, and Johnston's army, Connolly thought, must be "wending its way, weary and dispirited, toward that mythical ditch of which we have heard so much." In contrast, in good country with fine weather, everything was "going well with the Yankees in Georgia."

The 22nd of May, a Sunday, was "a bright, sultry, lazy day" in Kingston, with "scarce a breath of air stirring, and mules, Negroes, soldiers, everybody lolling in the shade." Orders to pack twenty days' rations had been issued; Sherman would be marching again in the morning. The 9th Ohio went home, its three years of service completed. Two days previously this German regiment had been skirmishing with the gray-backs; now Connolly watched "the sturdy Germans" as they "filed out from our camp, their old, tattered, battle worn flags fluttering like rags," their step "proud and soldierly," their "bronzed cheeks . . . wet with tears." The country south-ward from Dalton had begun to impress the major as "more like our northern farming country." Farmhouses looked "neat and comfortable," the barns "well built and capacious," and the women had lost "that yellow, smoky, snuff dipping appearance that characterizes so many of those of Tennessee and northern Georgia." Where was Sherman really going? Rumors were contradictory. Some said Atlanta, some Savan-nah, some Milledgeville, Macon, and Mobile. Connolly was anxious to see all these places, but meanwhile he hoped that his wife would send him twenty postage stamps in her next letter.

On a Sunday afternoon in camp Sherman liked to sit with his back against a tree. Sometimes, in the winking moments between sleep and wakefulness, details of a plan fell naturally into place. Sometimes he thought of Ellen, pregnant for the sixth time; sometimes of the old West Point days lived with classmates against whom the Union now fought. But today he remembered when in 1844, as a young lieutenant stationed for a time at Augusta, he had been sent to Marietta, Georgia, to assist Inspector General Churchill in taking testimony con-cerning losses of horses and accoutrements by the Georgia Volunteers during the Florida War. He had ridden the distance on horseback, and he could still visualize many of the topographic features that distinguished the country about Kenesaw, Allatoona, and the Etowah River. The Indian mounds on the Etowah, he remembered, were called the "Hightower"; the rugged hills of Allatoona Pass would be difficult for an army to force.

Sherman rubbed his back against the tree. Yes, he knew a bit about the Georgia terrain in which he soon would be tussling with "Old Joe."

3. "GOOD LUCK, YANK!"

TED UPSON felt satisfied that he had acted fairly. Covering the picket lines one night near Dallas, he found a youngster sleeping at his post. The penalty for sleeping on picket was death, but Ted wasn't going to tell on the kid. Still, he hoped that the others who knew would keep their mouths shut. To Ted the incident proved that "a fellow gets in a tight place sometimes trying to do his duty!"

But Ted had been in plenty of tight places since reaching Dallas. The generals simply planned the war; the soldiers fought it. At best Ted could understand but vaguely the over-all strategy of which he had been a part—a pawn moved forward in a general's gambit. The hand behind the move belonged to Sherman, who had determined to turn Johnston's strong position at Allatoona Pass by slipping from Kingston to Marietta by way of Dallas. The strategy was bold—and devilish from the start. Now the Yankees must leave their railroad, plunge through a densely wooded country, depend on the wagons for supplies, and trust to communications by crossroads or by couriers through the woods. A Confederate cavalry picket, captured at Burnt Hickory, carried papers revealing that Johnston at Allatoona had guessed Sherman's plan.

A chilling, sinister uneasiness accompanied this revelation, for now any of the Union columns could walk into an ambush.

Part Three: SHERMAN RUNS THE ENDS!

Sherman studied his maps and scouting reports. His finger traced the line where Pumpkin Vine Creek, a tributary of the Etowah, flowed north and west on the other side of Allatoona range. At Dallas, standing east of the creek, his finger stopped at a concentration point for roads leading in many directions. To hold Dallas would be tantamount to threatening Marietta and Atlanta, but to reach Dallas the Federals must regain use of the railroad "at least as far down as its *débouché* from the Allatoona range." Shadowy risks and uncertainties hovered over the map, but still the decision must be reached—somehow Johnston had to be forced out of Allatoona.

On the 25th of May every Union column moved steadily on Dallas. McPherson, on the right, neared the town of Van Wert; Thomas pounded straight down the center along the main road with Joe Hooker's division in the lead; and Schofield covered the left rear. The Federal forces, Connolly reported, approached the country of the Georgia gold mines where "the cripples and poor men who have not been conscripted are out gold washing among the mountain streams, to get gold dust enough to buy corn with." Hooker led three divisions by as many roads toward Dallas. The sky was overcast, the sun drew water, the daylight darkened. In this forbidding setting a Confederate cavalry force waited at Pumpkin Vine Creek, felt for Hooker's columns, skirmished bitterly, and then retreated behind a burning bridge. Hooker's boys quickly extinguished the fire, and a division under Geary chased the gray-clad cavalrymen down a road leading due east toward Marietta. That Union spurt ended as precipitately as it began, running into a heavy Confederate infantry force moving down from Allatoona toward Dallas.

Right there the bullets began to hum. Sherman rode forward at a gallop, finding that important roads crossed near by. Natives called the place New Hope, taking the name from a Methodist meeting-house. Within hours the Yankees, fighting through dark thickets and darker woods, sprawling over roads that linked Allatoona with Dallas and Van Wert with Mari-

94

etta, had rechristened New Hope the "Hell Hole." Night came on as black as any Stygian underworld, rain poured down in torrents, Federal columns converged in confusion. Sherman stretched out on the ground beside a log and tried to sleep.

The general's eyelids drooped heavily when a gray, wan dawn crept along those Georgia roads. Almost everywhere Sherman looked, Confederate entrenchments ridged the countryside and Confederate heavy guns frowned menacingly. The battle opened furiously and the Yankees clearly were getting nowhere. Sherman studied the day's reports. McPherson had reached Dallas that morning, spreading his troops southeast and east of the town and placing Davis's XIVth Corps, joining him on the road from Rome, on his left. Schofield meanwhile closed up on Thomas's left, but Sherman's eyes narrowed at the three-mile gap that existed between the forces of Hooker and Davis.

Fretfully, Sherman tugged at his red beard. Quite obviously, Johnston had arrived in New Hope with all his army. The stage seemed set. If Sherman wanted the railroad, there was no reason why he couldn't fight for it as easily in the "Hell Hole" of New Hope as at Dallas. All he really needed now was to swing McPherson from Dallas to Hooker's right and let "Old Joe" have it proper. But the Confederates had other plans for McPherson. Now that Mac had reached Dallas he would find plenty there to entertain him. And so would Ted Upson, crawling up to the skirmish line at Dallas. A sharpshooter's bullet snipped the button off the side of Upson's cap.

Ted ducked his head. He scrambled back fast to tell Colonel Albert Heath that what he had seen wasn't very pleasant. Those Johnnys were sitting in a fort with heavy earthworks facing the Yankee front. Heath thought that he knew how to fix those graybacks. Soon the boys in the 100th Indiana were cutting trees and piling up the trunks in a straight line until they had constructed a solid fence three feet high. Next Heath set them to digging a ditch, two feet deep and about four feet wide, using the dirt for packing outside the wall. Poles notched on both sides went on top of the logs, and then headlogs were placed in the notches. Now the boys in the 100th could fire under the headlogs without exposing themselves. It was nice and cozy.

Some of the Indiana boys wondered why Heath had left a gap in the works at the end of the regiment, but when a couple of field guns rolled up Ted began to grin. How were the Johnnys going to like that? The guns were pushed through the gap and opened up on the Reb fort. The boom of those field pieces sounded real pretty, except to the Rebs, who grew madder and madder about the whole business. Ted heard the Rebs charging with a whoop, saw the fool Indiana gunners dive back behind the works, and, poking his Henry 16-shooter under the headlogs, set to pickling Reb hides with volley after volley.

General Johnny Logan of the XVth Corps heard the rattle of the rifles. Hell's bells, lose a couple of field guns like that and next thing you knew they'd be blasting you out of your own position! Unless those Indiana boys had maggots in their brains, they'd get the hell out there and save those guns. Logan spurred his horse forward, jumping clear over the works of the 100th. The Johnnys had hitched prolonges on the field pieces and were trying to pull them away. Logan shouted for action. Out of the works came Ted and his buddies. The old Henry poured out its lead. Bayonets clashed. But those two guns were turned around and dragged back. The Federals didn't have guns to spare at Dallas.

The Rebs smarted. Back in the fort they began lobbing grapeshot down onto the 100th. Then, when they reckoned the Indiana boys had been softened up like crabs in a burrow growing new shells, the Rebs charged back after the guns. Soldiers dropped on both sides. The fighting grew mean. But the guns stayed put. Later, under a flag of truce, the Indianians went out and buried their dead in a long trench. Ted wrote in his diary: "We have been here for some time, but the Johnnys have not tried another assault, so we growl at each other and keep up an active skirmish fire on both sides."

Sherman's instructions reached McPherson to pull out of Dallas and swing around to Hooker's right at New Hope. That night Ted and his comrades tried it, but the Rebs suspected something unusual. The fighting blazed. With the bullets singing all around, Ted recorded that

. . . We were ordered back into our works. We got there pretty quick. The skirmishers came running in and then began the awfulest musketry firing I ever heard, and Gen Sherman says it was the heaviest fire he ever experienced. It was a continuous roar, dotted with the sharp explosions of the Artillery. It seemed for hours, though it only lasted about one. Gradually it died down. The skirmishers went out again, and this morning are popping away as usual. I believe it was a good deal of a scare and that the Johnnys were safe behind their works all the time.

With Hardee on the left near Dallas, Polk in the center, and Hood on the right near the New Hope meeting-house, Johnston had blocked Sherman's path to Atlanta. It had been Hood's skirmishers that had tangled with Hooker in the rain on the 25th. The Yankees assaulted again two days later, and once again, reinforced by spunky Pat Cleburne, Hood had made Sherman's boys dance. Through these stormy days, Sherman visited the lines, seeing "skirmishers dodging from tree to tree, or behind logs on the ground." The Yankee wounded piled up, and to General Howard "the very woods seemed to moan and groan with the voices of sufferers." Cleburne's official report would signal out Captain Key, who back at Dalton had writhed over Yankee yammering about miscegenation. By hand Key ran his artillery to a trench in the Confederate breastworks, emptied a murderous fire on the nigger-loving Yankees, and held the Yankee reserves, massed behind a hill, completely out of the fight by his bitter enfilading.

Confederate spirit ran high. Well-grounded rumors circulated through the ranks that Johnston had conferred with his lieutenant generals on the 28th, and that Hood would renew the attack in the morning. But daylight offered Hood a sight he didn't like—the Yankees dug in behind Pumpkin Vine Creek, a swamp in front of him. Hood hesitated. Hardee would report laconically: "The opportunity had passed." And so it had, for soon McPherson would shake loose from Dallas and by June 1st would join Hooker. Meanwhile Thomas and Schofield completed their deployments, slowly overlapping Johnston on his right and dropping the Federal left to the railroad, with Acworth, eight miles away, as the closest point. Johnston could move or be damned. Sherman described his view of the situation:

> . . . without attempting further to carry the enemy's strong position at New Hope Church, I held our general right in close contact with it, gradually, carefully, and steadily working by the left, until our strong infantry-lines had reached and secured possession of all the wagon-roads between New Hope, Allatoona, and Acworth, when I dispatched General Garrard's and Stoneham's divisions of cavalry into Allatoona, the first around by the west end of the pass, and the latter by the direct road. Both reached their destination without opposition, and orders were at once given to repair the railroad forward from Kingston to Allatoona, embracing the bridge across the Etowah River. Thus the real object of my move on Dallas was accomplished, and on the 4th of June I was preparing to draw off from New Hope Church, and to take position on the railroad in front of Allatoona, when, General Johnston himself having evacuated his position, we effected the change without further battle, and moved to

the railroad, occupying it from Allatoona and Acworth forward to Big Shanty, in sight of the famous Kenesaw Mountain.

In Dallas, as the first month of the Georgia campaign neared its close, Ted Upson heard the Yankee train tooting its whistle with lusty insistence. "You could hear the men cheer for miles," Ted said. On another occasion, slipping from behind some rocks beyond the skirmish line, Ted suddenly encountered a Reb.

"Say, Yank, got anything to trade?" the Reb asked. He "stood in plain sight without a gun."

Ted explained that he had left his haversack some distance back.

"Go and get it," the Reb said, and as Ted moved off "he still sat on a stone where I had left him."

But when Ted returned two other Confederates appeared. The Johnnys asked for coffee. Ted had a pound and swapped it for some dog-leg tobacco, but what pleased him more was a copy of a recent Atlanta paper. Ted and the Rebs chatted, then shook hands. As Ted made his way back to the skirmish line, a Reb called:

"Good luck, Yank! Come again some time. I hope you won't git hurt in any of our fights."

So did Ted. After he had read the paper, he carried it over to Logan's headquarters. For all the long years and all the dirty fighting, whether you called it the Rebellion or the War for Southern Independence, to the men in the ranks it remained a war between brothers.

By June 8 James Austin Connolly, near Acworth, was glad for the chance to write home "without the annoyance of being compelled to duck my head every few minutes, to let a straggling bullet whistle along." The Federals were within ten miles of Marietta; a rest for several days had been promised. Scraggly Georgia wheat had begun to change color; the corn stood about eight inches high. Mulberries were ripe, cherries only a week away from picking, apples and peaches forming on the limbs. Soon, Connolly thought, "we can live better than we do now," although with little prospect of changing the "Georgia lizards crawling down my boot legs and playing hide and seek in my pockets." Political pots, Connolly found, were simmering and boiling:

> . . . I learn this morning that Frémont has been nominated for President by the Cleveland convention. I hope he stands no show for election, but don't know whether he does or not. I want Abraham Lincoln for President, and think he will be, but we in the army are ignorant of what the politicians are doing or can do. . . .

The generals planned a war, and the soldiers fought it. The politicians fought it, too—but not always so cleanly.

4. THE BLOODLESS BATTLE AT BALTIMORE

SINCE the days of '61 when, as commander of the Department of Missouri, the haughty, imperious posturings of General John Charles Frémont in his headquarters at Planters' House had caused Sherman to sniff at the vultures gathering around the carcass, the American continent rarely entertained a group of more ill-assorted personalities than that which convened in Cleveland on May 31, 1864, to form the Radical Democracy. Suave political manipulators like Brigadier General John Cochrane of New York and stormy, militant abolitionists like Wendell Phillips of Boston, pink-cheeked crusaders like Elizabeth Cady Stanton fighting for woman suffrage and debonair adventurers like General Gustave Paul Cluseret who had marched to battle under Garibaldi were among the dissi-

dents meeting in Cleveland with only one unifying purpose—
to oust Old Abe from the White House.

Advanced publicity had claimed that thousands would pour
into the convention hall in Cleveland to hail the rise of the
new anti-Lincoln party, but not more than four hundred
attended any session. Undaunted, the Radical Democracy
drew up a platform favoring the Union, the suppression of the
rebellion without compromise, an expression of gratitude to
the army and navy, free speech, free press, habeas corpus, the
abolition of slavery, the right of asylum, the Monroe Doctrine,
a one-term Presidency, the confiscation of Rebel lands and
their division among the soldiers and sailors who served the
Union. Frémont, who had been the Republican candidate in
1856, resigned from the army to accept the nomination for
President on the understanding that he would withdraw if the
National Union Party meeting at Baltimore a week later
selected any candidate other than Abraham Lincoln. For
Frémont's running-mate the Radical Democracy turned to
John Cochrane, unaware that the President's secretaries,
Nicolay and Hay, could testify how en route to Cleveland Mr.
Cochrane had stopped at the White House to assure Mr.
Lincoln "of his continued friendship."

"Mr. Frémont's letter of acceptance," sneered the editor of
Harper's Monthly, "was every way remarkable." A glowing
example of duplicity, the editor implied, had developed when
"Mr. Frémont—the same that in 1861 had, without authority,
carried out the widest system of confiscation against Missouri
Rebels—said, also, that he was opposed to that part of the
platform in favor of the confiscation of Rebel property." The
editor of *Harper's Weekly* felt inclined to laugh off Frémont's
bid for the Presidency. Under a cartoon of Mr. Lincoln
greeting Messrs. Frémont and Cochrane this piquant conversation appeared.

FRÉMONT: "Well, Sir! I am nominated, you see."
COCHRANE: "Yes, Sir! WE are nominated."

Part Three: SHERMAN RUNS THE ENDS!

LINCOLN: "Well, gentlemen, and what then?"
FRÉMONT *and* COCHRANE: "Oh! nothing, Sir; nothing—
that's all!"

At the Cleveland convention a New York delegation had
thumped hard for General Grant as the presidential nominee,
but an officer of the Missouri militia had seized this critical
moment to move the selection of Frémont by acclamation
and had carried the day. Still Grant's name, once projected
into politics, remained appealing to many who opposed Lincoln. On June 4 in New York's Union Square twenty thousand
persons once more heard Grant extolled; but the orators on
this occasion, incited by the anti-Lincoln frothings of the *New
York Herald*, could not fool everyone. If Lincoln's popularity
began to slacken steadily in the days preceding the Baltimore
convention, no individual contributed more to the President's
plight than Ulysses S. Grant.

Grant floundered in Virginia. Day by day, mile by mile,
with teeming rains turning the roads of the Wilderness into a
network of swamps, Robert E. Lee grew in stature as a dangerous and treacherous antagonist. After the dismal agony of
Spotsylvania, with its frightful Union losses, Grant appeared
still to be advancing, but Lee's every withdrawal proved
prudent. Now "Uncle Robert" had grown wise to the cruel
effectiveness of breastworks, and wherever Grant reached for
him the soil of Virginia crimsoned with the Union dead.

General John Sedgwick of the VIth Corps, lying in state in
Dr. Holmes' embalming establishment on Washington's
Pennsylvania Avenue, represented but a symbol of the deeper
tragedy that had shaken the nation. Throughout the North, in
towns and cities, friends and neighbors stopped frequently to
visit distracted women whose trembling lips and reddened
eyes bespoke their loneliness for the husband and father who
had been lost; and a boy, hard-eyed, taking the news gamely,
as a soldier's son must, could make grownups turn away, wishing there never had been a war, a Negro, a Grant, or a Lincoln.

Except for the abolitionists, the Emancipation Proclamation somehow had changed the tone of the war for many people. Mostly they were inarticulate when it came to explaining the change, but some would blurt out that to die for the Union was one thing, to die for the nigger another. Grief often encouraged such talk. In grief it was difficult at times to understand how the two issues actually had grown together through military and political necessity; grief had a way of reaching out to place the blame on some mortal cause—on Grant, on Lincoln, on the Negro—since God is forever untouchable in that sense.

Then Grant met Lee at Cold Harbor. The first telegrams from the Army of the Potomac were overoptimistic. Cold Harbor after four days of bitter fighting had not destroyed Lee's army; once more, upon Lee's breastworks, fine Union soldiers had impaled themselves in disaster. It was perhaps as well for Mr. Lincoln that the true meaning of Cold Harbor had not become clear when the National Union Party, a coalition of Republicans and War Democrats, convened in Baltimore on the 7th of June.

Everyone knew before this two-day meeting that the Presidential nomination would go to Lincoln, and yet the convention of the National Union Party produced dramatic incidents that stirred the nation's emotions and re-emphasized the fundamental principles for which Grant struggled in Virginia and Sherman in Georgia. Even the sweltering heat, even the hubbub and commotion of the delegates scrambling for the ice water that boys carried through the aisles of the tightly packed convention floor, could not detract from the rousing sight of the Reverend Dr. Robert J. Breckinridge of Kentucky mounting the steps of the rostrum. Those who looked up at this white-haired, stiff-jawed, proud old preacher reminded each other in whispers that among the officers of the Confederate army fought two of his sons and a nephew. From the lips of the reverend doctor rolled bitter phrases that, like blasts of grapeshot and canister, shook the convention walls with their slow-measured, thoughtful impact. Dr. Breckinridge would follow the Union Party to "the gates of death." Every blow the Union struck, every battle won, every Rebel killed, to Dr. Breckinridge added a year or a century or perhaps ten centuries "to the life of the Government and the freedom of your children." The Constitution he would defend against any "who undertakes to trample it under foot"; slavery he would throw aside that all men might be free. So spoke a Breckinridge of Kentucky, a father who would point the guns of vengeance at his own sons, to save the Union and to re-elect Abraham Lincoln.

In the dispute over whether delegates from the Southern states should be seated and given the right to vote there was special tension. If Lincoln had exercised the choice he would have seated them all, for Lincoln never once conceded any legal actuality in secession. Would the convention support the same basic view? The seating of the delegation from Tennessee came as the essential test, and the correspondent of the *New York Tribune* wrote, with feeling for the drama in the moment:

> On the admission of the delegates from Tennessee, Louisiana and Arkansas, and Nevada, Nebraska and Colorado, the question was divided, and the vote of Tennessee taken first. She was rejected by decided and growing majority until New York gave her 44 votes. The Secesh applause was tremendous, and instantly infectious. Ohio voted 42 Yeas and right off enough states that had voted Nays caved in and changed their votes, each amid thundering applause, to reverse the action of the Convention and admit Tennessee delegates by a majority of 159.

In the end only the delegation from South Carolina, whose credentials were illegal, failed to be seated.

For the Committee on Resolutions grave Henry Jarvis Raymond, editor of the *New York Times*, now rose to read the Party's platform. Wherever Grant's or Sherman's armies fought, the Union Party gave them but one objective, to aid the Government "in quelling by force of arms the Rebellion now raging against its authority, and in bringing to the punishment due to their crimes the Rebels and traitors arrayed against it." No compromise would be made with the enemy, no terms offered other than unconditional surrender. The quiet cadences of Raymond's voice reached to the corners of the hall. Slavery had caused the Rebellion, slavery always "must be . . . hostile to the principles of Republican government," and national safety demanded "its utter and complete extirpation from the soil of the Republic. . . ."

Raymond could go no further. Cheers shook the walls of the convention. Over the yells, the stamping feet, the clapping hands, Raymond's voice finally proclaimed that the National Union Party favored an amendment to the Constitution whereby the people "shall exterminate and forever prohibit the existence of slavery within the limits or the jurisdiction of the United States." The applause bordered on pandemonium. A kind of drunken relief crept into the demonstration. For so long abolition had been the treacherous mistress, the dangerous bawd; now, wrapped in the sober robes of political destiny, abolition walked with quiet dignity, fingering her beads and with each offering a prayer for human freedom and equality. Once Lincoln's law partner, Billy Herndon, had hurried Abe away from a meeting for fear the abolitionists might seem to have cornered him; once Allen Pinkerton had whisked Lincoln through Baltimore in the dead of night to escape the threat of a hostile attack; and now in Baltimore, at a convention nominating Lincoln for President, both fears were dead. The war had brought the nation to a climactery. Bullets and ballots were to be fused into a single weapon.

Later, when the cheers subsided and the back-slapping ceased, Raymond called for the National Union Party to thank the soldiers and sailors "who have periled their lives . . . in vindication of the honor of the Flag," to recognize President Lincoln's own singular service "under circumstances of unparalleled difficulty" in defending the nation against "its open and secret foes," to chastise by implication the critics and opponents within Lincoln's own official family by deeming "it essential to the general welfare that harmony should prevail in the national councils," and, among other major points, to endorse the Monroe Doctrine and "the speedy construction of a railroad to the Pacific." Raymond sat down, flushed, hot, and pleased; around him, the correspondent from the rival *Tribune* reported, were "the wildest outbursts of enthusiasm."

Now at high pitch, the convention turned to nominating its candidates. A maneuver to name Lincoln for President and Hannibal Hamlin for Vice President by acclamation was beaten. The candidates, Raymond insisted, must be picked separately, and by recorded vote of the states. Delegate Burton C. Cook rose to his feet and roared: "Mr. President, the State of Illinois again presents to the loyal people of the Nation for President of the United States, Abraham Lincoln— God bless him!" The balloting began. The tally piled up unanimously for Lincoln until the vote reached Missouri. Although boos rang out, Missouri cast its ballot according to instructions: twenty-two votes for Ulysses S. Grant. At the end of the roll call Lincoln had received 497 votes, Grant 22. Missouri moved that the choice be declared unanimous.

"The enthusiasm was perfectly indescribable," declared the *Tribune* correspondent, "the whole Convention being on their feet shouting, and the band playing 'Hail Columbia.'" To everyone's surprise the Vice-Presidential nomination went to Andrew Johnson of Tennessee instead of to Maine's Hannibal Hamlin. The delegates packed up and went home, believing that they had done a fine job. Secretly, Abraham Lincoln did not think that he could be re-elected.

Grave disappointments, shattering challenges would soon close over the President and leave him at times morose and dispirited. The truth of Cold Harbor could not be concealed; cries of "Grant the butcher" were heard frequently. One grim June day followed another. Men who met casually on the street or at luncheon, men who read their newspapers thoughtfully, men who gathered on the dusty porches of suburban homes or lounged against the railings of country stores came to understand as clearly as the man in the White House what had happened.

In early May the Army of the Potomac had crossed the Rapidan in good heart and fine fighting trim. Now almost fifty thousand effectives had been lost. To the disappointments of Spotsylvania and Cold Harbor, Petersburg must be added. There would be no quick, smashing victory at Petersburg; only a siege, perhaps long-drawn, certainly brutal, promised to budge Lee's army from its newest breastworks. Meanwhile Franz Sigel had bogged down in his campaign through the valley and Ben Butler was stalled along the James. Discouragement edged the voices discussing these obvious realities.

In the military frustrations of Virginia the politically minded saw shadows of various shapes falling across the nation's future. The ward heelers of the Democratic Party, rallying in hamlet and city for the national convention at Chicago in August, spoke openly of the failure of the war and of the wisdom of a negotiated peace. Before the Chicago convention, correspondence would pass between Confederate representatives and Horace Greeley, editor of the *New York Tribune*, stating that men were in Canada authorized to open negotiations for peace if they could be assured safe conduct to Washington. Mr. Greeley packed his suitcase and set off to Niagara Falls to explore the matter. Societies, some sinisterly secretive, some blatantly open in their hostile opposition to Lincoln and the war, claimed growing memberships as 1864 moved into the hot summer months. Under such names as the Knights of the Golden Circle and the Sons of Liberty these groups of malcontents impressed many loyal Unionists as functioning in the manner of a fifth column. In many cases only God could know what was the true objective of these societies. Did they give aid and comfort to the enemy? Were their ranks riddled with spies? Did some of their members dream not only of a South split from the North but also of a Confederacy of Northwestern States divided from both?

No matter what answer one gave to these questions, no matter how lightly or how seriously one regarded the activities of the Golden Knights or of the Sons of Liberty, the symptom they represented could not be denied. Within the body of the Union cancerous cells had grown, and as the exertion of the war dragged on, wearing down the nation's resistance, the sores began to twitch and to ache. The Cleveland convention had sanctioned the war and rejected Lincoln. The Baltimore convention had reaffirmed a will to follow Lincoln and the cause of the Union, as Dr. Breckinridge had said, to "the gates of death." But would that will endure once the Chicago convention had crystallized and made respectable a militant opposition to the national government and its policies? For Lincoln the pondering of these thoughts brought lonely hours; his faith wavered.

In Richmond, however, any comfort that Jefferson Davis derived from these events had to be equated against what was happening in the West. During the month of May, by tactical brilliance, Sherman's armies had moved nearly a hundred miles, from Chattanooga to Big Shanty. Dalton, Resaca, Cassville, Allatoona, and Dallas were lost. Sherman still seemed as anxious to fight as Johnston appeared not to be. At his rosewood table Davis stared gloomily through the window. His distrust of Johnston's generalship mounted steadily. With increasing persistency the image of Sam Hood stalked through his meditations. Was Sam the answer? For Davis the war also approached a climactery, in part political, in part military, in part psychopathic.

Joseph Emerson Brown, four times governor of Georgia, who hated profanity and alcohol only less than he resented interference with his sovereign authority, long had been a heavy cross for Jefferson Davis to bear. Brown's manner and actions in dealing with Richmond consistently suggested that Georgia not only had seceded from the Union but also could secede from the Confederacy if circumstances so warranted. Every requisition for state troops found Davis and Brown quarreling over who should have the right to appoint officers, and as late as March 1864, in a speech in Milledgeville attacking the President's right to suspend the writ of habeas corpus, Brown snarled that "there is a point beyond which freemen will not permit encroachments to go." Brown called on his listeners to "hurl from power those who deny the fundamental principles upon which their own liberties rest."

Thus spoke Brown in March, unconvinced that any real military emergency threatened Georgia; now, with Sherman's army on the march, Brown was telling Davis how to run the war. Get Forrest out of Mississippi and Morgan out of Kentucky, ran the gist of Brown's advice, for of what earthly good were these silly sorties in stopping Sherman? Brown wanted cavalry and guns from the President for the militia he had called out on May 18 and 21; the arrival of the guns and not the horsemen did not mollify the Governor of Georgia. Everything about the situation had been misjudged in Richmond, Brown contended, and if the President's unreliable information regarding the strength of the contending armies resulted in the loss of Atlanta, "posterity may have reason to mourn over the error." The President's patience for once proved thinly veiled. Pugnaciously, he telegraphed the Governor of Georgia either to reveal his own "better knowledge" or to tend to his own business; and he would advise Brown not to "assume" that he knew the value of military operations "in distant positions."

But Davis, although clearly nettled by Brown, was more upset by Johnston. Let "Old Joe" argue until doomsday that in falling back in good order from Dalton through Big Shanty he had achieved a tactical success by drawing Sherman further away from his base while keeping the fighting strength of the Army of Tennessee intact, such arguments would seem to Davis, as they would sound to Sherman, the sheerest eyewash. The ominous shadows of Kenesaw Mountain were at

Johnston's back; beyond this range were the meandering banks of the Chattahoochee River and Peachtree Creek; and beyond these the homes and marts of Atlanta. Where was the strategical success to turn into the tactical triumph? This query gnawed at Davis with every thought of Georgia. How much longer should he depend on Johnston? With an army superior in numbers to that which Lee commanded in Virginia, when did Johnston intend to stand and *fight*?

Davis hesitated. But more and more his mind came back to Sam Hood. If the President had talked to the men in the Army of Tennessee he might have wondered if Sam could have served him any better than "Old Joe." For all that the President might wish to castigate Johnston, he could not deny that the general was liked by his soldiers. Could as much be said for Sam Hood? How many felt with Lieutenant T. B. Makall after Cassville that whereas Hood "talks about attack and not giving ground, publicly," behind the scenes he "quietly urges retreat"? These were mean words, branding Hood as two-faced and tricky; was the dislike for Hood deepening to the point where such comments were given ready currency?

Jefferson Davis's own neurasthenic tendencies prevented him from judging how much Hood may have been tortured by mental anguish. Sam's artificial leg helped him in the saddle; walking, it was only a hindrance. Sam's sensitivity of temperament must have made of his suddenly acquired handicap both an enemy and a friend. Outwardly, there could be something gallant about a cork leg; a man swung along, head high, making a go of it, cheerful and admired. Inwardly, a man recognized that a weakness existed and learned that long after the flesh had healed the spirit remained bruised. Like every person who ever had faced the need to surmount a suddenly acquired handicap, Sam Hood exhibited typical characteristics: the secret misgivings that often brought hesitancy in a crisis, the compensating compulsiveness of personality which must force others into roles of dependency, the inherently schizophrenic balance between instinct and duty which taxes strength and sanity in normal men and among the handicapped so often becomes abnormally magnified. The very environment of body in which Hood's personality now dwelled could have created confusion and conflict. How much, how little of these possibilities did Jefferson Davis comprehend? Or Joe Johnston? Or Sam Hood?

A German military authority, Count Karl von Clausewitz, who believed that war was "not merely a political act, but also a real political instrument," had written further that when a commander's

> . . . influence ceases and his own spirit is no longer strong enough to revive the spirit of others, the masses, drawing him with them, sink into the lower region of animal nature which recoils from danger and knows not shame.

For Lincoln and Davis, for Brown and his cohorts, for Johnston and Hood, was the count's Teutonic philosophy possibly prophetic?

The Union armies under Sherman verged on Marietta, Georgia. Soon the nation would learn if Clausewitz were right when he declared that "war is the continuation of politics by other means."

5. "THE BURROWING YANKEES"

FROM Big Shanty on the 10th of June many things could be "distinctly seen with the naked eye." The signal stations, the fresh lines of parapets, the heavy masses of Johnston's infantry clearly revealed to Sherman how securely the Confederates had dug in on Kenesaw, Pine Mountain, and Lost Mountain. For once the redbearded Federal general must admit that "Old Joe" had "chosen his ground well" and "with deliberation had prepared for battle." Still, as Sherman turned his horse back toward headquarters, he felt singularly undisturbed. Johnston's line must cover at least ten miles, and forces of only sixty thousand, which was the estimate Sherman then made of the fighting strength of the Army of Tennessee, couldn't hold that long a line successfully. However, it would be silly to forget that Johnston's "naked eye" could observe as much as his own. Any movement of the Federals must be executed cautiously. But Sherman's mind, as he jogged along, placed his forces in positions of complete maneuverability. On the left McPherson would continue to follow the railroad that curved around the north base of Kenesaw. Thomas in the center, where he had been since the jump-off from Chattanooga, but now nicely "obliqued to the right," could deploy below Kenesaw and face Pine Mountain (which Sherman always thought of as a hill). Schofield, "somewhat refused" on the "general right," would look south toward Lost Mountain. Content, Sherman ate a hearty breakfast.

Next morning the general's good spirit remained. The bridge over the Etowah had been repaired, a supply train rumbled up practically to the skirmish line, and the locomotive, detached, ran on to the water tank for refilling. Right there Sherman learned how keenly observant Confederate eyes could be. Within seconds enemy gunners lobbed shells down on the locomotive. But the engineer was a hard little nut who when he set out to get water wasn't easily distracted, and while the hose gushed into his dry boiler he screamed his whistle defiantly. The men in the skirmish line shouted and cheered. Sherman grinned. Did anybody doubt that the Yankees lacked the spirit to carry them over the mountains to Atlanta? Still tooting, the locomotive clambered back to its waiting cars.

Sherman's principal concern those June days became the rain, slashing down in torrents, soaking blankets and clothing, turning fields and woods into quagmires after the passage of a few wagons. By the 11th of June it had rained steadily for nine days without any promise of a let-up. In action, on a march, rain exerted a favorable effect on troops, Sherman believed, but "in the woods, where all is blind and uncertain" it seemed "almost impossible for an army covering ten miles of front to act in concert during wet and stormy weather." Then on the 14th the rain at least slackened, and Sherman saw the Federals entrenched along a line conforming to the irregular positions of the enemy. And the 14th brought good news—cavalry that he had ordered out of Memphis had so stirred up the situation in Mississippi that there wasn't the remotest chance of Forrest slipping away to operate behind the lines in Tennessee.

Sherman strained to start things popping at Kenesaw. Perhaps, like James Austin Connolly, he had grown irked with the "linen coated gentlemen and gaily dressed ladies" who each day drove out from Marietta and looked "with disdain on the burrowing Yankees in the valley below." "Deluded creatures," Connolly would snort, wondering if they had never heard of Missionary Ridge; and Sherman, reconnoitering his lines and looking for a spot to break through between Kenesaw and Pine Mountain, felt as eager as Connolly to unleash his "burrowing Yankees" on the "beauty and fashion of Marietta."

Abreast of Pine Mountain that 14th of June, Sherman observed a Rebel battery on the crest, a fresh rifle-trench halfway down the incline. Through his field glasses he also detected a group of Confederates watching him as coolly as he scanned them. For some reason this indiscretion rankled; Rebels, by God, must be taught to keep under cover in the sight of Yankee guns; and to Howard he gave orders to throw three volleys up that hillside. The artillery unlimbered, and Sherman rode on. But Bishop Leonidas Polk, who had been standing with Hardee and Johnston watching Sherman, couldn't hustle even under fire. Both the Bishop's dignity and corpulence made him a stately walker while his friends scattered, and an unexploded shell from the second or third Federal volley ripped through the Bishop's breast. Polk died almost instantly.

A sad day had come to the Army of Tennessee. In the army's darkest hour, Polk's influence had given Johnston the command and revived the spirit of the man in the ranks. Polk, baptizing Hood and Johnston, had joined the army's cause with God's. To Hardee fell the grievous duty of acquainting Davis with this disaster. "Mr. President," Hardee would write, ". . . it may be gratifying to you to know that only a day or two before his decease in speaking of you, he remarked, that the longer this war lasted the more he had cause to admire your foresight, & particularly your just judgment of men." In so far as "no General needs good corps commanders more than Johnston," Hardee hoped that Davis would send the best man he could find to replace Polk, perhaps even finding a better general than Hindman, whom Hardee favored, or Stewart, whom Johnston and Hood desired.* Almost archly, Hardee wrote: "You sent us a splendid man in Hood," but within short weeks Hardee and Hood would be openly snarling at each other. Of the future Hardee could not comment optimistically: "The enemy won't attack us in our entrenchments, and we are not disposed to attack him in his, so if the present system continues we may find ourselves at Atlanta before a serious battle is fought."

Sherman, however, entertained no intention of continuing "the present system." Johnston, anxious to tighten his lines, abandoned Pine Mountain without a fight, precisely as Sherman might have hoped. Now Thomas and Schofield had "gained about two miles of most difficult country," and McPherson's left "lapped well around" the north end of Kenesaw. Prisoners fell to the Federals like a windfall of apples, among them the entire regiment of the 14th Alabama.

* Major General Loring, next in rank, temporarily succeeded to the command of Polk's corps.

Still Sherman's right threatened the railroad below Marietta, and once more Johnston felt compelled to contract his lines, giving up Lost Mountain and covering Marietta "and all the roads below."

On the 17th and 18th of June the rain torrented harder than ever. Concentrated on Kenesaw, Johnston had dug into a position that a depressed Sherman felt would be "as dangerous to assault as a permanent fort." Yet Sherman was determined to make the best of a bad situation. Garrard's cavalry guarded his supply depot at Big Shanty, McPherson worked further around to the right, Thomas moved up in greater strength. And to match the slave labor that built Johnston's breastworks Sherman evolved a plan. Freedmen who escaped to the Federal lines were organized into a pioneer corps, fed out of regular army supplies, and promised ten dollars a month. At night, while Sherman's troops slept, these pioneer detachments piled headlogs and dug trenches; in the morning the soldiers filled the entrenchments and the freedmen went behind the lines to sleep.

So through the endless driving rains of mid-June, parapet was thrown up to face parapet, enemy regiment moved up within gunshot and earshot of enemy regiment, Federal field piece rolled into place to duel with Confederate field piece. Day and night cannonade and brisk musketry fire rattled through the gloomy forest, and more than one officer slept with his sword buckled on. To keep up morale, regimental quartermasters came into the lines, distributing new pants, hats, and shoes to the men crouching behind the breastworks. A captured Rebel officer provided a good laugh for "the burrowing Yankees." Connolly would relate that about two hours before the Rebel's capture

. . . Gen. Cheatham and staff rode along their lines, announcing to each regiment that the Yankee railroad to Chattanooga had been destroyed by their cavalry, and that the Yankees would be compelled to retreat very soon to get something to eat. Just as Cheatham was making this announcement to this Colonel's regiment, one of our trains from Chattanooga came thundering along into our lines, whistling and screaming like an engine gone mad; the whistle and rumble of the train could be heard by this regiment almost as distinctly as by our men, and, as the Colonel said, "Cheatham dried up." . . .

The quickening tension of the battle threatening at Kenesaw left its mark alike on trooper and general. Cheatham's bald-faced story caused a grin, but a grin was badly needed to ease nerves that had tightened and stomachs that sometimes rolled queasily. Sherman found handling Joe Hooker a special problem. On the 22nd Joe informed Sherman that three corps were in front of him, that he had fought off two heavy attacks, that his extreme right flank had become dangerously exposed. Why in God's name Hooker reported this information to Sherman and not to Thomas, under whom he served, was almost more than Sherman wished to understand. Hooker's trick of "switching off," of "leaving wide gaps in his lines, so as to be independent, and to make *glory* on his own account" had to be stopped!

Sherman bristled. Hooker couldn't forget that before Gettysburg he had commanded the Army of the Potomac, and Sherman was equally resolved not to forget how disastrously Joe had fought at Chancellorsville. Hooker had damned little reason for looking down his nose at Thomas, Schofield, or McPherson. Maybe Joe had fought well in the Battle above the Clouds, but it was time Joe pulled his head down out of those clouds. It was sheer rot to claim three corps were in front of him; Johnston's whole army only consisted of three corps! Schofield likewise seethed at Hooker; hell, he had repulsed the attacks Joe claimed and Schofield would take Sherman out in the field and show him his dead lying further

out than any of Hooker's. Sherman sailed into Joe and Schofield added an oar; the words grew sharp, for the mood of
Kenesaw had begun to blister.

And not on the Federal side of the lines alone. That attack
on the 22nd, in which Hooker had pictured himself a hero,
had been led by Sam Hood. Still fretful of the swing of the
Federal right toward the railroad, Johnston had sent Hood
down to the Marietta and Powder Spring Road to stop the
movement. Hood recounted a gallant story of the fight.
Hindman's and Stevenson's divisions, Hood said, not only had
repulsed the enemy but had followed him to a line of light
entrenchments and driven him from it. The fire of an entrenched artillery unit had caught Hood there and forced him
to withdraw. Johnston accepted this report, but with tongue
in cheek. He kept inquiring what really had transpired there
on the Marietta and Powder Spring Road and in time * gave
a different version of the action:

> . . . It appeared that our troops had not fallen back
> merely to escape annoyance, but that, after the Federal
> infantry had been driven back to and then beyond the
> line of breastworks, Lieutenant-General Hood deter-
> mined to capture the entrenched artillery referred to in his
> brief report. It crowned a high, bare hill, facing the inter-
> val between his right and the left of Hardee's corps. To
> direct his line toward it, a partial change of front to the
> right was necessary, and that slow operation, performed
> under the fire of a formidable artillery, subjected his two
> divisions to a loss so severe that the attempt was soon
> abandoned—I am uncertain whether by the decision of
> the commander, or the discretion of the troops themselves;
> not, however, until they had lost about a thousand men.

Still, writing Davis somewhat belatedly of Polk's death,
Hardee that day would call Hood "a splendid man." But
the fundamental clash in temperament between Johnston and

---

* Actually this account was published after the war.

Hood would be revealed in the incident—"Old Joe" intent on sparing blood, Sam Hood more reckless and headstrong in seeking victory.

On the 23rd Sherman telegraphed Halleck in Washington: "Our lines are now in close contact, and the fighting is incessant, with a good deal of artillery-fire. As fast as we open one position the enemy has another all ready, but I think he will soon have to let go Kenesaw, which is the key to the whole country." The weather had cleared; the roads were drying up fast. The trouble with Hooker seemed to bring Sherman's mind to a decision. It would be better to act than to waste energy on internal wrangling. At a meeting of his three commanding generals he expressed the belief that, like it or not, they would have to attack fortified positions. Thomas, Schofield, McPherson agreed. "I reasoned," Sherman said, "if we could make a breach anywhere near the Rebel centre, and thrust in a strong head column, that with the one moiety of our army we could hold in check the corresponding wing of the enemy, and with the other sweep in flank and overwhelm the other half." June 27th was picked as the day for the grand finale on Kenesaw; at eight o'clock that morning the Union troops moved; and Sam Watkins of the 1st Tennessee would remember that for two hours "every man in our regiment killed from onescore to fourscore, yea, fivescore men," for "all that was necessary was to load and shoot." And still they came, Watkins said.

Few Confederate generals excelled Samuel G. French in possessing the kind of disposition requisite for sitting on one of the two chief hot-seats at Kenesaw that morning. Sam French, a native of New Jersey, was the son of a Quaker. Apparently Sam's father had been a "sporting Quaker," who could forget his religious scruples in his delight over his son's appointment to West Point. In Sam's class at the Academy had been another lad called Sam—Sam Grant, who was registered as Ulysses S. through a Congressman's mistake despite the fact that Grant had been christened Hiram Ulysses—and French with his fellow classmates insisted on dubbing Grant "Uncle Sam" or plain "Sam" for short. Sam French had fought with Hood under Longstreet and knew his way around in a military sense. Typical of Sam French would be his laconic diary entry when ordered to hold a reserve for Hardee: "I have to hold a reserve for everybody but myself." On the morning of the 27th French needed all the reserves he could beg, borrow, or steal.

The traveler who approaches Kenesaw from Marietta finds that Little Kenesaw, which is hooked to the main mountain, drops off on the southwest into a sort of ravine. Beyond this ravine the ground rises slightly, forming a hill that slopes downward, again on the southwest, to face the road from Marietta. Ector's brigade of Texans and North Carolinians covered the crest of Little Kenesaw for French that morning; and Cockrell's brigade of Missourians manned the entrenchments across the ravine to the foot of the hill. Walker's division of Georgia militia—courtesy of Governor Brown—covered another hill across the Marietta Road. French's entire force numbered fewer than 3,500 men, and Cockrell's Missouri brigade, where General Morgan L. Smith would strike with 5,500 Federals, could claim about 1,000 effectives. Sam French stamped around; any way he looked at it, he could be in a hell of a fix.

Under orders from John Logan of the XVth Corps, Morgan Smith had massed for the attack during the night. Morgan Smith wanted most the hill that Cockrell held and, forming Lightburn's brigade of two thousand muskets in two lines, picked a little orchard, about four hundred yards to the right of the hill, as the point for launching an assault on that flank. Simultaneously another brigade of about the same strength under Giles A. Smith would strike directly at the hill, and Colonel Walcutt with 1,500 men from Harrow's division was to move for the gorge, lap the mountain on the left of the hill, and capture the works in front. Walcutt would move first, since Morgan Smith believed that "the enemy could not depress their artillery sufficiently to fire on him," and the first enemy fire that Walcutt drew would be the signal for Lightburn and Giles Smith to advance.

Walcutt pressed forward, cursing the dense underbrush that made it impossible for the skirmishers to keep in front of his lines. Advanced rifle-pits, dropped about four hundred yards from the Confederate main works, fell easily. But now a dark, swampy ravine stretched ahead. With fixed bayonets, their hearts in their throats, Walcutt's boys plodded on. The sides of the ravine were steep and rugged; trees had been felled as an added impediment; and no advance on the main works could be made with regularity. Then Confederate lead, hot and deadly, came down in a shower. "Officers and men," Morgan Smith reported, "fell thick and fast." But the advance pushed on, until "within about 30 feet of the enemy's main works the line staggered and sought cover as best they could behind logs and rocks." As the engagement quickened, Cockrell would report, some of his Missourians "fired sixty rounds to the man."

The 55th and 111th Illinois from Giles Smith's brigade "fell on and inside the works," but Lightburn's boys were having a hell of a time. In the swamp through which Lightburn pressed, officers and men sank to their knees. Thickets closed around them and an enfilading fire permitted Lightburn at no time to come closer than one hundred and fifty yards to the orchard and the works beyond. A colonel from the 57th Ohio fell with a wound that would mean a leg amputation, another from the 83rd Indiana with his shoulder cut away. Bayonets clashed, men screamed and cursed and clawed and cried, and the terror of Kenesaw spread like a mist over the ravine, behind the logs hugged by trembling men, and into the blazing rifle-pits. Lieutenant Colonel Robert A. Fulton of the 53rd Ohio reported:

> The Rebels fought with a desperation worthy of a better cause. The conduct of our soldiers and officers on this occasion needs no comment; never did men show more

gallantry, mounting the works, shooting the enemy, and beating them over the heads with the butts of their guns.

From Little Kenesaw, Sam French looked down on the battle raging around him and thought it "one of the most magnificent sights ever allotted to man." Over on Kenesaw, Thomas pounded at Cheatham, and between the two actions —one boiling on the left, the other erupting at his feet—Sam surveyed a "hundred and fifty thousand men arrayed in the strife of battle on the plain below." For miles "the blue smoke of musket" marked the Confederate lines, and above it, like great cumulus clouds, rose "the white smoke of the artillery." The wind broke rifts through the smoke; "the battle, in its entirety," Sam said, "became a pageantry on a grand scale."

Ever since Sam had lodged on Kenesaw he had been building up a peeve that was being wonderfully released. Day after day of skirmishing that had not even omitted the Sabbath had caused French to write his Southern wife: "Sherman has no respect for the Fourth Commandment." Now Sam may have begun to wonder if the Federal commander had any more respect for human life. Sherman's dead at Kenesaw were strewn across swamp, ravine, plain, and mountainside. When Cockrell asked for reinforcements Sam gave him part, then all, of Ector's Texans and North Carolinians. Perhaps the charging men under Ector remembered how the Yanks used to call across to the outposts: "Hello, Johnny, how far is it to Atlanta?" The answer then had been: "So damn far you'll never get there," and the Texans and North Carolinians, joining Cockrell's Missourians, blazed away at the tormentors who once had shrieked that when they reached Atlanta they'd be having "a big dance with your sister!" Well, they could have their big dance now to the hum of singing bullets at their britches! Under orders from Johnny Logan, Morgan Smith pulled his bleeding boys back from the assault on Little Kenesaw.

The attack on Cheatham fared no better. The boys in the Army of Tennessee came off the best as they scampered up the mountainside as though they were stalking Indians in the tradition of the West. When they glanced back and saw Thomas's lads in the Army of the Cumberland marching up those slopes in formal columns they could thank God they had hugged the boulders and tree stumps. Those fool Cumberlanders looked like a throwback to the British at Bunker Hill except that the Rebs weren't waiting to glimpse the whites of their eyes before blasting away with their muskets. Three times Ted Upson of the 100th Indiana charged the rise of Kenesaw. "We were in a bad fix," Ted said. "We could not go ahead and we could not get back." A rock twenty feet ahead, too high to scale, gave a sort of cover: "The Johnnys might have killed every one of us as we hugged its base, but they only yelled and threw stones at us." Night seemed a long time coming, then Ted and the other tired, discouraged kids from Indiana crept back to the Federal lines. The rumor persisted that there wouldn't have been a fight at Kenesaw if Sherman hadn't been piqued because the country's attention seemed focused on Grant's Army of the Potomac. His own army, Sherman was reported to have told Johnny Logan, "was entirely forgotten, but now it would fight."

Johnston, watching the Yankee assaults against Cheatham rolling in waves and breaking in foams of blood upon the mountainside, calculated that more of Sherman's "best soldiers lay dead and wounded than the number of British veterans that fell in General Jackson's celebrated battle of New Orleans." Johnston's hand wiped the grime and sweat from his face. Who said he couldn't fight? In Johnston's estimation, Sherman's veterans "had encountered *intrenched* infantry unsurpassed by that of Napoleon's Old Guard, or that which followed Wellington into France." For Ted Upson the strangest experience of bloody Kenesaw came the next day, when under a flag of truce:

Details from both Armies were made and gathered up the dead, of which there were a great many, and at suitable places buried them. The Confederates in one, our men in another big grave—side by side, wrapped in their blankets. Our graves were marked by a piece of board from hard tack boxes with name, Company, and Regt where we could make them out—which we could not always do. Their watches or other articles of value [were] taken charge of by an officer to be sent home. A prayer was made by a Chaplain of either Army and the graves filled up. After this was done we filled in the rest of the time allowed with visiting between the officers and men of both Armies, all showing kindly interest in each other. When the gun was fired that announced that the truce was ended we parted with expressions of good will such as:

"I hope to miss you, Yank, if I happen to shoot in your direction," or "May I never hit you Johnny if we fight again." All went back to their lines and in a short time the pickets were merrily popping away at each other.

Eight hundred and eight Confederates died that day; Johnston believed the Federal loss was 6,000, but Sherman cut this figure to 2,500 killed and wounded. Sherman would list his total losses during the month's fighting for Kenesaw at 7,530 in killed, wounded, and missing; Johnston would claim that for the month beginning June fourth his total loss was 3,948, omitting the "missing." The month of June had taught Sherman a lesson. He was through abandoning his flanking movements for a frontal attack.

Again, although Thomas shook his head at the risk, Sherman decided to leave the railroad and wrote Halleck on July first:

General Schofield is now south of Olley's Creek, and on the head of Nickajack. I have been hurrying down provisions and forage, and to-morrow night propose to move McPherson from the left to the extreme right, back of General Thomas. This will bring my right within three miles of the Chattahoochee River, and about five miles from the railroad. By this movement I think I can force Johnston to move his whole army down from Kenesaw to defend the railroad and the Chattahoochee, when I will (by the left flank) reach the railroad below Marietta; but in this I must cut loose from the railroad with ten days' supplies in wagons. Johnston may come out of his intrenchments to attack Thomas, which is exactly what I want, for General Thomas is well intrenched on a line parallel with the enemy south of Kenesaw. I think that Allatoona and the line of the Etowah are strong enough for me to venture on this move. The movement is substantially down the Sandtown road straight for Atlanta.

Johnston lost no time quitting Kenesaw and running to beat Sherman across the Chattahoochee. By the 4th of July, Yankee pickets roamed at will along the crest of Kenesaw.

No one was happier to move on than Ted Upson. In the old Seminary Building near Marietta young Upson was set to guarding a difficult batch of prisoners—four hundred young women who had been working in a factory at Rossville making cloth for the Confederate government. Some of these girls were tough, knew what the men wanted, and, Ted confessed, it was "a hard job to keep them straight." He added: "General Sherman says he would rather try to guard the whole Confederate Army, and I guess he is about right."

6. NO. 1 VERSUS NO. 44

AFTER Kenesaw, only one objective remained: for Sherman, the capture of Atlanta; for Joe Johnston, the city's defense. With Lieutenant General Alexander P. Stewart taking over the command of Polk's corps, the Confederates now fell across the Chattahoochee, and, Johnston said: "engineer-officers joined in the work of strengthening the intrenchments of Atlanta with all the Negro laborers that could be collected." Obviously Sherman must approach from the side of the Augusta and Marietta roads, and Johnston fled to a "position on the high ground looking down into the valley of . . . [Peachtree] creek from the south."

Very likely, as "Old Joe" fell back, he felt that he was drawing Sherman's army to the precise spot where he wanted it, backed against the Chattahoochee with the muddy channel of Peachtree Creek still to cross. Perhaps Johnston felt at last that the bitter retreats through Dalton, Resaca, and Cassville, and the savage fighting at Kenesaw, had resulted in the right situation. Let Sherman come to "Old Joe" across Peachtree Creek and there might, indeed, be some reason to the past seventy days as the Army of Tennessee had staggered back a hundred miles from Dalton to the Chattahoochee! Now Johnston would prove that for all of Sherman's fine flanking maneuvers his army remained unbeaten and unbeatable.

On the 14th of July, Joe Johnston and the men in the Army of Tennessee received an unexpected visitor in General Braxton Bragg. The purpose of Bragg's appearance, as Johnston understood it, was "to ascertain what re-enforcements for *me*" could be furnished, but soon Bragg would be telegraphing Davis in Richmond that, as far as he could determine, Johnston had no plans for the future, that among Johnston's three lieutenant generals (Hood, Stewart, and Hardee), the latter alone in any way favored Johnston's policy, and that everything—"Position, numbers, and morale"—now favored the Federals. Bragg felt that "General Hood would give unlimited satisfaction" if Davis wished "any change," and, indulging in the double-talk that had distinguished Bragg following the debacle at Missionary Ridge, he added that Davis must not misunderstand him in thinking Hood was "a man of genius, or a great general." To Bragg, Hood simply was "far better in the present emergency than anyone we have available."

In Richmond, Jefferson Davis knew that he must replace Johnston. He had come to a point where trying to explain to his cabinet—or to himself—what he was going to do about Johnston's eternal, infernal retreats had become impossible. Davis would ask Lee, how can there be any question but that Johnston intended to abandon Atlanta? Johnston must be replaced, Davis told Lee, but "who should succeed him?" Hood? Even Lee's tactfulness in conceding that Hood "is a good fighter," couldn't keep him from remarking guardedly that "I have had no opportunity of judging his action when the whole responsibility rested on him." Hardee, Lee thought, was much to be preferred as commander. So Davis faced his choice. Lee wouldn't endorse Hood, and leaned toward Hardee. Bragg suggested Hood, but with his tongue in his cheek. Hardee still wanted Johnston. What Jeff Davis did under these circumstances might have been expected long ago. A telegram from the Adjutant General in Richmond told Johnston:

> I am directed by the Secretary of War to inform you that, as you have failed to arrest the advance of the enemy to the vicinity of Atlanta, far in the interior of Georgia, and express no confidence that you can defeat or repel him, you are hereby relieved from the command of the Army and Department of Tennessee, which you will immediately turn over to General Hood.

Promptly "Old Joe" replied:

Your dispatch . . . received and obeyed. Command
has been transferred to General Hood. As to the alleged
cause of my removal, I assert that Sherman's army is
stronger, compared with that of [the Army of] Tennessee,
than Grant's with that of [the Army of] Northern Virginia. Yet the enemy has been compelled to advance
more slowly to the vicinity of Atlanta than to that of
Richmond and Petersburg, and penetrated much deeper
into Virginia than into Georgia. Confident language by a
military commander is not usually regarded as evidence of
competence.

Johnston, obviously peeved, refused to believe that comparisons were odious—even comparisons with Robert E. Lee.
And once that "Old Joe," hurt to the quick, decided he was
no longer wanted, he couldn't quit the Army of Tennessee
quickly enough. The orders dismissing him had been dated
July 17; the next day Johnston delivered his address of farewell
to the men he had found so miserably huddled in their winter
huts at Dalton. To "the Corn-fed" the removal of Johnston
came almost as a last blow. Sam Watkins of the 1st Tennessee
said "I saw, I will say, thousands of men cry like babies—
regular, old-fashioned boohoo, *boohoo*, BOOHOO." Sherman, on
the other hand, who believed that "the character of a leader
is a large factor in the game of war," must confess that "I was
pleased at this change." McPherson, Schofield, and Hood had
been in the same class at West Point. McPherson had graduated No. 1 in his class, Schofield No. 7, Hood No. 44. In one
sense, the battle for Atlanta had become a question of mathe-
matical averages.

But mathematics would never decide the issue. War was a
human equation. The sultry days of mid-July settled down
over central Georgia. A redheaded general studied his maps
and wondered. A general on a cork leg looked up at the stars
and dreamed of his two great leaders, Jackson and Lee. Another general, disheartened, dispirited, traveled the road to

Macon. Each of these men were principals in the drama about to unfold.

And so, too, was a girl who had not yet reached her tenth birthday. And a woman who would go to a funeral. And a banker, a governor, and a Union general whose ambitions would be focused on an August day in the Wigwam in Chicago. And a man in Meadville, Pennsylvania, who would scribble a message on a window. And a major who would write his wife, and a foot soldier who would hold the hand of a dying boyhood friend, and a general who would be afraid to attack intrenchments—

Each would be part of the drama. Meanwhile the hot sun in the cloudless sky above Atlanta, Georgia, would reach out to touch each. That sun would shine down on trench and headquarters tent, on city street and country road, on a child playing and on a woman thinking of her husband. History, like love, levels all ranks.

July came and passed. But everywhere the Federal soldiers looked they saw something they preferred next to—if not before—dead Confederates.

Ripe blackberries.

PART FOUR

✶✶✶✶✶✶✶✶✶✶✶✶✶✶✶✶✶✶✶✶✶✶✶✶✶✶✶✶✶✶✶✶✶✶✶✶✶✶✶

"And Fairly Won"

—the battle for Atlanta

1. ATLANTA HONORS A GENERAL

THE body of Bishop Leonidas Polk, reaching Atlanta, lay in state in St. Luke's Church. Grief spread an unnatural hush over the city. To Sallie Clayton, in her home on Marietta Street, the war had brought its saddest day. The girl ate breakfast without interest, and, looking through the window, the beauty of the magnolia blossoms made her young heart ache. Around General Polk's casket in front of the chancel in St. Luke's, where kindly Dr. Quintard hovered constantly, magnolia blossoms had been banked. Over the casket the flag of the Confederacy had been draped, but the blossoms, by their beauty, emphasized the solemnity of the moment. "In that day and generation," Sallie remembered, "it was the first and only time for some years to come that flowers were used in Atlanta on a funeral occasion."

Early that morning Dr. Quintard had opened the doors of St. Luke's to the hundreds who already thronged the streets and waited patiently to pay their last respects to the gallant Polk, and before noon the queues before the church would number in the thousands. Sallie's eyes gazed through the window; the melancholy sweetness of the flowering magnolias reached her; but the girl lingered at the table. She must go to St. Luke's and pay her own silent tribute to the dear old general, but for the instant she seemed lost in the memory of how the war had affected Atlanta.

In the early spring of '61, "before leaving for the army became general," when there were still parties and picnics in Ormond's Grove at the foot of Washington Street or by the mineral spring near the Macon Depot, Sallie's existence had revolved around the Atlanta Female Institute. How attractive the restrictions of the institute seemed now: to be seated at your desk promptly at eight-thirty, to keep in style by wearing a straw shaker bonnet drawn over the face, and to maintain a discreet silence if accused of stealing an apple from the trees growing in the front schoolyard or of chewing the sweet-gum oozing from their trunks! But the coming of the war had brought a change so that Sallie thought her life had been like a play with the curtain ringing down on "Life, Joy, and Mirth" and rising again to "Gloom and Sorrow, Suffering and Death."

A Southern girl, knitting three socks a day for the soldiers, rolling bandages and scraping lint, soon demonstrated that she wasn't the "frivolous, helpless creature" most Northerners imagined! The senseless talk she heard about Southern girls being waited on hand and foot by Negroes made Sallie bridle. Such talk proved how much the North knew about anything! To listen to the prattle Yankees believed, you'd think every Negro in the South called white girls "Chile" or "Honey," when, as a matter of fact, the use of pet names was restricted to Negro women of maturity and experience who could wrap bright-colored turbans around their heads as "marks of aristocracy."

Exciting days followed the firing on Sumter. The first military company to leave Atlanta, Sallie remembered, was the Gate City Guards, en route to Pensacola. Then "companies from all parts of the state began to pass through Atlanta and . . . would be in camp here for a few days." The Fulton Dragoons, Atlanta Grays, Irish Volunteers, and the German-born Steuben Yaegers were among the trim-clad companies that paused at the camping grounds near Walton Spring before passing on to the front. Soon a large recruiting camp opened at Big Shanty and Sallie liked to go with the parties from Atlanta to watch the parades of volunteers "beautifully uniformed in dark green with gold trimmings and large dark hats with drooping white plumes."

The tempo of the war increased. General John H. Morgan,

riding, raiding, and fighting across a thousand miles of Indiana and Ohio until he almost reached the border of Pennsylvania, created a legend of bold rashness that captivated Confederate imaginations. The swashbuckling Morgan, imprisoned in Ohio, escaped by tunneling under a stone wall, and "about the greatest day ever seen in Atlanta," Sallie said, witnessed the reception for Morgan at the old Trent House. The crowds gawped and cheered and the general passed through the streets in a carriage from which the horses had been unhitched so that husky Atlantans might have the honor of drawing it. Sallie felt enraptured, and, looking "upon the gallant General that day," who could "dream that in one short year his brilliant career would be brought to a sudden close"? *

Other raiders whom Sallie saw in Atlanta were the henchmen of Captain James J. Andrews, but the city's mood was quite different that day. A Union spy, Andrews appeared at Big Shanty on an April day in 1862, and, with twenty-one cohorts who had assembled at various points along the railroad north from Atlanta, stole the engine "General" and two boxcars while the railroad crew and passengers were breakfasting. Andrews's plan was to race to Chattanooga, cutting telegraph wires and burning bridges so that communications with Atlanta would be completely disrupted; but the quick wit of Captain W. A. Fuller, a conductor on Governor Brown's Western and Atlantic Railroad, brought about Andrews's failure. Impressing a hand-car and crew, Fuller hastened across the Etowah to where the yard engine "Yonah" was puffing at the siding of some iron mines. At Adairsville, Fuller changed to a new engine, the "Texas," and pounded on, running backward, at a mile a minute. Andrews abandoned the "General" at the Georgia-Tennessee state line and fled into the woods, but seven of his "bridge burners" were cap-

* In 1864, on another raid into Kentucky, Morgan was surrounded in a home at Greenville and shot trying to escape. Lincoln despised the marauder Morgan as "a nigger-driver"; Sallie's hero, in Lincoln's estimation, was "low, mean, cowardly."

tured, brought back to Atlanta, and sentenced to hang. Sallie tried to dissuade the young Semmes boys from attending the execution, but go they must. Two of the seven ropes broke, requiring "a second hanging," and that night the boys wished they hadn't watched the dangling bodies at the gallows. Their "howls," Sallie said, "were loud enough to have brought out the entire police department," and "one poor little fellow insisted that all seven of the men were sitting on the foot of his bed."

The odor of the magnolia blossoms filled the room. Sallie stirred. How many now were the memories of the war years! One of the strangest was of the party that had set out from Atlanta to visit Bragg at Missionary Ridge. Sallie had gone along for "the grand sight of the opposing armies"; Bragg had entertained the ladies courteously and, insisting that the party stay all night, had "promised to take us the next day to Lookout Mountain, and let those who wished to do so, fire cannon." Bragg won his point; soon after breakfast, Sallie remembered, "we began preparing for the trip to Lookout Mountain." Bragg sat at his desk writing autographs. Ladies or no ladies, to the foot soldiers in the Army of Tennessee Monday was wash day, and Sallie saw the unmilitary picture of men fighting dirt in a washtub.

The ride to the mountain passed pleasantly, but ended abruptly. In cussed Yankee fashion, the Federals started shelling Lookout. Sallie had no wish "to be one of the dead women to roll out of one of the ambulances." The shells kept dropping and five words summarized everyone's deepest wish: "I want to go home!" Back at Missionary Ridge, Bragg still insisted that the ladies stay for dinner, but within ten minutes changed his mind. A battle had started! Sallie's party fled homeward through a camp "of wild confusion" where "the men were seizing their arms, and were almost running over one another, in their hurry to reach the front." Boxes, benches, camp stools were swept aside. Sallie could run, too.

Missionary Ridge, Sherman on the march, the war drawing

closer to Atlanta, and now Polk lying in state in St. Luke's! Sallie could put off the sad moment no longer; she would go to the church. Passing through the crowed aisles, standing at last before Polk's casket, tears filled her eyes. "Many, very many," she noticed, "paused long enough when the casket was reached to stoop, for it was quite low, and take a leaf, or flower, or twig." The beauty of the morning, she thought, "seemed a mockery to the gloom and sorrow of Atlanta."

But soon Atlanta would know several such mornings after Kenesaw, and Johnston's dismissal as commander of the Army of Tennessee. Polk's body in St. Luke's was but an omen. Now Sallie would grow accustomed to the noise of the connonading, "and if anyone who wanted to hear it would go into a quiet place the sound of musketry was quite plain." On every train residents scurried away from the city. Sallie's last day in school found the teacher "questioning us as to our understanding of the position of our forces above the town." Thus school ended for a girl who never "had expected to be graduated at the mouth of cannon." A short reading of the Scripture followed, and the class knelt in prayer. "We had little hope of ever meeting again," Sallie recalled. That night she left Atlanta for Augusta.

2. "THE LEE AND JACKSON SCHOOL"

"Old Joe" had gone to Macon. To Captain Tom Key of Pat Cleburne's division every man in the Army of Tennessee "looked sad and disheartened," for all "felt that evil would result from the removal of Johnston." The General's address of farewell, Key believed, had "touched every heart," and every man had become convinced "that his favorite general had been grievously wronged." A day later Key found the men in the Army of Tennessee still clinging hopefully to the rumor that Johnston remained in command, but whereas this report "cheered the despondent hearts," Key suspected a ruse "to prevent desertions and to cause the troops to fight with their former bravery in the now approaching conflict."

A sick emptiness gnawed at the edges of Sam Hood's stomach. He didn't want the command! The "manifold difficulties and trials which beset me at the period" were enough! The order from the Secretary of War removing Johnston from command left Sam as stunned and confused as the weariest soldier he was now expected to lead. Pride-swallowing was not one of Hood's most graceful gifts, but his "appeals" to Johnston "to pocket all dispatches from Richmond" grew "urgent and repeated." If Johnston would stay and fight the battle of Atlanta, Sam would be satisfied simply to retain command of his own corps. Bitterly, in after years, Hood recalled that Johnston

> . . . deserted me the ensuing afternoon. He deserted me in violation of his promise to remain and afford me the advantage of his counsel, whilst I shouldered all the responsibility of the contest.

Hardee, who neither liked nor trusted the military judgment in Richmond any more than he did Hood's, remained convinced that the changes of position made by Johnston from Dalton to Atlanta were "deliberate, and without loss, disorder, or discouragement." Under Johnston's leadership, Hardee one day would write his old commander, the troops were "in buoyant spirits" and "speaking for my own corps, I have no hesitancy in saying that I should have led them into action with more confidence at the close than at the beginning of the campaign." * Lieutenant General Alexander P. Stewart, who had joined the Army of Tennessee after Shiloh, when

---

* The date of the letter from Hardee to Johnston containing these opinions was April 20, 1868; that from Stewart, subsequently quoted, was February 11, 1868.

it "was then mostly without discipline," also believed that Johnston was "the only commander . . . whom *men* and *officers* were disposed to trust and confide in without reserve." Stewart said significantly: "You know how I felt when you showed me the order relieving you. . . . The Army of Tennesee *loved* you as an army of brave men will love . . . *skill, pluck,* and *honor.*"

Sam Hood could not escape the disappointment, resentment, and distrust surrounding him, even among his lieutenant generals. It was difficult, he confessed, "to imagine a commander placed at the head of an army under more embarrassing circumstances." After all, he was "comparatively a stranger" to these officers and men now so ardently wedded to Johnston's policy of "the timid defensive," and he must expect that they "naturally regarded with distrust a commander likely to initiate offensive operations." Hardee had been on the point of resigning, and only Hood's appeal to Davis to continue Johnston in command until after the battle of Atlanta had mollified the old man so that he had decided to remain with his corps. But nothing basic in their conflict had been resolved. Hood could not conceal his contempt for "Johnston's mode of warfare," which formed "so strong a contrast to the strategy and tactics practiced in Virginia, where far more satisfactory results were obtained than in the West." As a warrior, Hood always would call himself a devoted pupil of "the Lee and Jackson school."

On the evening of the 18th of July, the unhappy Hood, facing the torments of his unwanted command, still seethed at the thought of Johnston "comfortably quartered at Macon." Scouting reports told Hood that McPherson's and Schofield's corps were "tearing up the Georgia Railroad" between Stone Mountain and Decatur and that Thomas's army "was hastening preparations to cross Peachtree Creek, within about six miles of Atlanta." The Confederate general set grimly to the task of "hunting up" the positions of Stewart's and Hardee's corps so that he might establish communications with this part of his army! Hood's thin-lipped mouth tightened. Johnston had "disappeared so unexpectedly" that he did not know where Hardee's and Stewart's men were posted, and it would not be until years afterward, he declared, when reading Sherman's *Memoirs*, that he would learn how early that morning McPherson had come so close to Atlanta that "a few enterprising scouts thrown out . . . in the direction of the Macon Railroad might have captured my predecessor on his retreat to Macon." Any tears Sam might have shed at that eventuality certainly would have waited for a later day! On the 18th he did not even know of the presence of the Federals in Decatur, "almost at the gates of Atlanta," intelligence surely that "must have been communicated to General Johnston by the cavalry." Next day Hood's official report would recognize for the first time McPherson's whereabouts, adding evidence, he said, to "the trying position in which I was placed at this juncture."

Still, dark though the emergency appeared, Sam Hood would be damned if he were licked. The stanch advocate of the "Lee and Jackson school" was determined to act quickly and boldly, even if outnumbered in force and depressed by the fact that he believed his men "downcast, dispirited, and demoralized," as a result of "day after day [turning] their back on the enemy" till now they were across the Chattahoochee "with one-third of their number lost." Grandly, Hood would say: "Our troops had awakened in me heartfelt sympathy"; now they must be given the sort of quick, imaginative stroke that would revive their fighting quality!

Through the night of the 18th and the morning of the 19th Hood formed his line of battle facing Peachtree Creek, his left resting near Pace's Ferry Road and the right covering Atlanta. Confederate scouts reported Thomas building bridges across Peachtree Creek, and said that "McPherson and Schofield were well over toward, and even on, the Georgia Railroad, near Decatur." The blood surged in Hood's veins. For once, by God, Sherman had violated "the established maxim,"

. . . in separating his corps, or armies, by such distances as to allow me to concentrate the main body of our army upon his right wing, whilst his left was so far removed as to be incapable of rendering timely assistance.

Had Sherman forgotten that "an army should always be held well within hand, or its detachments within easy supporting distance"? Here, Hood felt, he was

. . . afforded one of the most favorable occasions for complete victory which could have been offered; especially as it presented an opportunity, after crushing its right wing, to throw our entire force upon its left.

Such a blunder, Hood thought excitedly, "affords a small army . . . the sole chance of success when contending with a vastly superior force."

Sam saw his great moment almost within grasp. Stewart's corps on the left, Hardee's in the center, and Cheatham's on the right frowned down on the Federal positions at Peachtree Creek. Hardee and Stewart were "to observe closely and report promptly the progress of Thomas in the construction of bridges across Peachtree Creek and the passage of troops," while Cheatham would "reconnoitre in front of his left . . . erect, upon that part of his line, batteries so disposed as to command the entire space between his left and Peachtree Creek [thereby isolating the forces of McPherson and Schofield from those of Thomas, and] finally, to thoroughly entrench his line."

Hood couldn't see why he should fail! When Thomas partially had crossed the creek and "made a lodgement on the east side within the pocket formed by Peachtree Creek and the Chattahoochee River," the men under Hardee and Stewart, falling upon Thomas, would "crush Sherman's right wing" in the narrow corridor between the creek and the river! For either McPherson or Schofield to assist Thomas without recrossing the creek would require a ten- or twelve-mile march to reach Thomas's bridges, and, to make certain the harassments of such a march would be doubly devilish, Hood sent the Georgia militia to reinforce Cheatham's right. Hardee, Stewart, and Cheatham met at Hood's headquarters. The attack, Sam told them, would be launched on the 20th, at one o'clock in the afternoon. Everything on the Confederate side of the creek was ''to be taken at all hazards''; each general would hold a division in reserve, and:

> . . . Owing to the demonstrations of the enemy on the right, it became necessary to extend Cheatham a division front to the right. To do this, Hardee and Stewart were each ordered to extend a half division front to close the interval.

Here, Hood must admit, was the possible joker; if in the ''confusion and delay'' that could follow, Hardee failed ''to see that the left did not take more than a half division front,'' disaster could result! But Sam, ignoring this risk, clung to the hope that he might catch the Federals throwing up breastworks and strike them ''in that state of confusion to enable our forces to rout them by a bold and persistent attack.'' Sam, trying to reckon on everything as he endeavored ''to surprise the enemy in their unsettled condition,'' overlooked—as once, quite understandably, Braxton Bragg had done at Missionary Ridge—that in George H. Thomas he was pitted against one of the toughest fighting generals in the Union army.

For the impatient, impulsive Sherman, Thomas's methodical habits at times proved an annoyance, but Halleck would counsel his old friend: ''Thomas is . . . a noble old warhorse. It is true, as you say, that he is slow, but he is always sure.'' On the 19th, as Thomas crossed Peachtree Creek, Sherman had been fooled, for his three armies, converging on Atlanta, had met ''such feeble resistance that I really thought the enemy intended to evacuate the place.'' Caught off guard, Sherman recognized far too complacently that ''there was quite a gap between Thomas and Schofield, which I endeavored to close by drawing two of Howard's divisions nearer to Schofield."

Next day, the 20th, shortly after noon, Sherman rode with Schofield close to the center of the Federal lines, when the redheaded general heard "heavy firing in front of Thomas's right, which lasted an hour or so, and then ceased." Soon Sherman learned that the Confederates "had made a furious sally" on Hooker's XXth Corps, partially on Johnston's Division of the XIVth Corps, and on Newton's Division of the IVth Corps. The Federal troops, crossing Peachtree Creek and deploying, were "resting for noon, when, without notice, the enemy came pouring out of their trenches down upon them, they became commingled, and fought in many places hand-to-hand." Thomas stood near to the rear of Newton's division. Here the "Rock of Chickamauga," the general whose troops had routed Bragg at Missionary Ridge, climbed a spur overlooking Peachtree Creek. Six Federal field guns placed there caught his eye and he took personal command. There the battle raged; there the issue must be—and would be—decided.

Although, in Sherman's *Memoirs*, the battle had begun "shortly after noon," Hood's main attack, timed for 1:00 p.m., actually had been delayed three hours. Still, the surprise of the attack by Hardee on the unprepared Thomas had achieved an almost immediate breakthrough, and Thomas, falling back, saw his left turned. Sam Hood's great moment drew closer. But with Sam Hood, from the day he joined the Army of Tennessee, something always went wrong. This time a division in Hardee's corps seemed at fault. Hardee's attack limped, like Sam Hood walking on his cork leg, and the muskets and the artillery of the Union raked his faltering lines. Confederate General Winfield S. Featherston remained "struck with surprise" that at the time Hood's attack was launched neither artillery nor small arms "were heard on our right, save a feeble skirmish." Featherston wondered if no enemy had been met; later, instead of the "brilliant" victory Featherston believed would have resulted "had the attack on the right been vigorously made," he must admit that "the orders seem to have been misunderstood . . . or for some cause not fully carried out." Hood's opinion was that "in lieu of moving the half division promptly to the right, attacking as ordered, and supporting Stewart's gallant assault, the troops of Hardee— as their losses on that day indicate—did nothing more than skirmish with the enemy." Unfair though the accusation might appear, Hood always would believe that Hardee's men had, when they discovered that "they had come into contact with breastworks, [laid] down, and consequently, this attempt at pitched battle proved abortive." Hood obviously preferred to blame Hardee rather than to praise Thomas for what happened at Peachtree Creek that afternoon.

Standing on that spur above the creek with his six field guns, Thomas demonstrated how well he had learned the art of the artilleryman during the Mexican War, at the battle of Buena Vista. To rake opposing lines with canister and grapeshot was a battery's job. Thomas stood there, immovable, stuck to the ground like a tree, and didn't care if Hardee had been reinforced by Stewart. Hood could say that Hardee "lay down," but Thomas, hearing those guns roar, smelling the smoke that came back on the wind with an acrid odor, didn't care. Let them "lay down" or be mowed down—it was quite the same to Thomas. The day for Hood, under Thomas's roaring guns, had been lost; his casualties were five thousand—perhaps higher. Hooker, fighting in open ground and losing about fifteen hundred men, would suffer the heaviest Federal losses that 20th of July. The Rebel loss to Connolly "was terrible," and the men around him believed that the Confederate casualties may have been as high as eight thousand; but the next day Atlanta papers, Connolly said, reduced this figure to six thousand. In comparison, the aggregate Federal loss "was between two and three thousand." For Sherman, however, the real triumph of the action at Peachtree Creek would rest in the fact that his army "had successfully met a bold sally, had repelled it handsomely, and were also put on guard."

3. "BLEEDING, WOUNDED, AND RIDER-LESS"

SAM HOOD wasn't convinced that he had failed. He was "determined to make all necessary preparations for a renewed assault, to attack the Federals in rear and flank, and endeavor to bring the entire Confederate Army into united action." If Atlanta were to be saved, "even for a short period," the "most active measures" had become "urgent." McPherson's left flank, Wheeler told Sam, "was standing out in air, near the Georgia Railroad between Decatur and Atlanta," while "a large number of the enemy's wagons had been parked in and around Decatur." Sam's memory went back to Chancellorsville and to Second Manassas, where Jackson had swung away from the main army and struck the Federals in the rear. Now Sam would march his army "under cover of darkness" around McPherson's "exposed flank" and attack as old Stonewall would have assaulted!

Still, Hood wasn't fooling himself about the kind of adversary McPherson would make. After all, Sam and Mac had been classmates at West Point, and "often, when we were cadets," Hood would write, "have I left barracks at night to participate in some merry-making, and early the following morning have had recourse to him to help me over the difficult portions of my studies for the day." Cheerfully Sam admitted, at West Point and afterward, that, unlike McPherson, he "was more wedded to boyish sports than to books." And, oddly enough, across enemy lines at about this time Sherman was hearing McPherson revive recollections of Hood at West Point and agreeing that "we ought to be unusually cautious and prepared at all times for sallies and for hard fighting, because Hood, though not deemed much of a scholar, or of great mental capacity, was undoubtedly a brave, determined, and rash man."

With Hardee's and Stewart's corps resuming "their former positions," Hood sent his chief engineer to inspect the works toward Peachtree Creek which Johnston had ordered built for the defense of Atlanta. These entrenchments, Hood grew convinced, were "too close to the city . . . located upon too low ground . . . totally inadequate." With Sherman's line extending from near Decatur practically to the Dalton Railroad north of Atlanta, "an entirely new line" must be constructed "upon more elevated ground." The new works were to be dug and ready for the troops by the night of the 21st, Hood ordered; and Hardee was told to move first into the new entrenchments since he "commanded the largest corps" and his "troops were comparatively fresh, as they had taken but little part in the attack of the previous day." * Except that Schofield and McPherson "had advanced slightly toward Atlanta," Sherman's position remained unchanged. Sherman's "strange blunder in separating Thomas so far from Schofield and McPherson" remained unrectified, and Hood felt that before his opponent could correct this mistake he must assume his own risk. Frankly, Hood admitted that

> . . . To transfer after dark our entire line from the immediate presence of the enemy to another line around

---

* Hood, writing some years after the events, would remember that Pat Cleburne, explaining the failure of the attack at Peachtree where Hardee, Stewart, and Cheatham had been ordered to take everything on the Confederate side of the creek "at all hazards," would reveal that "Hardee rode along the line, and, in the presence of those around him, cautioned him to be on the lookout for breastworks." Thus, Hood implied, boldness had been replaced by timidness. Hardee's words, Hood thought, "were almost equivalent to an order to take no active part in the battle." If it were not for Hardee's popularity with his troops and the "further demoralization which I feared might ensue" Hood would have asked for Hardee's removal from command then and there. Cf. Hood's *Advance and Retreat*, pp. 185–7.

Atlanta, and to throw Hardee, the same night, entirely
to the rear and flank of McPherson—as Jackson was
thrown, in a similar movement, at Chancellorsville and
Second Manassas—and to initiate the offensive at daylight, required no small effort upon the part of the men
and officers.

Hood hoped not only to bring on "a general battle" but
also to gain "a signal victory to our arms." Time began to
count—almost to the second. A note from Sherman warned
McPherson on the 21st that he must not "extend so much by
his left." McPherson should be able to see that Sherman had
not "troops enough to invest the place, and I [Sherman]
intended to destroy utterly all parts of the Augusta Railroad
to the east of Atlanta, then to withdraw from the left flank and
add to the right." Hood desired nothing more than to stop
Sherman from "extending his left toward our main line of
communications," for otherwise "Atlanta was doomed to fall
at a very early day." Sam drew a breath—and perhaps
prayed to Lee and Jackson—then "soon after dusk" sent
Hardee's corps "to move south on the McDonough Road,
across Entrenchment Creek at Cobb's Mill, and to *completely*
turn the left of McPherson's Army and attack at daylight,
or as soon thereafter as possible." Wheeler's cavalry, familiar
with the roads that must be employed in this "swing away
from the main body of the army" would guide Hardee. Cheatham would support him by "driving the enemy down and
back upon Peachtree Creek, from right to left," the Georgia
Militia would join the attack, and Stewart, on the left, would
"keep a strict watch on Thomas." The task given to Hardee
was considered by Hood "a very simple one" in which "he
had simply to follow the guides furnished him to Decatur
and attack." Hood suddenly had gained new confidence, for
into his headquarters walked General W. H. S. Walker to say
that he was with Hood "in heart and purpose," and that he
"intended to abide by me through all emergencies." A

voluntary expression of confidence from a senior officer was as sweet to Sam as the kiss of any Richmond belle he ever had known!

On the morning of the 22nd Sherman and McPherson discussed many matters, including "the chances of battle, and of Hood's general character." Schofield dressed forward his lines, and Thomas, farther to the right, apparently had become engaged. McPherson seemed in fine spirit, "well pleased at the progress of events so far," and he told Sherman that from Leggett's Hill he could see "the high smoke-stack of a large foundry in Atlanta" that "he intended to knock down." McPherson, dressed handsomely with "boots outside his pantaloons, gauntlets on his hands" and wearing "a sword-belt, but no sword," raised his head with Sherman's at the sound of "an occasional gun back toward Decatur." The lively skirmishing where Schofield and Thomas stood made sense, but what did *this* mean? Sherman pulled out his old pocket compass. Obviously "the firing was too far to our left rear to be explained by known facts." McPherson galloped off. Within minutes "McPherson's horse came back, bleeding, wounded, and riderless." Later the general's dead body would be "laid on a door wrenched from its hinges" in Sherman's headquarters at the Howard House. Around his figure raged the savage Battle of Atlanta of July 22nd. Before the day ended, said Colonel Robert Ingersoll, "the third Iowa Veteran Battalion literally fought itself out of existence." General Strong, McPherson's chief-of-staff, would remember how "batteries and regimental colors were lost and won again and again," and General Giles A. Smith saw "men . . . frequently bayoneted across the works."

South of the Atlanta and Augusta Railroad—almost halfway between Atlanta's present "Five Points" and the town square in Decatur—Captain Tom Key of Pat Cleburne's division moved into the fight with Hardee's corps. "About noon," Key wrote in his diary, "the enemy opened his artillery upon our advance, throwing spherical case along the road on which we were advancing." Cleburne's boys drove on toward the Yankee earthworks "under the fire of artillery and minié balls," and Key must admit that "the fire was so galling many faltered in the charge." The Yankees had cut off saplings and bushes, bending them over and "leaving the butt or stump two feet high." There were cozier perches for an abdomen.

But the Confederates came on, anyhow; works were taken, lost, retaken; Key, with his eye on four Napoleon guns that had been abandoned,

> . . . called to the men of the battery for volunteers to go with me across the fortifications and turn the enemy's guns upon them . . . with a cheer I led them at a double quick through the abatis to the Yankee guns. However, while my men had one gun in the road in full view of a second line of works of the enemy, and were running up to commence firing, the Yanks from behind the second works poured such a volley of musketry upon those brave cannoneers that they were compelled to abandon the gun and leave the road. The Yanks reenforced and came back with a charge, and I thought it advisable to retire . . . in hasty steps and not in good order, knowing that artillerists are defenseless unless they can get their guns in an effective position. . . .

So the battle began to seesaw. Half an hour later Cleburne had driven the Yankees back into their works. And through it all, Key would remember that marching up to the battle "we had a conversation . . . upon religious matters, speaking of the consolation that a Christian enjoys even in the midst of imminent danger." The "imminent danger" proved plentiful. Said Giles Smith's official report:

> . . . Rebel commanders with [their] men . . . were not infrequently occupying one side of the works and our men the other. . . . The flags of the two opposing regiments would meet on the opposite sides of the same

works and would be flaunted by their respective bearers in each other's faces. . . .

Bending over McPherson's body, searching for the sign of life that no longer remained, Sherman remembered that so many shots struck the building "I feared [it] would take fire." The reports that came to Sherman "from all parts of the field revealed clearly what was the game of my antagonist, and the ground somewhat favored him." McPherson's line of battle, flung across the railroad, followed a ridge with a valley in front "between him and the defenses of Atlanta," and another valley behind him was clear, "but to his left rear the country was heavily wooded." The Confederates had approached under that cover of forest, struck the rear of Giles Smith's division, captured Murray's battery, and overrun several hospital camps. Meanwhile the Confederate right struck Dodge's troops of the XVIth Corps "in motion," but halting and facing to the left, the XVIth was neatly "in line of battle" and "not only held in check the enemy, but drove him back through the woods." Sherman recalled:

> . . . About the same time this same force had struck General Giles A. Smith's left flank, doubled it back, captured four guns in position, and . . . almost enveloped their left flank. The men, however, were skillful and brave, and fought for a time with their backs to Atlanta. They gradually fell back, compressing their own line, and making a junction with Leggett's Division of the XVIIth Corps. . . . One or two brigades of the XVth Corps . . . came rapidly across the open field to the rear . . . forming a strong left flank. . . . The enemy attacked, boldly and repeatedly . . . and on that ground a bloody battle raged. . . .

Sam Hood waited. About ten or eleven o'clock that morning he heard skirmishing on Cheatham's right. Then, after "a considerable time," he discovered

. . . with astonishment and bitter disappointment, a line of battle composed of one of Hardee's divisions advancing directly against the entrenched flank of the enemy. I at once perceived that Hardee had not only failed to turn McPherson's left, according to positive orders, but had thrown his men against the enemy's breastworks. . . .

Hood squirmed. Now the whole result was in doubt! Hardee's disregard "of the fixed rule in war that one danger in rear is more to be feared than ten in front" could lose everything! Simply by "moving a little further to the right, and attacking in rear and flank instead of assaulting an entrenched flank" Hardee could rout McPherson's army! Sam waited in miserable anxiety. The sounds from the direction of Decatur were not right. Wheeler's guns roared, yes; but not with the continuous clatter of musketry that would mean Hardee "advanced and drove the enemy down Peachtree Creek between our general line of battle and that formidable stream." The sound of the musketry came only "at intervals." Hood could stand it no longer and sent a staff officer to learn what had happened.

The answer was simple. Entrenchments. Partial success. Delay. Cheatham was sent to keep the Yankees from concentrating on Hardee; but Cheatham was forced to retire under "a heavy enfilade fire," and so, too, was the Georgia Militia that attempted to support him. Hardee "bore off as trophies eight guns and thirteen stands of colors" and Cheatham "captured five guns and five or six stands of colors," but Sam Hood's more telling description of the Battle of Atlanta would be: "the non-fulfillment of the brilliant result anticipated." Federal losses for the day would be set at thirty-five hundred and, Sherman said, the "estimated loss of the enemy," was "at least" ten thousand.

McPherson's command, given temporarily in battle to Johnny Logan, went permanently to Howard, and Joe Hooker resigned in a peeve. On the 28th, at Ezra Church, "close by the Poor-House," Howard's Army of the Tennessee would encounter its first battle under his command and would come off well. Johnny Logan's official report spoke of "lines . . . only protected by logs and rails, hastily thrown up in front of them," of "six successive charges . . . made, which were six times gallantly repulsed," "of troops . . . [that] could not have displayed greater courage, nor greater determination not to give ground. . . ." Ezra Church was a "feeling" action, resulting in an attack on a flank "well posted and partially covered" and it was part of a developing scheme Sherman must devise to "compel Hood to come out from behind his fortified lines to attack us at a disadvantage." The truth was, Sherman hadn't expected the fight at all, but Howard had. The action proved entirely indecisive; blood spilled needlessly, because such was the shape of war—Hood's shape of war, if not "Old Joe" Johnston's. But the affair at Ezra Church would at least fix in Hood's mind what he believed were the principal weaknesses of the army he commanded:

> . . . one corps struggled nobly, whilst the neighboring corps frustrated its effort by simple inactivity; and whilst the entire Army might fight desperately one day, it would fail in action the following day. Stewart's gallant attack on the twentieth was neutralized by Hardee's inertness on the right; and the failure in the battle of the twenty-second is to be attributed also to the effect of the "timid defensive" policy upon this officer, who, although a brave and gallant soldier, neglected to obey orders . . . and swing away, totally independent of the main body of the Army.

Ezra Church's bloodletting was one more example to Hood of the inability among his troops "in bringing about united action."

Sam Hood dug into his entrenchments around Atlanta and brooded over his own problems. Hurt and bruised, he refused to concede defeat. Sherman, having fought four times in July—on the 4th at Kenesaw, the 20th at Peachtree Creek, the 22nd before Decatur, and the 28th at Ezra Church— needed a rest. "The month," he would remember, "though hot in extreme, had been one of constant conflict." Meanwhile Joe Hooker, disgruntled because he had not received Mc- Pherson's command, would make a speech in Cincinnati. Sherman, by Hooker's estimate (and Sherman's own report- ing), had "run up against a rock at Atlanta," and "the country ought to be prepared to hear of disaster from that quarter."

In part, at least, Joe Hooker spoke with some sense of reality at Cincinnati.

4. "IT WILL BE A USED-UP COMMUNITY"

AUGUST, hot and sultry, broke over the encamp- ments outside Atlanta. Sherman considered his position "healthy," with an "ample supply of wood, water, and pro- visions." The troops, he said, "had become habituated to the slow and steady progress of the siege," but Henry O. Dwight told the readers of *Harper's*, from "here in the trenches before Atlanta, on this 15th day of August," how greatly the war had changed since Sherman's men had left Tennessee in early May. The pomp and show of war, Dwight said, had become "a matter of poetry rather than of fact"; the men be- fore Atlanta were "dusty, ragged, and unshaven," but what could one expect when a soldier "is reduced to marching in line-of-battle through swamps, thickets, and brier patches, and then sleeping night after night on the bare ground with only heaven's clouds for an overcoat"? Dwight believed that:

. . . Had the army been as experienced at Shiloh as it is now, Beauregard would have come up and broken his army to pieces on our fortifications, instead of finding our whole army lying exposed to his attacks on the open field. At Fort Donelson, too, where we had to attack fortifications, we ourselves had no sign of a work upon which we could fall back after each day's repulse; nor did the enemy seem to realize the value of his own works, for instead of quietly awaiting the attack, he threw away his army by fighting outside his works.

"To fight with movable breastworks, to save every man by giving him cover," had become the principle of the campaign before Atlanta. The first duty after a halt was to create "defensive fortifications" no matter how "rude" as long as they enabled "us to hold ground against any force." Every man had become an engineer. Whenever a position was reached, "The front rank take all the guns and remain on the line, while the rear rank goes off in double-quick to collect rails, logs, rocks, anything that can assist in turning a hostile bullet." In five minutes after a halt, Dwight declared, a barricade would be ready, "bullet-proof and breast-high," and "you can hold your line against an attack by three times your number." Barricading had become an art:

. . . A ditch is speedily made on the inside to stand in. The earth is thrown on the outside of the barricade, and the ditch deepened, so that, standing inside, your head will be protected by the parapet . . . with a step inside to stand on when firing, and a ditch to stand in while loading. If you are in the woods you want to give range to your rifles, and have all the thick undergrowth and small trees cut away for fifty paces in front. By felling these all the same way, the bushy tops all turning outward, and trimming off the smaller twigs and leaves, and tangling the tops together, you have a formidable abatis, through which it will be next to impossible to advance alone, let alone against the showers of bullets from your men at short range. . . .

Early in the campaign the men learned that the headlogs on a parapet, if struck by a cannonball, toppled on the heads of the men inside, so poles were placed to guide the rolling of the logs in a sensible direction. One idea bred another; next stakes were being "set in the ground with their sharpened points directed outward at an angle of forty-five degrees, and so close together that a man cannot pass between them." A strong wire was stretched in front to "trip all comers," and Dwight could "imagine how astonished will be the Rebels in charging the works to be suddenly tripped up and to fall forward on the sharp palisades." All a man needed for real comfort in such a parapet were a couple of howitzers throwing "nearly a bucketful of small balls at a charge."

Dwight described what it was like to attack an enemy behind his breastworks:

. . . You make up your mind to assault the enemy's work. You have formed line of battle, with a second and third line behind you for support. You march forward filled with the determination to accomplish the object, yet feeling the magnitude of the undertaking. Two hundred yards brings you to the picket-line, and here the opposition commences. You dash across the space between the two lines, you lose a few men; and the enemy's pickets, after making as much noise as possible, run back to their main works. By this time the enemy are sure you are really coming, and open on you with artillery, besides a pretty heavy fire of musketry. This artillery throws the shells screaming through your ranks, producing more moral than physical effect, or throws shrapnel which, bursting in front, scatter myriads of small bullets around. You commence to lose men rapidly. The ball is opened. "Forward, double-quick!" again; and while the whole line of the enemy open fire from behind their works, your men, mindless of this—mindless of the death intensified, the bullets and the shells, they dash on with wild cheers.

The abatis with its tangled intricacy of sharpened branches snares your line. Tripping, falling, rising to fall again, the men struggle through this abatis . . . though the moments are drawn out interminably, and though in each step are left brave men to pay for the ground. You get through a part of you and still rush on: the firing grows more fierce and the men grow more desperate. Your three lines have been almost reduced to one, and you strike another line of abatis. In this abatis are the palisades, which must be uprooted by force before a man can pass. You stumble, fall, tear your flesh on these stakes, and must stop to pull them up—stop, when every instant is an hour —stop, when you are already gasping for breath; and here open up the masked batteries, pouring the canister into that writhing, struggling, bleeding mass—so close that the flame scorches, that the smoke blinds from those guns. Is it any wonder that your three lines are torn to pieces, and have to give back before the redoubled fire of an enemy as yet unimpaired comparatively? And then the slaughter of a retreat *there!* Oftentimes it is preferable to lie down and take the fire . . . until night rather than lose all by falling back under such circumstances.

What an assault meant, Henry Dwight said, was "a slaughter-pen, a charnel-house, and an army of weeping mothers and sisters at home." On the 22nd of July, when Hardee struck the Federals both in flank and rear, the men found that they could fight either inside or outside the works, "looking for all the world like a long line of these toy-monkeys you see which jump over the end of a stick," and from that experience "they fortified not only the front, but facing the rear and every way, so that they could hold out if surrounded."

Hand-to-hand fighting, Dwight declared, while frequently mentioned in the dispatches, was "of very rare occurrence." Still he would remember one instance in the fighting on July 22nd when "a man was actually well-nigh dismembered, the

Rebels pulling his feet, to take him prisoner, and our boys pulling his head to save him." The sharpshooters were more to be feared, digging their pits with bayonet and tin cup, and inventing their own tricks: "Sometimes they will raise a tremendous shout, and when the enemy bob up to see what is going on they give them a telling volley, and then roll over and kick up their heels with joy." Behind the lines were the cooks, ambulance nurses, stretcher-bearers, shirks, and sometimes surgeons, technically called "bummers," generally scorned, although often "missiles passing over the front lines must fall somewhere." Fortifications built behind the lines were known as "Bummer's Roosts." A cook coming into the trenches with hot coffee ran the same teasing, day after day:

"Hey, bummer! Run quick, bummer!"

"A man was just killed there, bummer!"

Through August men built their bunks in the parapets outside Atlanta. Inside the city Carrie Berry would keep a diary reflecting through the keen eyes of a child the pattern of existence within a city under virtual siege. On August 3 the girl would write:

> This was my birthday. I was ten years old. But I did not have a cake times were too hard so I celebrated with ironing. I hope by my next birthday we will have peace in our land so that I can have a nice dinner.

Day by day entries in the diary of ten-year-old Carrie would reveal the slowly accumulating torment of life inside Atlanta:

> Aug. 4. The shells have been flying all day and we have stayed in the cellar. Mama put me on some stockings this morning and I will try to finish them before school commences.
>
> Aug. 5. I knit all morning. In the evening we had to run for Auntie's and get in the cellar. We did not feel safe in our cellar, they fell so thick and fast.

Aug. 6. We have ben in the cellar all day. Cousin Henry Beatty came this evening and brought some Yankee coffee for me to grind for him, some he had captured yesterday in a skirmish.

On Sunday, August 7, Carrie went to church for the first time in a month. Monday proved fine—"We have not had many shells today." But on August 9:

We have had to stay in the cellar all day the shells have ben falling so thick around the house. Two have fallen in the garden, but none of us were hurt. Cousin Henry Beatty came in and wanted us to move, he thought that we were in danger, but we will try it a little longer.

Rain on the 10th made the day gloomy, even with few shells. Again, next day, the Federal cannons unlimbered, forcing the Berrys to their cellar, and little Carrie wished they "would quit . . . so that we could get out and get some fresh air." Friday, the 12th, was fine, with no shells and time for Carrie to knit "on my stocking," and Saturday also passed quietly, so that, the girl would record: "We have all ben very buisy trying to work some while we could get out in safety." But the child's mind remained uneasy. "We will have shells to night," she thought; "We can hear muskets so plane." The shells that night "averaged one every moment." Tremblingly, she waited; every shell, she feared, must "come through and hurt some of us"; but nothing happened. Maxwell Berry, the girl's father, worked all through Sunday strengthening his cellar while his daughter turned philosopher: "I dislike to stay in the cellar so close but our soldiers have to stay in ditches." Then on Monday:

. . . after breakfast Zuie and I were standing on the platform between the house and dining room and a very large shell filled with balls fell by the garden gate and bursted. The peices flew in every direction. Two peices went in the dining room. It made a very large hole in the garden and threw the dirt all over the yard. I never was so frightened in my life. Zuie was as pale as a corpse and I expect I was too. It did not take us long to fly to the cellar. We stayed there till nearly dinner and no more fell so we came out again and stayed out till night though we had them all day but they did not come so near us again.

But the fear remained. Now, on the following day: "a large peice came through Mama's room directly after we went to bed and fell on the little bed and I expect if we had been sleeping there some of us would have ben hurt." Cousin Eddie tried to cheer Carrie, declaring that he did not think "the Federals would be here much longer to torment us." Carrie hoped he was right: "We are getting very tired of living so." And yet a child's world was quickly adaptable, as Carrie's diary demonstrated on the 18th:

When I woke this morning I thought the hole town would be torn up. The cannons were so near and so loud but we soon found out that it was our guns so we have ben very well content all day. . . .

At Grandpa's—"the only place I had to run to"—Carrie spent a day knitting on her stockings. But in her mind dark phrases formed: ". . . shells all day . . . a rainy morning . . . our cellar is not safe." The problems of war, for a ten-year-old girl, suddenly faded with the prospect of moving to a new house on Alabama Street between Pryor and Central Avenue. Now she helped: "Mama pact up to move . . . we have a nice large cellar. . . . Mama says that we make so much noise that she can't here the shells." A day of moving, filled with excitement and adventure, and then the dark phrases creeping back into Carrie's mind: ". . . Mama is fretted to death all the time for fear of fire. . . . I get so tired of being housed up. . . . I have ben wanting to go home all day to get some grapes but it has ben too dangerous."

So, for Carrie, life in Atlanta conformed to the ugly siege-guns behind the Federal picket-lines. Sherman would feel that "the field-batteries were in select positions, covered by handsome parapets, and occasional shots from them gave life and animation to the scene." His men, he said, were "as snug, comfortable, and happy, as though they were at home." Minor cavalry skirmishes filled the general's mind, a sort of luxury after the hard march from Chattanooga. He decided that "cavalry could not, or would not, make a sufficient lodgement on the railroad below Atlanta, and that nothing would suffice but for us to reach it with the main army." Schofield, on the right, received this job. The XIVth Corps, co-operating with Schofield, was under General John M. Palmer, who claimed to outrank Schofield. Sherman thought Palmer was "a man of ability, but was not enterprising," and there was a limit to how much vanity Sherman could stand. The XIVth Corps, in his opinion, had sustained "fewer hard knocks than any other corps," but now he had work for it. Atlanta, "full of founderies, arsenals, and machine-shops," would represent, if captured, "the death-knell of the Southern Confederacy," and the vital objective to this accomplishment, as Sherman saw it, was possession of the Macon railroad, on which Hood's main source of supplies depended. With this prize in mind, Sherman ordered Schofield "to make a bold attack on the railroad, anywhere about East Point," and asked Palmer to report to Schofield for duty. Temperaments clashed; Palmer demurred; and Sherman accepted his resignation, supplanting him with Brigadier General Jefferson C. Davis. The corps Davis took over had been formed by Thomas, and, like him, was "always safe, slow, and sure." Sherman could stand anything but personal bickering; it was enough, as he would wire Halleck, to "keep hammering away all the time, and there is no peace, inside or outside Atlanta." Again, he would tell Halleck:

> . . . I am too impatient for a siege, and don't know but this is as good a place to fight it out on, as farther in-

land. One thing is certain, whether we get inside of Atlanta or not, it will be a used-up community when we are
done with it.

One day a Yankee brigade would strike a Confederate outpost and lose about five hundred in killed and wounded; the
next day, when the Federals came back, the outwork would be
abandoned. But this was part of the military design forming
before Atlanta, Sherman said, as "the Rebels were extending
their lines, parallel with the railroad, about as fast as we could
add to our line of investment." Then the Parrott thirty-
pounders were received and rolled into position. Sherman
would report:

> . . . for a couple of days we kept up a sharp fire from
> all our batteries converging on Atlanta, and at every avail-
> able point we advanced our infantry-lines; but I was not
> willing to order a direct assault, unless some accident or
> positive neglect on the part of our antagonist should reveal
> an opening. However, it was manifest that no such open-
> ing was intended by Hood, who felt secure behind his
> strong defenses. . . .

The success of Hood's cavalry in damaging the railroad on
which the Federals depended—the Confederate Wheeler,
operating from around Macon, had raided as far as Resaca—
convinced Sherman that Hood "would attempt the same game
against our rear." Annoyed, Sherman placed his own cavalry
divisions to meet this danger, and on August 10th telegraphed
Grant that since July 28th Hood had not "attempted to meet
us outside his parapets" and in so far as it was necessary "to
possess and destroy effectually" the Rebel communications
"I may have to leave a corps at the railroad-bridge, well intrenched, and cut loose with the balance to make a circle of
desolation around Atlanta." Two days later Sherman received the heartening news that Farragut had entered Mobile
Bay, "a most valuable auxiliary to our operations at Atlanta,"

159

and on the same day Sherman learned that he had been commissioned a major general in the regular army, "which was unexpected, and not desired until successful in the capture of Atlanta."

Day by day the new major general felt more satisfied that Hood "would hold fast" even though Federal artillery battered down "every house in the town." By some decoy Hood must be brought out to fight the Yankees "on something like equal terms," unless of course the whole army was employed to raise the siege and attack Hood's communications. Sherman had waited long enough. On Saturday, the 13th, while little Carrie Berry wrote in her diary that "we have had a very quiet day," the XXth Corps started drawing back to the railroad bridge at the Chattahoochee, where it could guard Federal trains, hospitals, spare artillery, and the depot, and the rest of the army began to "move bodily to some point on the Macon Railroad below East Point."

Hood's cavalry, under Wheeler, remained a thorough nuisance. At Tilton Square above Resaca, Wheeler's horsemen captured a thousand Federal beef-cattle; next Wheeler appeared before Dalton, demanding the surrender of the town, but the appearance of a couple of thousand Yankees, hurrying along the rails from Kingston, convinced Wheeler to strike out for Cleveland. Another Confederate cavalry detachment popped up in force at Allatoona and the Etowah bridge; for days railroad and telegraph communications with Nashville were disrupted. Sherman grew suspicious. Had Hood committed *all* his cavalry to raiding the railroads? Sherman prodded to find out, detaching Garrard's and Kilpatrick's cavalry for strong reconnaissances. Kilpatrick easily skipped up and back to Fairburn Station on the West Point road. There was nothing to it. Delighted, Sherman sent him off to break up the Macon railroad about Jonesboro. Hood soon would learn, Sherman thought, that two could play this cavalry game, but Hood had better watch his step. If the Federals gained control at Jonesboro, what choice had Hood

but to evacuate Atlanta? The city would fall and Hood himself would stand the chance of being caught "in the confusion
of retreat"!

From the 18th to the 22nd, with two brigades of Garrard's
cavalry in reserve as a support, and with the infantry and
artillery awakening all along the front, Kilpatrick "made the
complete circuit of Atlanta." Three miles of railroad had been
destroyed at Jonesboro; maybe the Rebs could repair it in ten
days. A division of infantry and a cavalry brigade had been
met; three battle-flags and seventy prisoners were the proof of
that pudding. A battery had been captured and three guns
destroyed; and one had been brought back as a trophy.
Trains coming into Atlanta from the south on the next day,
however, reaffirmed Sherman's belief that "cavalry could not
or would not work hard enough to disable a railroad prop-
erly." The damage Wheeler had done about Resaca and
Dalton had now been repaired, and Wheeler was so far away
he had become useless to Hood. On the evening of the 24th
Sherman wrote a telegram to Halleck:

> Heavy fires in Atlanta all day, caused by our artillery.
> I will be all ready, and will commence the movement
> around Atlanta by the south, tomorrow night, and for
> some time you will hear little of us. . . . The Twentieth
> Corps will hold the railroad-bridge, and I will move with
> the balance of the army, provisioned for twenty days.

On the 26th Carrie Berry rejoiced that "Cousin Henry
came in this morning and told us we need not fear the shells
any more." The Yankees, Cousin Henry declared, had left
their "brest works," and Carrie wrote: "We have had such a
delightful day. We all wanted to move to day but we will wait
till tomorrow and see if the Yankees have gone." On the 27th
the Confederate infantry came out of Atlanta and found
the Federal camps abandoned. The South rocked with the
news that Atlanta had been saved; ladies came by railroad
from Macon to join the celebration; and happily Carrie

"moved home this morning" and became "buisy trying to get things regulated."

So did August approach its climax, but its surprises had not ended. In a quiet Pennsylvania town a sinister portent already been seen, and a man would set off from that town for Philadelphia bearing a dreadful letter. In Chicago a general would rise to threaten the future of the Lincoln administration and a spy would write Jefferson Davis that a political compromise had been reached to "let the South go." Sherman meanwhile marched the twenty miles to Jonesboro.

5. "IT ALL MEANS PEACE"

ON A windowpane in Meadville, Pennsylvania, appeared a crudely written inscription:

Abe Lincoln
Departed this
Life Aug. 13th 1864
By the effects of
Poison.

Along the streets of Meadville, at the time of this ominous scribbling, moved the brooding figure of John Wilkes Booth. The actor's purpose in being there, it was said, was simply to attend to some oil-stock investments.

Later Booth would arrive in Philadelphia to visit his sister Asia and her husband, comedian John Sleeper Clarke. Some United States bonds and some oil-stock certificates would be in an envelope that Booth gave to Asia. Also, there would be a letter, addressed "To whom it may concern," and declaring "Right or wrong, God judge me, not man. For be my motive good or bad, of one thing I am sure, the lasting condemnation of the North." Just when in 1864 Booth composed his long, rambling, mentally confused letter none but he would ever know. He would write in one paragraph:

> I love peace more than life. Have loved the Union be-
> yond expression. For four years have I waited, hoped,
> and prayed for the dark clouds to break, and for a restora-
> tion of our former sunshine. To wait longer would be a
> crime. All hope for peace is dead. My prayers have
> proved as idle as my hopes. God's will be done. . . .

So, in part, ran the secret letter; so, in quiet ugliness, grew the secret resolve. But August of 1864, "the darkest month of the war," would breed distrust, dissension, and rebellion in many places throughout the North. And not so pathetically tortured as the mind of John Wilkes Booth were all the minds that felt the hope for peace would be dead as long as Lincoln remained in the White House. The fiasco at Niagara Falls, where Horace Greeley had gone to meet a Confederate dele-gation in what *Harper's Monthly* would describe as "a singular but abortive effort . . . to open negotiations for peace," had ended bitterly. Clement C. Clay of Alabama and James P. Holcombe of Virginia, spokesmen for the delegation, informed Greeley that "they were not accredited agents of the Con-federate Government to submit propositions for peace [*Harper's* reported], but they were in its confidential employ-ment, were familiar with its wishes, and would be furnished with authority to act." They asked for safe conduct to Wash-ington and Richmond. Greeley conveyed this request to Lincoln, who replied:

> Any proposition which embraces the restoration of
> peace, the integrity of the whole Union, and the abandon-
> ment of slavery, and which comes by and with authority
> that can control the armies now at war against the United
> States, will be received and considered by the Executive
> Government of the United States, and will be met by
> liberal terms on substantial and collateral points, and the

bearer or bearers thereof shall have safe-conduct both ways.

Messrs. Clay and Holcombe found Lincoln's rejoinder completely unsatisfactory. It was the same old Lincoln policy, they implied, permitting

. . . no bargaining, no negotiation, no truces with the Rebels except to bury their dead, until every man shall have laid down his arms, submitted to the Government, and sued for mercy.

Leslie's Weekly in its issue for August 4 commented: "Peace must come through the powerful negotiations of Gens. Grant and Sherman," and Sherman would say: "The only principle in this war is, which party can whip. It is as simple as a schoolboy's fight." Lincoln, however, was not easily deceived by the surface manifestations, and, reflecting on Clay and Holcombe and their colleagues at Niagara Falls, asked: "Does any one doubt what they *are* empowered to do is to assist in selecting and arranging a candidate and a platform for the Chicago convention?" In a letter to Abram Wakeman, postmaster at New York, the President continued:

. . . the present presidential contest almost certainly will be no other than a contest between a union and disunion candidate, disunion certainly following the success of the latter. The issue is a mighty one, for all people, and for all times. . . .

On August 29 in the Wigwam in Chicago, where in June of '60 "Old Abe Lincoln came out of the wilderness" to win the Republican nomination for President, the Democratic National Convention met to draw the "mighty" issue. Wealth and power smiled down at the delegates as the meeting was called to order by August Belmont. Before the convention stood the financial influence of the director of the American branch of the Rothschild bank, the social prestige of the presidency of the American Jockey Club, and the political might of the chairmanship of the Democratic National Committee. None of the smile remained in Belmont's voice when he told the delegates that "four years of misrule by a sectional, fanatical, and corrupt party had brought our country to the verge of ruin." If Lincoln were re-elected, Belmont warned, through a "want of patriotism and unity," only "disastrous consequences" could follow.

Next William Bigler, former governor of Pennsylvania, mounted the rostrum to accept the gavel as temporary chairman. Mr. Bigler expanded Mr. Belmont's rousing theme:

> . . . The men now in authority, through a feud which they have long maintained with violent and unwise men at the South, because of a blind fanaticism about an institution in some of the States, in relation to which they have no duties to perform and no responsibilities to bear, are utterly incapable of adopting the proper means to rescue our country from its present lamentable condition.

To the Honorable Horatio Seymour, governor of New York and permanent chairman of the convention, fell the pleasure of finally annihilating the Lincoln administration. Step by step, Governor Seymour declared, "they have marched on to results from which at the onset they would have shrunk with horror." With war desolating the land, with bankruptcy imminent, "They will not let the shedding of blood cease even for a little time, to see if Christian charity or the wisdom of statesmanship may not work out a method to save our country." Doubtless to Mr. Belmont's satisfaction, Governor Seymour had now succeeded in placing Christ in Mr. Rothschild's counting-house. By the refusal of Lincoln's administration even to listen "to a proposal for peace which does not offer what this Government has no right to ask," Seymour thundered on, it had "hampered its own freedom of action by unconstitutionalities." The soldiers and sailors had done all they could; and wise statesmanship, had it existed to secure the fruits of their victories, would have restored peace; but:

> . . . This Administration can not save the Union. We can. We demand no conditions for the restoration of the Union. We are shackled with no hates, no prejudices, no passions. We wish for fraternal relations with the people of the South. We demand for them what we demand for ourselves, the full recognition of the rights of the States.

That the platform of the Democratic Party must support an unequivocal peace plank became more apparent as the hours of fiery speech-making mounted. When at last that plank was presented to the convention any chance of compromise with the moderate elements had been overwhelmed:

> *Resolved,* That this Convention does explicitly declare, as the sense of the American people, that after four years of failure to restore the Union by the experiment of war, during which, under the pretense of a military necessity higher than the Constitution, the Constitution itself has been disregarded in every part, and public liberty and private right alike trodden down, and the material prosperity of the country essentially impaired, justice, humanity, liberty, and the public welfare demand that immediate efforts be made for a cessation of hostilities, with a view to an ultimate convention of all the States, or other peaceable means, to the end that, at the earliest practicable moment, peace may be restored on the basis of the federal Union of States.

Accurately the *New York Daily Tribune* predicted on the 30th of August that the Presidential candidate of the party would be General George B. McClellan, and where, asked the *Tribune,* could anyone find a nominee better able to represent a Democracy "which maintains that the weak, ignorant and simple are, because of their weakness, the rightful as well as natural prey of the cunning and the strong"? That the "Union has 'no right to coerce a State,' however much that State may coerce the Union," the editor said, "has been the first article of their creed ever since it became evident that such coercion of the States might work to the downfall of Human Slavery." To some, the *Tribune* admitted, "the support of McClellan for President must be a bitter dose," but:

. . . It *will* be swallowed. . . . True, he volunteered for the War; but he did so to save Slavery from the effects of its own suicidal madness, not to punish it for its treason. True, he commanded for a time the Union Grand Army; but no Rebel slaveholder ever justly complained that his chattel was invited by this General to exchange the service of treason for that of his country; and no outnumbered Rebel force ever justly complained that its retreat was hurried or seriously annoyed by McClellan or anyone under his command. True, he made war on the Rebels; but he made it so gently, so considerately, so languidly, that they habitually praised his generalship while it lasted, and regretted it when it was no more. . . . He is not Union General enough to hurt him with the Rebels, who will help him all they can in the canvas, even though it be necessary for that purpose to make a show of denouncing and decrying him; but he is General enough to catch a number of votes from soldiers who served under him and liked his easy campaigning and courtier-like ways. . . . the slave power has never had a more docile tool. . . . he is as devoted to the propping up and the perpetuation of the tottering fabric of Human Bondage as Jeff. Davis himself, and a "Peace" Copperhead who affects hesitation or coyness as to his support, ought forthright to be kicked out of the party and ordered to stay out.

Sadly the *Tribune* predicted that McClellan would "poll the full party vote," and whereas the *Tribune* never had been known to "regard Mr. Lincoln as a great man . . . no candid observer who knows both will pretend that Gen. McClellan is his equal in ability." McClellan was "timid, hesitating, negative," and

> . . . a plaything in the hands of some of the worst and most dangerous men in the Republic, who hope to achieve power . . . and then to lay the country at the feet of Jeff. Davis, begging him to indicate the constitutional and other changes that will reconcile him to the task of governing the whole Union . . . and thus to place the heel of the Slave Power on the neck of prostrate Freedom and the inalienable Rights of Man.

Jefferson Davis's "personal observers" had wandered down the aisles of the Wigwam and loitered in the lobbies of Chicago hotels, and soon from Jeffersonville, Virginia, one [L. Ditzler] would write the President that he had just arrived from the convention with "all the proceedings," and "I'm glad to assure you, McClellan is pledged to *Peace*." Seymour, said the President's correspondent, had been "the leading man of the *doubtful* wing of the party," and had given the Western men "the pledged assurance that McClellan was for peace." The end-the-war-at-any-cost leaders, like Clement L. Vallandigham of Ohio, were "enthusiastic for the Candidate," which, Davis must understand, was

> . . . of itself evidence of the assurance they have of peace. *It all means peace*—let the South go. So they all understood it. I'll send you on the papers and some others to show the general tone there, and of the Democrats. I'm so fatigued from my travels, I have to rest a few days—a week—ere I go to Richmond. I'll call on you as soon as I arrive, and relate the tone of things as I saw them in England, New York, and the Great West. The North is clear of all soldiers—Ky. empty—concentrated under their two great armies. The draft, if enforced, *will be resisted*.

From this report Jefferson Davis had cause to believe that on the 29th and 30th of August in Chicago the Confederacy had won one of its greatest victories. The very note on which the Democratic National Convention ended should have cheered Richmond, for an motion of Governor Charles A. Wickliffe of Kentucky the Democrats voted to "remain as organized," subject to recall by the national executive committee at any time "circumstances may occur between this [meeting] and the fourth of March next." Composed now of a tight regrouping of Peace Democrats, War Democrats, Know-Nothings, Whigs, and extremists of various ambitions, the party that for thirty years before Lincoln's election in 1860 had ruled the Government stirred with the confident hope that its power would be restored. Even to John C. Frémont and John Cochrane of the Radical Democracy it soon became clear that if the Republicans remained split "the result of the Presidential election is at least doubtful," and they would withdraw as candidates in favor of Lincoln, not because they had grown to love Old Abe more but because, *Harper's* reported, "The Chicago platform is simply separation; McClellan's letter of acceptance re-establishment with slavery."

With narrowing eyes, William Tecumseh Sherman read the dispatches from Chicago. Grant's army appeared "checkmated about Richmond and Petersburg," his own army "to have run up against an impassable barrier." One thought grew in his mind. Success to Federal arms at that instant had become "a political necessity" and "it was all-important that something startling in our interest should occur before the election in November."

Within four days Sherman succeeded in mitigating much of the triumph that the Belmont-Seymour-Vallandigham coalition had achieved in their nomination of McClellan at Chicago!

6. "THE SALUTE WILL BE FIRED . . . AMID GREAT REJOICING!"

ON THE 29th of August, while Mr. Belmont arose to welcome the delegates to the Wigwam, Sherman found that by "making a general left-wheel, pivoting on Schofield," Thomas and Howard had reached the West Point Railroad, extending from East Point to Red Oak Station and Fairburn. During the hours while Belmont, Bigler, and Seymour inveighed against the Lincoln administration, Sherman watched as the track of the West Point Railroad was "heaved up in sections the length of a regiment, then separated rail by rail." Ted Upson of the 100th Indiana had learned well the technique of destroying a railroad:

> . . . The way this is done is to string the troops out along the track, two men to a tie. The men stick their guns with their bayonets on into the ground close behind them so as to have them handy in case of an attack, and then at a "Yo heave!" every man grabs a tie and lifts. Up comes the whole track and slowly tips over. Then with sledge hammers, hand spikes, or any thing else handy, the ties are knocked loose from the rails, the fish plates unbolted, the pine ties made into piles, set on fire, and the rails laid on top. When they get red hot in the center about twenty men get hold of the ends and wind them edgewise around a telegraph pole or small tree. That fixes them. The deep cuts we fill with brush and tree tops and put shells in them that will explode if the Johnnys try to clean them out.

Sherman would have added that "the explosion of one such shell would have demoralized a gang of Negroes, and thus would have prevented even the attempt to clear the road." But Ted would have shaken his head. Before the Indiana boys

170

started to work they had been "issued a ration of whiskey" and most of them had refused it. If they were going to be killed, Ted said, "they wanted to die sober."

Schofield meanwhile thrust forward the XXIIIrd Corps in "a bold front" toward East Point, "daring and inviting the enemy to sally out to attack him in position." On the 30th, while the Democrats in the Wigwam ballotted for McClellan, Schofield moved to Mount Gilead Church and then to Morrow's Mill across from Rough and Ready. On Schofield's right, Thomas moved by crossroads from Red Oak to the Fayetteville Road, "within easy support"; and Howard aimed straight for Jonesboro. The day, Sherman would remember, was "hot but otherwise very pleasant." At noon he and Thomas stopped to rest at Shoal Creek Church. The infantry had halted in the road, stacked their arms, and napped in the shade, fetched cornstalks from a field to feed their horses, or loaded their arms with "roasting-ears, then in their prime." Hundreds of fires dotted the roadside. Sherman recognized "a most kindly relation" that existed between Thomas and his men. Now Thomas stopped to converse with a soldier who, down on his knees, was roasting corn.

"What are you doing?" Thomas asked.

"Why, general, I am laying in a supply of provisions."

"That is right, my man, but don't waste your provisions."

As the generals walked on, Sherman heard the soldier mutter: "There he goes, there goes the old man, economizing as usual," and Sherman thought: "Economizing with corn, which cost only the labor of gathering and roasting!" Sometimes it was difficult for Sherman to understand Thomas. What a fusspot!

Howard's guns sounded off to the right front, but now, Sherman reflected, the left, where "I was expecting at each moment to hear the sound of battle" was filled by "an ominous silence." Night closed in quietly, and in the morning "all moved straight for the railroad." Schofield reached the road near Rough and Ready, Thomas at two points between

Rough and Ready and Jonesboro. Howard, however, ran straight into an entrenched foe.

Since the 25th, Sam Hood had been expecting trouble. For over a month now, Sherman had been "continuously moving toward our left and thoroughly fortifying, step by step, as he advanced in the direction of the Macon Railroad." That night Sherman withdrew from Hood's immediate front, but Hood wasn't fooled by the "many idle rumors." Inside Atlanta some would believe, as little Carrie Berry wrote in her diary, that the Yankees "were on the way back to Tennessee," but Sam Hood knew better. Sam's scouts prowled the front to keep him "advised of the slightest change in the enemy's position" and General Francis C. Armstrong and his cavalry were ordered to keep a sharp watch on the West Point Railroad. On the 27th Armstrong reported Sherman in force at Fairburn; "it became evident at once," Sam wrote, "that General Sherman was moving with his main body to destroy Macon [rail] road, and that the fate of Atlanta depended upon our ability to defeat this movement."

Sam grew rattled and scared, and his general attitude had become, in the opinion of one biographer, that he would be "damned if he left Atlanta, double-damned if he stayed and submitted to siege." Certainly his actions supported this estimate, for now while he rushed Reynolds's and Lewis's brigades to Jonesboro to support Armstrong, and asked General Maury to assist General Adams in guarding the defenses at Opelika, the chief quartermaster, ordinance officer, and commissary were

> . . . given most explicit instructions in regard to the disposition of their respective stores. All surplus property, supplies, and so forth, were ordered to the rear, or to be placed on cars in readiness to move at any moment the railroad became seriously threatened. General Armstrong was instructed to establish a line of couriers to my headquarters, in order to report every hour, if req-

uisite, the movements of the enemy. In fact, every precau-
tion was taken not only to hold our sole line of communication, but also, in case of failure, to avoid loss or
destruction of stores and material.

Irresistibly, Sherman tightened his squeeze. Sam **Hood**
sweated. The fall of Atlanta was not his chief fear, but "the
recurrence of retreat, which I full well knew would further
demoralize the Army and renew desertions." A portion of
Brown's division was hurried to protect the road at Rough
and Ready, and Hardee, in the vicinity of East Point at this
juncture, "was instructed to make such disposition of his
troops as he considered most favorable for defence." Every
clomp of Sam's cork leg filled the night of the 29th with sinister
echoes as he waited for Generals Jackson and Armstrong "to
report the different positions of the corps of the enemy."
Damn Sherman, but he had placed his army well, for had he
he not been "doubly protected by the Chattahoochee" with
its "deep intervening creeks and ravines" supporting "the
wall of parapets behind which he had thus far manoeuvred"
Sam could have moved out from East Point "and have at-
tacked his Army whilst effecting these changes of position."
By the morning of the 30th, cavalry reports removed the last
doubt—"the enemy would strike our road at Jonesboro."
Hood could vacillate no longer. Now—or never—he must find
"the last hope of holding on to Atlanta."

Hardee stood at Rough and Ready with S. D. Lee's corps,
near East Point, on his right. Armstrong made a prediction
that a Federal corps would cross Flint River, near Jonesboro,
and fall on Lewis's brigade. By six o'clock that evening the
crossing had been made, Lewis engaged, and "the signal for
battle" given. Sam Hood snapped out his orders. Hardee,
with Lee to follow, must flee to Jonesboro and, with his force
and Lee's, attack early on the morning of the 31st and "at all
hazards" must "drive the enemy . . . into the river in their
rear." Sam could see how nicely his plan could work. As

though he were playing chess, he set up the moves in his mind: Hardee's attack succeeds; Lee moves back to Rough and Ready; Stewart with the militia form on Lee's right, near East Point; and "the whole force" moves "the following morning," attacking "the enemy in flank" and driving "him down Flint River and the West Point Railroad." Meanwhile, like well-placed pawns, the cavalry would hold in check the Federal corps stationed at the railroad bridge across the Chattahoochee near the mouth of Peachtree Creek, "whilst Hardee advanced from his position near Jonesboro, or directly on Lee's left." In the game for Atlanta, that would be checkmate!

Sam remained in Atlanta with Stewart and Smith of the militia, "anxiously awaiting tidings from Jonesboro." Hardee had been told the night before "that the fate of Atlanta rested upon his ability"; now had he struck with the first morning light? No word came and the telegraph wires were down. Unable to stand the suspense any longer, Sam sent a courier with orders to pull back Lee's corps and march them to Rough and Ready. Still no word. Something had gone wrong. Sam could feel the ugly apprehension growing inside him. Then news filtered through. Hardee's attack, ordered for morning, had not been made until two o'clock in the afternoon—after the Federals had been allowed "to strongly entrench!"

James Austin Connolly would tell what happened:

. . . it was a glorious battle! But this Division suffered terribly. There was no chance for flinching there. Generals, Colonels, Majors, Captains and privates, all had to go forward together over that open field, facing and drawing nearer to death at every step we took, our horses crazy, frantic with the howling shells, the rattling of canister and the whistling of bullets, ourselves delirious with the wild excitement of the moment, and thinking only of getting over those breast works—great volleys of canister shot sweeping through our lines making huge gaps, but the blue coated boys filled the gaps and still rushed forward right into the jaws of death—we left hundreds of bleeding comrades behind us at every step, but not one instant did that line hesitate—it moved steadily forward to the enemy's work—over the works with a shout—over the cannon—over the Rebels, and then commenced stern work with the bayonet. . . .

Captain Tom Key, commanding a battery with Pat Cleburne's division, knew how great a fool Hood had been, drawing back Lee's corps from Hardee's already outnumbered forces. Hood, believing Sherman still in front of Atlanta, would learn too late that except for the XXth Corps the entire Federal army had been concentrated on Jonesboro! The end came swiftly for Key's artillerymen as

. . . the immense numbers and overwhelming forces of the Yankees ran upon the works, sweeping over the right of [General Daniel C.] Govan's fortifications, striking the line at both batteries, and capturing the general and several hundred of his gallant Arkansans. The cannoneers continued to pour canister upon the enemy until they were within ten steps of their guns, and all of Key's battery were captured except twelve men. . . . Our lines fell back about 200 yards and then rallied and checked the enemy until re-enforcements were brought up. I was at Captain Goldthwaite's battery at the moment of the charge that carried our lines, and I caused the available guns of his battery to bear upon the Yanks. The defense of the Confederates were noble, but they were too weak to contend against such numbers. . . .

In the great moment of victory Major Connolly would recollect:

. . . finding myself in a tangled lot of soldiers, on my horse, just against the enemy's log breastworks, my hat

175

off, and tears streaming from my eyes, but as happy as a
mortal is ever permitted to be. I could have lain down on
that blood-stained grass, amid the dying and the dead
and wept with excess of joy. I have no language to express
the rapture one feels in the moment of victory, but I do
know at such a moment one feels as if the joy were worth
risking a hundred lives to attain it. Men at home will
read of that battle . . . but they can never feel as we felt,
standing there quivering with excitement, amid the
smoke and blood, and fresh horrors and grand trophies
of that battlefield. . . .

And yet even victory can demand a dreadful price. For Ted
Upson of the 100th Indiana, word came that an old home-
town friend, William Sharp, had been "terribly wounded."
Ted said:

> . . . It pretty near broke me up. He knew he had to
> die but did not seem to worry about that so much, but
> whispered that he wished he had been a better boy, that
> he had not been as good as he ought to have been. I tried
> to say something to comfort him; told him that it would
> be made all right; that God would take all things into ac-
> count. He wanted some one to pray with him. No one
> seemed to want to, our Chaplain was not with us. . . .
> Sick Billy was dying, so I just dropped down by his side
> and asked God to take care of all his wayward boys and
> help this one who so badly needed help. He held my
> hand and seemed to feel better and then his life slipped
> away so quietly we hardly knew he was gone. The boys
> did not laugh at me as I expected they might, and I am
> glad I did it. . . .

Sherman, standing near by as Connolly and his comrades
in Davis's divisions swept forward "over some old cotton
fields," would exclaim that they "went over the Rebel parapet
handsomely." He watched Govan's brigade captured, the

two Rebel batteries of ten guns each knocked out. Now Sherman checked Davis and ordered Howard to send two divisions of the XVIIth Corps "round by his right rear, to get below Jonesboro, and to reach the railroad, so as to cut off retreat in that direction." Also, Sherman said, "orders after orders" were dispatched to hurry forward General T. R. Stanley "so as to lap around Jonesboro on the east" in the hope of capturing all of Hardee's corps. Even Thomas was sent after Stanley and, Sherman said, for "the only time during the campaign I can recall seeing General Thomas urge his horse into a gallop." Night came on before Stanley could be stopped from deploying his troops on Davis's left. By then Hardee had escaped.

Sherman felt restless. Slocum, commanding the XXth Corps at the Chattahoochee bridge, had been told "to feel forward occasionally toward Atlanta, to observe the effect when we had reached the railroad." Sherman couldn't sleep. Toward midnight Atlanta reverberated with "sounds of exploding shells, and other sounds like that of musketry." Still "so restless and impatient" he must do something, the general walked to the house of a farmer close to his bivouac. Together, farmer and general listened to the explosions in Atlanta, twenty miles to the north. Both agreed the sounds were "just like those of a battle." Then the night grew quiet but toward four o'clock in the morning the explosions started again. Slocum, hearing those same sounds, moved up rapidly—and entered Atlanta unopposed!

Sam Hood suddenly decided he couldn't leave quickly enough. Too late he had sent both Lee and Stewart back to reenforce Hardee, but when they reached Jonesboro "the contest had ceased." With the Federals in undisputed possession of the Macon railroad, the sooner Hood could get out of Atlanta the better he would like it. In Andersonville prison were thirty-four thousand captive Federals, and unless Hood placed his army between Sherman and Andersonville Sam shuddered at what it might mean if this large body of prisoners

were turned loose "to wreak its ill-will upon our people."
With Lee's corps protecting the Confederate flank, Hood began the march out of Atlanta to Lovejoy Station along the
McDonough Road, at 5.00 p.m. on September 1. Fifteen years
later, publishing *Advance and Retreat*, Hood still could not understand why "Sherman should have occupied himself with
attacking Hardee's entrenched position, instead of falling
upon our main body on the march around to his rear."

But Sherman was satisfied with what had been accomplished. Slocum's note announcing the evacuation of Atlanta
impressed Thomas as "too good to be true." Thomas examined the note to be sure it was genuine, then, by Sherman's
report,

> . . . snapped his fingers, whistled, and almost danced,
> and, as the news spread to the army, the shouts that arose
> from our men, the wild hallooing and glorious laughter,
> were to us a full recompense for the labor and toils and
> hardships through which we had passed in the previous
> three months.

To the nation by wire went the message: "Atlanta is ours,
and fairly won!" Northern loyalists, like Thomas, "snapped
their fingers, whistled, and almost danced," and flung this
news into the faces of the McClellan men returning from
Chicago. From the White House a grateful Lincoln sent
Sherman "the national thanks," declaring that "the marches,
battles, sieges, and other military operations, that have sig-
nalized the campaign, must render it famous in the annals of
war." From City Point at nine o'clock on the evening of
September 4, Grant would wire Sherman: "In honor of your
great victory, I have ordered a salute to be fired with *shotted*
guns from every battery bearing upon the enemy. The salute
will be fired within an hour, amid great rejoicing."

7. "THOUGH MINE BEAT FASTER FAR THAN THINE"

THE last Confederate soldiers were leaving Atlanta. Through the darkness, as they retreated, they sang *Lorena*, the ballad of a love that "a *duty*, stern and pressing, broke." No song through all the weary war years would the South take more dearly to its heart. And in this sad moment, with Atlanta lost, no song could capture so well the melancholy heartbreak of defeat:

> A hundred months have passed, Lorena,
>   Since last I held that hand in mine;
> And felt the pulse beat fast, Lorena,
>   Though mine beat faster far than thine;
> A hundred months, 'twas flowery May,
>   When up the hilly slope we climbed
> To watch the dying of the day,
>   And hear the distant church bells chime.

The feet tramped on, the song faded on the stirring breezes, and Atlanta, like Lorena, lived with "the hopes that could not last."

Carrie Berry had just finished dinner on September 1 when "Cousin Emma came down and told us that Atlanta would be evacuated this evening and we might look for the Federals in the morning." The news seemed to spread with the wind; soon "the hole town found it out and such excitement there was." Every footfall, every creaking tree-branch, every neighing of a horse awoke the same half-frightened anticipation. Had the Yankees come? But the evening passed quietly for Carrie. The stockings she had started before the shelling were finished at last. On the 2nd Carrie would confess to her diary:

> We all woke up this morning without sleeping much last night. The Confederates had four engenes and a long

train of box cars filled with ammunition and set it on fire last night which caused a grate explosion which kept us all awake. It reminded us of the shells—of all the days of excitement, we have had it to day. Every one has been trying to get all they could before the Federals come in the morning. They have been running with saques of meal, salt and tobacco. They did act rediculous breaking open stores and robbing them. . . .

Mary Rawson Ray's husband fought with the 1st Georgia Volunteers. Where John was Mary did not know, when on the afternoon of September 1 Hood began evacuating Atlanta. Tight-lipped, Mary wrote in her diary that "The gentlemen who did not wish to fall in the hands of the Federals might have been seen . . . in company of the last of the soldiers, wending their way slowly out of the now desolate city." With dread, Mary watched the sun fading, and "the sable shadows" of night creeping into the city. The silence had become oppressive. At nine she went to bed, but the explosion of the ammunition trains brought her running to the window. Breathlessly she thought that

> . . . The heavens were in a perfect glow, while the atmosphere seemed full of flaming rockets. Crash follows crash and the swift moving locomotives were rent in pieces . . . while the sparks filled the air with innumerable spangles. . . .

Then a bright light flared in another part of the city where other government provisions were being burned. As Mary looked, the dawn began to rise in gray mists. Anxiety closed heavily over her heart. Wherever she turned, whatever she tried to do, the fear was there—of Sherman and his men, "caring naught for justice or humanity." Every story she had heard of Yankee indignity—and they had been many—haunted her mind. There were rumors that Hood had left a few cavalry "to dispute every inch of ground through the city," and that fact became a torment. More fighting! More bullets and shells! Time dragged, filled with uneasiness. At dinner her father said simply that the Federals had taken possession of the city. Mary could hardly believe him. There had been no disorder, no loud exulting, no threats and sneers! But later she admitted:

> . . . Atlanta was taken possession of quietly. About ten o'clock in the morning the mayor [and] two councilmen with the principal citizens went out to invite them in. After some hesitation they marched in under the command of General Slocum. . . . Immediately upon entering the town the stars and stripes were seen floating from the flag pole on the Franklin Building. Father's store was used as a signal station. The signals were given with a blue flag having a large white star in the center and in the evening they used beautiful lanterns which were moved in different directions. . . .

That night Mary wrote that "the moon once more shines over sleeping, silent Atlanta."

But troubles and annoyances mounted steadily in the days that followed. On a rainy Saturday she watched General Geary set up his headquarters in the old schoolhouse. "The beloved old playground" was filled with tents, the shade trees cut down, "Miss Maria's and Miss Ann's cherished pet flowers trampled," and Mary "shed tears to think of the desolation." Sunday saw the soldiers filling "our own beloved churches," and, spiritually revived, the Yankees raided the potato patch. That night "the cows were gone." When a group of prisoners were marched into the city and taken to the freight depots "a great many of the ladies" defiantly "visited them carrying delicacies." Rumors persisted that Sherman intended to move all civilians out of the city, giving them the choice of going "farther down in Dixie" or attempting "the ice and snow of a Northern winter." Neither Geary nor Slocum knew anything about the command; Mary waited anxiously for a definite

denial. A Yankee law forbade any person to sell cotton or tobacco. Mary thought: "Ill-fated weed, though loved and
longed for by Yankee soldiery, you seem as ever to be only a
source of trouble to those who possess and use you!" On the
8th Sherman reached Atlanta. Everything became worse.

The general settled himself in the house of Judge Lyons,
opposite one corner of the Court House Square. The brigade
of the Massachusetts 2nd and 23rd Regiments occupied the
square, and the general felt that this brigade had two of the
finest bands in the army. To Halleck a few days before he had
written: "If the people raise a howl against my barbarity and
cruelty, I will answer that war is war, and not popularity-
seeking." In this spirit, he faced the problems of dealing with
an occupied Atlanta:

> . . . Hundreds of sutlers and traders were waiting at
> Nashville and Chattanooga, greedy to reach Atlanta
> with their wares and goods, with which to drive a profit-
> able trade with the inhabitants. I gave positive orders
> that none of these traders, except three (one for each
> separate army), should be permitted to come nearer than
> Chattanooga; and, moreover, I peremptorily required
> that all the citizens and families resident in Atlanta should
> go away, giving to each the option to go south or north,
> as their interests or feelings dictated. I was resolved to
> make Atlanta a pure military garrison or depot, with no
> civil population to influence military measures. I had
> seen Memphis, Vicksburg, Natchez, and New Orleans,
> all captured from the enemy, and each at once was gar-
> risoned by a full division of troops, if not more; so that
> success was actually crippling our armies in the field by
> detachments to guard and protect the interests of a hostile
> population.

Sherman knew his measure "would be strongly criticized,"
but the people of the South could read into it

. . . two important conclusions: one, that we were in earnest; and the other, if they were sincere in their common and popular clamor "to die in the last ditch," that the opportunity would soon come.

One of the very last ditches in which the Confederacy wanted to die was in Europe. In London the Confederate government published *The Index*, which, said its masthead, "was established in May 1862, in the darkest hour of Confederate fortunes, by earnest friends of Southern Independence, with the distinctly expressed object of being the representative, in English journalism, of a gallant and struggling people appealing to the world not only for political, but still more for moral recognition." *The Index*, struggling with "the callous indifference of the British Government" and "the perplexity, to the European mind" of the problems raised by "four millions of the African race, intermingled with a population of the highest Caucasian type," must now struggle as well with the problem of General Sherman and his army.

"The rumours of a pitched battle and a defeat of the Confederates before Atlanta we do not credit," *The Index* told its European audience in early August. It was not at all likely that "Hood would force on a general action by attacking the Federals in their entrenchments." Hood's dash, *The Index* predicted, "may yet produce the most brilliant results." Sherman, at best, faced "the tedious process of regular siege operations," a delay that "may be fatal to him," for "it is not possible that Sherman's army can subsist wholly in front of Atlanta in a country which has been drained for the last six months by the troops of the Confederacy." Measured, thoughtful, cautious, the propaganda technique of *The Index* emphasized quiet confidence.

In September *The Index* must face the fact that Atlanta had fallen. Nothing had been lost, really; "there is only one city the less to defend." Atlanta would prove to be "of fictitious rather than of real value" to the Federals. Sherman had entered "a comparatively deserted town," and "he finds it, as Butler found [New] Orleans, inhabited solely by old men, women, and children." Set down in "a hostile community," he now must fight "for every twenty miles he may wish to travel, east, west, or south. . . . If he is enabled quietly to go into winter quarters at Atlanta, this is about as much as he can expect." Perhaps that result was worth "all the frenzy of Mr. Lincoln's Cabinet and the New York press." *The Index* shrugged: "Johnston was prepared to evacuate the city two months ago, and to throw it into the hands of the Federals as a matter of policy. Sherman, however, has gained his prize. It remains to be seen what he will do with it."

If the "English and Southern writers" who produced *The Index* wished a real lesson in propaganda Sherman and Hood proceeded to supply it. Both seized their pens and filled long pages in virulent debate. The correspondence opened when through James M. Ball and James R. Crew, citizens of Atlanta, Sherman requested a truce at Rough and Ready to provide facilities for transporting the families of Atlanta who preferred to go South. The city must be evacuated in "the interest of the United States," Sherman said, and Hood in reply could not see, if this were so, that "I have any alternative in this matter." But Hood certainly held his own opinion of Sherman's decision:

> . . . the unprecedented measures you propose transcend, in studied and ingenious cruelty, all acts ever before brought to my attention in the dark history of war.

Sherman's temper rose. If Hood wished to speak of "studied and ingenious cruelty," he had better reserve his remarks for someone who had not that very day seen how:

> . . . You yourself burned dwelling houses along your parapet, and [how] . . . You defended Atlanta on a line so close to town that every cannon shot and many musket-shots from our line of investment, that overshot their mark, went into habitations of women and children. . . .

"Talk thus to the marines, but not to me," sneered Sherman, the neck under his collar growing warmer over:

> . . . You who, in the midst of peace and prosperity, have plunged a nation into war—dark and cruel war— who dared and badgered us into battle, insulted our flag, seized our arsenals and forts that were left in the honorable custody of peaceful ordnance-sergeants, seized and made "prisoners of war" the very garrisons sent to protect your people against Negroes and Indians, long before any overt act was committed by the (to you) hated Lincoln Government; tried to force Kentucky and Missouri into rebellion, spite of themselves; falsified the vote of Louisiana; turned loose your privateers to plunder unarmed ships; expelled Union families by the thousands, burned their houses, and declared, by an act of Congress, the confiscation of all debts due Northern men for goods had and received! . . .

Hood answered Sherman with no less spirit, refuting every one of his charges in detail. He would thank Sherman not to "presume to sit in judgment between me and my God," when, as a matter of fact:

> You came into our country with your army, avowedly for the purpose of subjugating free white men, women, and children, and not only intend to rule over them, but you make Negroes your allies, and desire to place over us an inferior race, which we have raised from barbarism to its present position, which is the highest ever attained by that race, in any country, in all time. . . .

To Sherman's taunt, "Let us fight it out like men," Hood replied darkly, "We will fight you to the death! Better die a thousand deaths than to submit to live under you or your Government and your Negro allies!"

The moment was scarcely propitious for the mayor of Atlanta and two councilmen to petition Sherman to revoke his order of evacuation. Among "many poor women . . . in advanced state of pregnancy," among others "whose husbands for the greater part are either in the army, prisoners, or dead," and among still others who could not "live through the winter in the woods," the mayor and councilmen said that the "aggregate consequences" of the general's order would be "appalling and heart-rending." Tartly Sherman responded:

> You might as well appeal against the thunderstorm as against these terrible hardships of war. . . . I myself have seen in Missouri, Kentucky, Tennessee, and Mississippi, hundreds and thousands of women and children fleeing from your armies and desperadoes, hungry and with bleeding feet. . . . Now that war comes home to you, you feel very different . . . when peace does come, you may call on me for any thing. Then I will share with you the last cracker. . . . Now you must go, and take with you the old and feeble, feed and nurse them, and build them, in more quiet places, proper habitations to shield them against the weather until the mad passions of men cool down, and allow the Union and peace once more to settle over your old homes at Atlanta.

All of this correspondence Sherman forwarded to Halleck in Washington, who approved the course taken. "Old Brains" couldn't see why the Federals were required "to treat the so-called noncombatant Rebels better than they themselves treat each other." In Virginia, Halleck declared that within fifty miles of the Capitol, "they strip their own families of provisions, leaving them, as our army advances, to be fed by us, or starve within our lines." The answer to Halleck was very simple: "We have fed this class of people long enough."

Sherman and Hood also clashed on the exchange of prisoners. Hood wanted "out of the vast number of our men then held captive in Andersonville," a general exchange, but whereas Sherman knew of "the pitiable condition" of Federal prisoners there, he refused to exchange generally since the men released from Andersonville "would have to be sent to their own regiments, away from my army, whereas all we could give him could at once go into his immediate army."

In the midst of this squabbling, Lieutenant Colonel Horace Porter arrived from City Point with a letter from Grant. In Virginia, Grant confessed, he was "holding on quietly," waiting for the "advantage of recruits and convalesents" to strengthen a long line extending from Deep Bottom, north of the James, across the peninsula to south of Appomattox. Still, Grant said, he must extend to the left. Whereas this line was "strongly qualified," its very length required many men "in the aggregate." Meanwhile he planned an expedition against Wilmington and Fort Fisher to gain control of the harbor there the way Union iron-clads now held the harbor at Mobile. What to do with the forces under Sherman's command puzzled Grant. Where next? Mobile and Savannah, Macon and Augusta were places that came naturally into any military consideration. "My object in sending a staff-officer to you," Grant wrote, "is not so much to suggest operations as to get your views."

Sherman replied at considerable length, hoping that Grant's army would soon be so well reenforced that "with one part you can watch" Lee and "with the other push out boldly from your left flank," thus compelling the Confederates "to attack you in position, or accept battle on your own terms." With Mobile shut off, the first expeditious moment should see the occupation of the Alabama River and Columbus, Georgia. The "utter destruction of Wilmington" would cut off Confederate foreign trade, of first importance, and enable sending the fleet to the Savannah River. Then, Sherman thought:

. . . the reduction of that city is the next question. It once in our possession, and the river open to us, I would not hesitate to cross the State of Georgia with sixty thousand men, hauling some stores, and depending on the country for the balance. Where a million of people find subsistence, my army won't starve; but, as you know, in a country like Georgia, with few roads and innumerable streams, an inferior force can so delay an army and harrass it, that it would not be a formidable object; but if the enemy knew that we had our boats in the Savannah River I could rapidly move on Milledgeville, where there is an abundance of corn and meat, and could so threaten Macon and Augusta that the enemy would doubtless give up Macon for Augusta; then I would move so as to interpose between Augusta and Savannah, and force him to give us Augusta. . . . Either horn of the dilemma will be worth a battle. I would prefer his holding Augusta (as the probabilities are); for then, with the Savannah River in our possession, the taking of Augusta would be a mere matter of time. This campaign can be made in the winter.

To go farther into Georgia "without an object beyond" would be futile. Sherman suggested, with General Edward Canby holding the Mississippi, and sending a force to take Columbus, with Wilmington taken, and the fleet striking for Savannah and its river, then: "I should keep Hood employed and put my army in fine order for a march on Augusta, Columbia, and Charleston." The Confederacy could not hope to enter Missouri now, "except as raiders," and if Rosecrans wanted any of Sherman's troops for defense there he "should be ashamed." Secure Wilmington and Savannah, let Canby command the Mississippi and the country west, and: "I will send a force to the Alabama and Appalachicola, provided you give me one hundred thousand of the drafted men to fill up my old regiments; if you fix a day to be in Savannah, I will insure our possession of Macon and a point on the river below Augusta."

The vision had rooted. It would grow—in Grant's mind, in Sherman's. There would be debate over who saw the full image finally, but in the letter that Horace Porter carried back to Grant, Sherman would say: "They may stand the fall of Richmond, but not of all Georgia."

Halleck's love of gossip brought relief from these sobering reflections and the virulent haggling with Hood. Hooker, said "Old Brains," was spreading all manner of mean stories; and he inclosed "a specimen." Washington was a fine spot for Halleck to listen to political simmerings:

> . . . Mr. Seward's speech at Auburn, again prophesying, for the twentieth time, that the rebellion would be crushed in a few months, and saying that there would be no draft, as we now had enough soldiers to end the war, etc., has done much harm, in a military point of view. I have seen enough of politics here to last me for life. You are right in avoiding them. McClellan may possibly reach the White House, but he will lose the respect of all honest, high-minded patriots, by his affiliation with such traitors and Copperheads as B[igler], V[allandigham], W[ood], S[eymour], & Co. He would not stand upon the traitorous Chicago platform, but he had not the manliness to oppose it. A major-general in the United States Army, and yet not one word to utter against Rebels or the rebellion! . . .

Sherman settled down in Atlanta and listened to the bands across the Court House Square. Thomas, believing [as Sherman reported] that "it would not be prudent for us to go much farther into Georgia because of our long lines of communication," wanted to send his trains back to Chattanooga "for the convenience and the economy of forage." Sherman wondered then if the Federals could afford "to remain on the defensive, simply holding Atlanta and fighting for the safety of its railroad." That doubt would grow. Schofield went back to Knoxville, and Generals Logan and Blair "went home to look after politics." A sense of idleness affected everyone; many regiments had finished their terms of service and claimed discharges; so that "with victory and success," Sherman could not avoid noticing, "came also many causes of disintegration." From May 6 through the battles about Jonesboro, Sherman set his losses at 14,424 in killed, missing, and wounded, and those of Hood, in the same engagements, the Federals would compute to be 12,983.

At Rough and Ready all but a few families were evacuated to the south. The newspapers that came to Sherman, excepting a few like the hostile *Cincinnati Commercial* and the equally hostile *New York Herald*, filled him with pleasant hours of reading. There must have been some astonishment for Sherman to learn that a minor boom for him over McClellan had stirred a few Democrats in late August; but his antagonistic attitude toward Negro-recruiting, always intense, had not kept him from favoring emancipation and that fact alone had killed him as a potential candidate (to no one's greater satisfaction than his own). Sherman was to the end a general. A soldier. Sherman felt at home in Atlanta. He wanted his troops to feel the same. It was said afterward that his men fulfilled his wishes so well they stole the silver handles from Atlanta caskets.

PART FIVE

✳✳✳✳✳✳✳✳✳✳✳✳✳✳✳✳✳✳✳✳✳✳✳✳✳✳✳✳✳✳✳✳✳✳✳✳✳✳

"And Make Georgia Howl"
— the march to the sea

1. "AM ABLE TO WHIP ALL HELL"

In a tent on a hilltop one starlit night in early September, Major Connolly listened to "the mellow notes of a flute" floating "through the evening air from the camps beyond." Sentimentally, he wrote his wife:

> . . . How many hearts, hardened by years of toil and scenes of blood on scores of historic battlefields, are softened by the mellow twilight of this evening, and [how many are] their owners, sitting alone, in musing mood, looking at the stars in the Northern skies, and wondering what the dear ones beneath those stars are doing? . . .

In the "bright glow of victory" following the capture of Atlanta, Connolly confessed that "we are all . . . happy as lovers in their moneymoon" willing "to follow Sherman and Thomas to the ends of the Confederacy," for "the 'God of Israel' is wielding his sword in our behalf and we know no such word as fail."

Scornfulness crept into his thoughts at the mention of McClellan and the campaign of the Democratic Party. Who was McClellan but "a man of straw" set up "by Wood, Richmond, Seymour, Cox, *et id omne genus*, to enable them to steal into the Capitol and the Cabinet, and the foreign missions, patch up a dishonorable peace and pocket the spoils"? McClellan was a "verdant spooney whom old gamesters have inveigled into their snares"; the nation must know that Little Mac "lacks backbone" and that his nerves "are not strong enough for this storm." If anyone had a right to complain it was the soldiers in Atlanta. Their back pay amounted to thousands of dollars, but the soldiers were of one heart. They were for Lincoln, who had dared to say: "The Nation must live."

Inside the shattered city the child of a nation that here no longer existed, ten-year-old Carrie Berry, found during those early September days that "every one I see seems sad." The heartbreak and the uncertainty surrounding the girl's life could not be concealed: "We all commenced this morning to prepare for moving. We do not know how long we will get to stay here. We are all in so much trouble." Carrie saw her mother distracted to the point where she "can't do any thing," and even "Papa says he don't know where on earth to go." More cheerful than either parent, the child thought: "The citizens all think that it is the most cruel thing to drive us from our homes but I think it would be so funny to move."

Routine chores filled Carrie's days. The girl liked the "wirk" she must do, and at night tumbled into bed, tired and certain she would sleep "if the musquitoes don't bite me too much." One by one the days of September passed. Always, there were soldiers underfoot, "pacing backward and forward," and yet they impressed Carrie as "orderly" and she dared to admit to herself: "I think I shall like the Yankees." For the ten-year-old, life in the occupied city developed a pattern:

Sept. 14. . . . I got dinner by myself.

Sept. 16. I ironed till dinner and got through and I had a hollowday the rest of the evening. We have had a nice time playing. . . .

Sept. 18. This had ben a dark rainy day. We had stewed chickens for dinner.

Sept. 20. I went up to Auntie's this evening to see Willie. He is mighty cute and took three or four steps while I was there.

Rain fell almost constantly. The wash could not be hung out to dry, and a sore throat made the child miserable. Then a

favorite cousin died, and Aunt Healy, to whom the girl was
devoted, packed to move north. Carrie missed going to church,
but the Yankees had requisitioned all places of worship. For a
day the sun broke through the clouds and the child's spirit improved. Aunt Healy gave her "some quilt peaces and some
doll clothes." After that, even though Sundays dragged out
"long and lonely," she was busy "making my doll a frock." In
the cities of the North other ten-year-olds, tramping home
from Sunday school, whistled the tune of a new song, *How
Sherman's Veterans Took Atlanta.* Their young voices sang:

Now, glory to Sherman, and all his brave Veterans,
    Who won Georgia back to the Union again;
The Rebel strong-hold has our flag waving o'er it,
    And treason shall never touch it, nor stain!
From triumph to triumph advancing, full quickly,
    Our soldiers new honors and trophies shall claim
While Jeff. losing strong-holds one after another
    Will be hunted from Richmond and—give up his game.

Despite the rain, mid-September found Sherman's mood
mellow. With the telegraph and the railroads repaired, and
with Wheeler's cavalry driven out of middle Tennessee, Sherman could write that "matters and things had settled down in
Atlanta, so that we felt perfectly at home." This "period of
repose" suited Sherman's plans perfectly, for through various
emissaries he prodded Governor Brown with warnings that
unless Georgia "prevailed" upon its policy of "separate State
action" and withdrew from the Rebellion, the Union armies
"would be compelled to go ahead, devestating the State in its
whole length and breadth." As though playing directly into
Sherman's hands, Brown, sulking in his executive quarters at
Milledgeville, cast covetous eyes on the corn and sorghum
"then ripe and ready for the harvesters," and ordered the
Georgia militia sent home to "look for a time after important
interests, and prepare themselves for such service as may be

required when another campaign commences against other important points in the State."

Sherman felt almost gleeful. Would Brown come to Atlanta to meet him? The city would welcome Brown warmly, Sherman promised, with "as full and respectable an audience as any he had ever spoken to." Even Lincoln took heart, telegraphing Sherman that "I feel great interest in your dispatch, mentioning corn and sorghum, and the contemplated visit to you." The general at once responded to the President's wire:

> . . . Georgia can now save herself from the devastation of war preparing for her, only by withdrawing her quota out of the Confederate Army, and aiding me to expel Hood from the borders of the State; in which event, instead of desolating the land as we progress, I will keep our men to the high-roads and commons, and pay for the corn and meat we need and take.

Lincoln and Sherman waited; no reply came from Brown. For once, the governor had everyone stymied. After all, both Hood and Sherman were inactive; why was it necessarily treasonable to put his militia to work where they would do the most good? But nerves were taut, tempers frayed, and events hung on thin hairs. On the 21st of September, Sam Hood moved the Army of Tennessee from the Macon Road at Lovejoy's to the West Point Road at Palmetto Station. Hood's objective was to take the offensive against the railroads on which the Yankee hold on Atlanta depended, but to Sherman it seemed as though Hood were "stepping aside, and opening wide the door for us to enter Central Georgia." Did Sherman's eyes suddenly grow brighter? Did his tongue flick across his bearded lips as though already tasting blood? Sending Newton's division by cars to Chattanooga and Corse's division to Rome, Sherman telegraphed Halleck in Washington: "If I were sure that Savannah would soon be in our possession [by naval action], I should be tempted to march for Milledgeville and Augusta."

Sherman knew he must first secure what he had, but the vision had captured him. Almost as an afterthought, he informed Halleck that Jefferson Davis was reported in Macon. At City Point, Virginia, where Grant kept an eye on Lee and prepared a noose of his own with which to hang the Confederacy, frank disbelief greeted the intelligence that Davis was in Macon, and franker disbelief greeted Sherman's advice next day that the President had visited Hood at Palmetto Station. Then the proof arrived; on the 27th Sherman secured a printed copy of Davis's speech in Macon and considered it "so significant" that he ordered it telegraphed in full to Louisville and thence sent by mail to Washington.

In Columbia, South Carolina, Mrs. Chestnut read in *The Charleston Mercury*, with the feeling that it was "really touching," the account of the Macon address. "More in sorrow than in anger," Mrs. Chestnut wrote, *The Mercury* "declares there must be some hoax." Even to Sherman the Macon speech appeared incredible and he could only decide that Davis "seemed to be perfectly upset by the fall of Atlanta, and to have lost all sense and reason."

Jefferson Davis had arrived in Macon in a bullheaded mood, incensed by the constant harping in the press, on the street, and within the Army of Tennessee that Johnston should never have been replaced by Hood. Now the President lashed back, branding Governor Brown "as little better than a traitor," and seeming to some to include Joseph Johnston in the same class. Davis's dander was up and his guard down, so that with astonishing blandness he announced that Hood's next move would be to join Forrest in Middle Tennessee and leave "the Yankee army . . . to retreat or starve." Yet despite the stormy indiscretions so obvious within this speech, when Davis passed through Columbia a fortnight later Mrs. Chestnut would report that "the President's hand was nearly shaken off," and that she heard such comments as "I like the game look the fellow has." But Sally Preston would tell Mrs. Chestnut with the candor of an intimate friend:

> . . . They do things that our feminine common sense regards as madness, but they talk so well, and we listen until they almost fool us into believing they have some reason for the wild work. But say what you will, this northern movement of the Western Army is against common sense.

At City Point, Grant didn't entirely agree with Sally Preston. Quickly he advised Sherman: "I have directed all new troops from the West, and from the East too, if necessary, in case none are ready in the West, to be sent to you." Grant clung to the determination that Sherman should not be driven "from where you are," and Sherman, now that he was aware that Forrest already had appeared in middle Tennessee, could guess that Hood was "evidently edging off in that direction." There were those who believed that the raids of Nathan Bedford Forrest rarely achieved major results, but Forrest carried into battle a freebooting individualism that Westerners like Sherman and Grant respected. Forrest's reputation as a cavalryman rested on the belief that the commander who got there "fustest with the mostest men" won a battle, and Forrest and Hood, operating in unison, could offer considerable danger.

Sherman acted promptly. On the 29th Thomas was ordered back to Chattanooga, and the next day Morgan's division was hurried along the rails to join Thomas. Forrest intended to cut the road of the Federals, but even if he did, Sherman wired Halleck, "his cavalry will travel a hundred miles where ours will ten." Sherman begged Halleck to watch the Federal roads from the rear, adding almost wistfully: "I prefer for the future to make the movement on Milledgeville, Millen, and Savannah." Sam Hood now rested his army on the Chattahoochee twenty-four miles to the south with his right flung across the West Point Road. In annoyance Sherman confessed that Yankee spies could not penetrate Hood's camp at Palmetto Station; and to Halleck he admitted: "I can whip his infantry, but his cavalry is to be feared."

Inside Atlanta ten-year-old Carrie Berry sensed that some new movement of the armies impended. On the 3rd of October Carrie would write in her diary: "We heard that General Hood had got around toward Chattanooga tearing up the railroad. The Federals seemed very much troubled about it." Carrie started "a little worsted dress" for her sister, thinking "I love to sew for her because she loves me." The dress was finished next day, too quickly; twice, "so lonesome I can't stay at home," Carrie visited her aunt; above everything, the girl wished "it was so that I could go to school." Everyone felt the same fear. Would Hood come back "and commence shelling as the Federals did"? Carrie thought: "I never would stay and be shelled again if I could get away."

But Sherman worried little over Hood's returning to Atlanta. With nothing more than surmise to go on, Sherman believed that by the first of October Hood had shuttled his infantry across the Chattahoochee near Campbelltown and held his cavalry on the west bank at Powder Springs. If Hood tries to get on our road this side of the Etowah, Sherman's mind reasoned, I'll attack him. But the general's real guess was that Hood would try for the unfinished railroad from Selma, Alabama, through Talladega to Blue Mountain. Common sense favored that move. At Blue Mountain, Hood would stand at a terminus sixty-five miles southwest of Rome and approximately fifteen miles southeast of Gadsden, where, Sherman calculated, "The Rebel army could be supplied from the direction of Montgomery and Mobile, and from which point Hood could easily threaten Middle Tennessee." The prospect of remaining on the defensive nettled Sherman. If Hood should attempt to straddle the Selma & Talladega railroad, he wired Grant at City Point:

. . . why will it not do to leave Tennessee to the forces
Thomas has, and the reserves soon to come to Nashville,
and for me to destroy Atlanta and march across Georgia
to Savannah or Charleston, breaking roads and doing ir-
reparable damage?

Moving quickly, prodding for a weak spot, Sam Hood be-
deviled Sherman wherever he could. Still trusting to surmise,
Sherman decided by the 3rd of October that the enemy would
"strike our railroad nearer us . . . about Kingston or Marietta." That same day Major Connolly noted that the Union
forces "struck tents at 1 o'clock p.m." and "marched until late
at night, through mud and rain." The troops, discouraged,
"lay down in the fence corners" and "without supper . . .
slept until morning." At daylight the Federals began crossing
the Chattahoochee on a pontoon bridge. Another day's
cheerless marching brought them to the military college at
Marietta, but before they could encamp orders came to resume marching, "all night, if necessary," until they reached
"Jack's House," a point about a mile in rear of the position
Connolly and his comrades had held the previous June at the
foot of Kenesaw. The night was dark, the roads muddy, the
rain still pelting down. Tired and hungry, the men floundered
on, cursing Hood and the war.

Sherman reached Kenesaw Mountain on October 5. Looking down, he "could see the smoke of camp-fire, indicating
the presence of a large force of the enemy, and the whole line
of the railroad from Big Shanty to Allatoona (full fifteen miles)
was marked by the fires of the burning railroad." Sherman
heard distinctly the reverberation of cannon. The smoke of
battle curled into the sky at Allatoona.

Where was Johnny Corse? Had Corse, who had been sent
down to Rome with his division on the same day that Newton's division enrailed for Chattanooga, received his orders in
time, and had Allatoona been adequately garrisoned? On
these two questions Sherman hung in painful suspense. From

Kenesaw, looking northwest toward Allatoona, every order Sherman issued must run the risk of coming too late and of supplying too little. The XXIIIrd Corps under General Cox sped west along the Burnt Hickory Road with instructions to burn houses or piles of brush as it advanced so that Sherman would know where the head of its column stood, for the general clung to the hope that he could "interpose this corps between Hood's main army at Dallas and the detachment then assaulting Allatoona." The rest of the Federal army headed straight for Allatoona. Sherman had done all he could.

The morning stretched on endlessly. Johnny Corse was the kind of fighting general that Sherman liked. A hard-bitten, hard-swearing veteran of the Corinth and Vicksburg campaigns, Corse was the sort of mad-eyed young Army officer who, wounded critically at Missionary Ridge, had growled all through his rest leave, wanting to be back in action. Now Corse had his wish. A signal officer on Kenesaw brought Sherman a decoded flag message: "Corse is here."

Sherman ruffled a hand through his red hair. Through the remainder of the morning and until two o'clock in the afternoon, "when the smoke of battle . . . grew less and less," Sherman's nerves continued ragged. By four o'clock the smoke had blown away. Still Sherman waited, sustained only by the faith that Johnny Corse was a match for any of Hood's detachments. Then in the morning a courier arrived with a message from Corse:

> . . . I am short a cheek-bone and an ear, but am able to whip all hell yet!

Johnny Corse had wanted a fight. Sam Hood's army had not disappointed him.

2. "THE WILD ADVENTURE OF A CRAZY FOOL"

AT ALLATOONA that bloody 5th of October, Sam Hood gambled for stakes in part military, in part psychological. That Sam held command of the Army of Tennessee because Jefferson Davis insisted on it was no longer a secret; and that many of Hood's men no longer stifled their grumbling that they would be better off with "Old Joe" back in the saddle was equally well known. After the fall of Atlanta Hood had written a remarkably frank letter to Braxton Bragg, saying in part:

> I am officially informed that there is a tacit if not expressed determination among the men of this army, extending to officers and higher in some instances, as Colonel, that they will not attack breastworks. In this state of affairs I think my troops, for offensive operations, not more than equal to their numbers of the enemy. The enemy can thus hold me in check with a part of his force and is at liberty to detach strong parties to operate upon my communications and upon such points as Augusta, Columbus, Andersonville, &c. To save this country from being overrun it is necessary to crush Sherman. To accomplish this reinforcements should be sent me immediately.

Bragg forwarded Hood's letter to Davis and the President wrote across the back: "It is sad to hear such feeling as is described in any portion of our troops who are required to act offensively."

To anyone who would listen, Sam Hood said that he faced no problem greater than the task of restoring the army's "fighting spirit." If he could turn the enemy's right flank and destroy his communications, what choice had Sherman but to retire from Atlanta? Wheeler's cavalry in Georgia, or Forrest's in Tennessee, were not sufficient to achieve this goal, in Hood's judgment. "To accomplish anything," he would write in a report to the adjutant general, "it became necessary for me to move with my whole force."

For impulsive Sam Hood to arrive at even a partial decision was tantamount to having the deed half done. "Causing the iron to be removed from the several railroads out of Atlanta for distances of forty miles," he told the adjutant general, he anchored the left of his line so that it touched the Chattahoochee and thus covered the road for several days "to allow the accumulation of supplies at Blue Mountain and a sufficiency with which to continue the movement." On the 29th of September he moved his main army from Palmetto Station, crossing the Chattahoochee on a pontoon bridge at Pumpkin Town and Philip's Ferry, and advanced at once to Lost Mountain. Here Sam stomped around on his cork leg, eying the surrounding countryside and calculating his possibilities. On the 4th of October he saw a chance to strike the enemy's railroad at Acworth and Big Shanty, and Lieutenant General Stewart's corps captured "the garrisons at both places, consisting of some four hundred prisoners, with some animals and stores."

The action at Acworth and Big Shanty, however, could scarcely be called satisfying in the sense that it could build the "*morale*" Sam so consistently italicized in his own mind. In his letter to Bragg following the evacuation of Atlanta he had promised: "I shall use every effort to induce our men to believe that they can carry the enemy's hastily prepared works." Just a month had passed since this statement to Bragg, and for Hood no engagement he precipitated could be critical unless it achieved this result. His scouts, constantly on the prowl, brought word that "the enemy had a quantity of stores at Allatoona." Sam's heart quickened. If he destroyed the bridge over the Etowah and sent a division to Allatoona, he could sting Sherman's rump for fair! Here was the kind of action

Sam liked, one where he could strike fast and hard. The general he selected to lead the assault was crusty Sam French, the fighting son of a Quaker who had pummeled Morgan Smith's boys at Little Kenesaw.

Johnny Corse was not too happy over the situation at Allatoona. He had come down on the 4th of October from Rome —in twenty instead of the thirty railroad cars he had ordered —so that the total reinforcements he could add to the garrison of 890 men was another 1,054 effectives. At two o'clock in the morning Corse, cursing the freshets that had spread the railroad tracks and deprived him of a third of his forces, sized up the odds against him. If reports could be trusted, French commanded somewhere between four and five thousand troops, and his men already were "pushing the picket-lines warmly." Throughout the predawn hours French kept pressing the Federal skirmishers, bent on gashing an opening. Corse rushed the 18th Wisconsin to the support of one outpost, the 7th Illinois to the rescue of another.

A ridge running along both sides of the railroad cut provided a summit where Corse could make a stand. At daybreak Sam French unlimbered his cannon, and for two hours Confederate shells nicked and rocked the ridge to which Corse and the Federals clung. Meanwhile French worked an infantry brigade around the north of the Federal lines with orders to cut the railroad and telegraph. Thus entirely destroying Corse's communications, Sam French felt the fight had ended, and under a flag of truce he informed Corse that he was surrounded and should surrender to "avoid needless effusion of blood."

Johnny Corse snorted. "We are prepared for the 'needless effusion of blood,' " he shot back, "whenever it is agreeable to you."

From front, flank, and rear, French pounced on the Federals; his attack was aimed at a spur that covered the redoubt on the hill above the railroad cut. Here the nineteen hundred Texans of Young's brigade stormed along the crest, opposed by the less than six hundred men of the 39th Iowa and the 7th Illinois. More than a million Federal rations in the depot by the railroad was part of the prize at stake making French's eyes glitter. To make sure that the Texans couldn't fail, French sent another Confederate brigade, under Sears, to move in from the north, straddle the railroad on its left, and support Young. The "needless effusion of blood" began to stain the smoke-covered hills of Allatoona.

The stubborn fighting quality in Johnny Corse imbued his men. Savagely and bitterly the Yankees fought back, shrieking defiance across the lines and emptying their guns point-blank into the faces of the charging Confederates. Assault after assault of the angry Texans rolled up to the Union lines, then broke under the blazing muskets. A colonel of the 7th Illinois was twice wounded, and later even Corse would be shot across the face with a ball that cut his ear and rendered him insensible for half an hour. But these disruptions became mere flea-bites to the raging Yankee defenders. Not until Sears could bring his brigade to the active assistance of Young did the graybacks begin to swing the balance.

Now for a time, Corse admitted, "the enemy's line of battle swept us back like so much chaff." The 7th Illinois, harassed by Young and Sears, was being slashed to pieces and Corse doubted if he would bring a single man back into the redoubt. Then the 39th Iowa swung into the fight like husky farm boys reaping wheat. Corse reported exultantly: "Their hand-to-hand struggle and stubborn stand broke the enemy." The lines of the Confederates now had to be reformed; bleeding and triumphant, the Yankees staggered into the forts. Corse looked at his watch. Eleven a.m. The relentless assaults had been repulsed for nearly two and a half hours.

The two redoubts overlooking the Federal storehouse at Allatoona had been built by Sherman's engineers during the advance on Kenesaw four months previously, and each had been placed to help the other defensively by catching an attacking force in the flank with a crossfire. Those forts were

"impregnable," in Johnny Corse's estimation, but his indebtedness to Sherman's engineers could not match the gratitude he owed the battered remnant of the 39th Iowa who had
"so,completely disorganized . . . the enemy that no regular
assault could be made on the fort till I had the trenches all
filled and the parapets lined with men."

Sam French now resembled the Jeff Davis who had spoken
at Macon. Stung and angry, refusing to calculate the advantage he had lost, Sam threw caution aside. If Hood felt the
men in the Army of Tennessee were too squeamish to attack
"hastily prepared works," French proceeded to teach him
otherwise. Even Corse respected the Confederate grit. Each
piece French had seen smashed on the field became a vantage
point, as his men filled "every hollow . . . every hole and
trench, seeking shelter behind every stump and log that lay
within musket-range of the fort." The taste of blood was on
Corse's lips when he confessed: "We received fire from the
north, south, and west face of the redoubt, completely enfilading our ditches, and rendering it almost impracticable
for a man to expose his person above the parapet."

French ordered an attack. Gamely the Confederates
charged. But gameness wasn't enough when six guns of the
12th Wisconsin screamed death into the faces of any living
column "within one hundred yards of the works." A kind of
paralyzing despair gripped the men in both armies. Behind
the parapets every Yankee understood that to raise a head was
to leave it there, and the officers, Corse said, "labored constantly . . . nobly setting them the example." French refused to be shaken. Doggedly he pressed the attack, firing
continuously and intensely, "gradually closing around us
[Corse reported], and rapidly filling our little fort with the
dead and dying."

Noon passed. One o'clock. Johnny Corse, wounded and insensible, shook himself to consciousness to the sound of a
"Cease firing" order. He came up on his feet. Who the hell
was losing his head? With a little more time, reinforcements

would reach Allatoona. Tactfully Corse was told the truth. In the "face of the murderous fire of the enemy now concentrated upon us" the artillery had run out of ammunition! Johnny Corse lived the agony of the damned. Then a volunteer—he is nameless in the record—offered to go across the cut for the case shot and canister the Federals needed. When the volunteer returned, he carried a single armload of ammunition.

With a dull, persistent deathlessness, time ticked on. Two o'clock. Two thirty. Behind a small house on a ridge not more than one hundred and fifty yards beyond the fort, Johnny Corse saw the enemy massing. Corse ordered the dead and wounded moved aside, a gun pushed up to the embrasure commanding the house and ridge. With only a single armload of ammunition, no shot could be wasted! Corse's head, with half an ear missing, dropped in a nod. The gun roared. Up on the ridge that shell fell as though an angel had flown it to the mark. The gunners reloaded. Corse nodded again. Out from the embrasure the shell shrieked and plummeted. The fort rang with a cheer. By God, this was a taste of Little Kenesaw in reverse! How did old Sam French like it? In elation, Corse watched the Confederates scattering, torn not only by the expert artillery fire, but also by a "heavy and continuous musketry" from the parapets.

By four o'clock French admitted that he was licked, and his confused troops fled from the field, "leaving their dead and wounded." Later, by converging heavy cannon-fire on a blockhouse at Allatoona Creek some two miles from the depot, French fired it and captured a garrison of four officers and eighty-five men, but that seemed scant recompense for a full retreat down the Dallas Road. Hood wrote with sagacious restraint that French "received information which he considered correct, but which subsequently proved false," and "immediately withdrew his command from the place without having accomplished the desired object."

On October 6 Major Connolly wrote in his diary that "the

roads [were] so bad we didn't reach 'Jack's House,' which is
near Pine Mountain, until 11 o'clock today. Hood is scared of
us and trying to get out of our way." On the next day Connolly reached Lost Mountain; to the northwest, he could see

. . . Lookout Mountain, overhanging Chattanooga;
nearer to us was the range of Allatoona hills, and Allatoona Gap, where the battle of day before yesterday was
gallantly fought and gloriously won by Corse; east of us
and nearer to us Kenesaw with its dromedary humps
loomed up from the plain, and still nearer arose Pine
Mountain from the summit of which, last June, the soul of
the Rev. Bishop General Polk went to its long home.

The twisted memories of war had begun to accumulate.
Connolly would recall an old man who brought out "a little
basket of apples" as the Federals marched by. And October
8 would arouse the sudden recollection that "I was in my first
battle two years ago today at Perryville, Ky." Connolly
reached Allatoona five days after the battle. The town contained no more than "a dozen shabby farm buildings" and he
rode by moonlight through the Gap where Corse had fought.
He was thirsty, could find no water, so tried his first draught of
"persimmon beer." It was "poor stuff" and tasted like
"vinegar diluted with water."

October 11—Election Day in Ohio—brought excitement.
From twelve o'clock to three the Union columns, now across
the Etowah River, halted so that the Ohio soldiers could vote
and Connolly noted with satisfaction: "Very few Copperhead
votes cast at this road side election." He would think:

. . . This has been a funny campaign from Atlanta
north, the Rebels have been using our breastworks of last
Summer, and we have been using theirs.

To his wife next day Connolly wrote: "Am well, the army is in
fine condition, and before we get through with Mr. Hood he
will be out of business." Four days later Connolly hoped "to

force a fight out of them tomorrow . . . then good by Mr. Hood," but on the 17th all he could tell his wife was that

> . . . Sherman is really mad now because he was forced to march so far north again, and is determined to annihilate Hood and his army, if possible to reach him.

Sherman chafed. Chasing Hood this way had become nonsense. To attempt a defense of the long line of road from Chattanooga to Atlanta, Sherman wired Grant on October 9, could only mean that "we will lose a thousand men each month, and will gain no result." The vision revived. Let him "strike out . . . for Milledgeville, Millen, and Savannah," Sherman urged Grant, and "I can make this march, and make all Georgia howl!" Suppose he had no corn? With eight thousand head of cattle and three million rations of bread, "we can find plenty of forage in the interior of the State."

A characteristic exuberancy, certainly a tone of impatience, crept into the official communications Sherman now dispatched. In a telegram to Grant at City Point on October 11 he spoke of "smashing things to the sea"; a letter to Schofield at Chattanooga four days later boasted of making "the interior of Georgia feel the weight of war"; and to General Amos Beckworth, the chief commissary in Atlanta, Sherman wired on the 19th: "I want to prepare for my big raid." In a spirit of intimate comradeship that went back to the grim days following Shiloh, Sherman would write Grant: "If you can whip Lee, and I can march to the Atlantic, I think Uncle Abe will give us a twenty days' leave of absence to see the young folks." A child that Sherman had not seen had been born to Ellen in June.

Although Atlanta was lost, Sam Hood had seized a certain psychological advantage. Sherman may have sensed this fact more clearly than Hood, for in a telegram to Grant on October 9 Sherman complained: "With twenty-five thousand infantry and the bold cavalry he has, Hood can constantly break my road." On the 10th Hood appeared at Resaca, demanding the surrender of the town, and adding with happy insolence that "if the place is carried by assault, no prisoners will be taken." Colonel Clark R. Weaver, commanding the Federal detachment there, replied that if Hood wanted Resaca he "could come and take it." Hood, suddenly changing his mind, remained content with minor skirmishing, the destruction of the railroad for nearly twenty miles to Tunnel Hill, and the capture at Dalton of the entire regiment of Johnson's 44th United States colored troops.

Sherman grew increasingly ruffled at Hood's skipping around the country. Almost every letter Sherman wrote, every telegram he dispatched contained the same sentiment: "We must resume the offensive!" Sherman pressed on doggedly to Lafayette, hoping to catch Hood there and force a fight, but Hood escaped down the Cattooga Valley. "It was clear to me that he had no intention to meet us in open battle," Sherman grumbled, "and the lightness and celerity of his army convinced me that I could not possibly catch him on a stern-chase."

Hood's nuisance tactics continued. At Ship's Gap Sherman found the telegraph lines to Chattanooga broken, and sent couriers to ascertain what situation had developed there. Schofield, he learned, held the city and even had endeavored to co-operate with the forces opposing Hood. Sherman's eyes snapped angrily and the air crackled when he spoke. Nothing went as he wanted, either in central Georgia or in Washington. Why did Grant seem to evade definite approval of the proposed march? Even if Grant felt the scheme unwise at the moment, Sherman expected Grant to stand by him, for, as he would say: "I stood by him when he was drunk." Then a courier, sent by Halleck in Washington, reached Ship's Gap. Sherman's eyes scanned the message and lost their sullenness. Here at long last was the first intimation that "the authorities in Washington were willing that I should undertake the march across Georgia to the sea."

"Send me Morgan and Newton's old divisions," Sherman

wired Thomas in Nashville on the 16th. If Thomas would re-
establish the road, Sherman would follow Hood wherever he
went. The divisions would be sent and the road repaired,
Thomas responded next day, adding that:

> . . . Mower and Wilson have arrived and are on their
> way to join you. I hope you will adopt Grant's idea of
> turning Wilson loose, rather than undertake the plan of a
> march with the whole force through Georgia to the sea,
> inasmuch as General Grant can't cooperate with
> you. . . .

Sherman's mood brushed Thomas's objections aside. He wrote
Schofield at Chattanooga that same day: "It is folly for us to
be moving our armies on the reports of scouts and citizens."
He would follow Hood "till he is beyond the reach of mis-
chief."

Chasing Hood down the Chattooga Valley as far as the
neighborhood of Gadsden, Sherman halted near the Coosa
River to forage off the rich countryside. He hoped next to
catch Hood at Gaylesville, Alabama, but when he reached
there on the 21st Hood had hurried on toward Decatur. A
Gaylesville, General Joseph A. Mower arrived and received
command of a division of the XVIIth Corps and, at Grant's
direction, General James H. Wilson appeared to take command of Sherman's cavalry.

Wilson, the youngest army commander in American
history, possessed a high-bridged nose sniffling for trouble and
action. Strongly opinionated, at times openly contemptuous of
army high brass, there was doubtless much truth in the report
that on first meeting Grant young Wilson had remarked the
stoop-shouldered little man looked more like a storekeeper
than a general. Grant grew devoted to Wilson. In the pinch
of battle Wilson could throw away the rule book and impro-
vise as he fought, and to the conqueror of Donelson no trait
could make a general more endearing. In Grant's judgment
Wilson "by his own personal activity" would increase the

effectiveness of Sherman's cavalry by fifty per cent, and Grant urged Sherman to send Wilson south with the cavalry, for Wilson and his horsemen, Grant contended, would accomplish as much as Sherman could with the main army.

Sherman, who had been thinking and talking and writing "march to the sea" for weeks, had no intention of entrusting the vision to Wilson. The very air could have grown electric. Wilson's private opinion of Sherman was that he trifled too much with minutiæ and lacked "combativeness." In turn, Sherman could have responded curtly—and with the tart implication that if the shoe fit, Wilson could wear it—that he "had not so much faith" in the cavalry as Grant. But the meeting between Sherman and Wilson soon reached the friendliest terms. The condition of Sherman's cavalry completely depressed Wilson. The horses were run down, perhaps another evidence that Sherman was right in thinking of General Kilpatrick as "a crazy damn fool." A compromise suited both generals. Wilson would select horses for forty-five hundred men to remain with Kilpatrick and operate with Sherman, while Wilson returned with the rest of the horses to Nashville and reorganized the cavalry there to act under Thomas in the defense of Tennessee. The decision proved climactic. If there were going to be a march to the sea, Sherman would make it! In a confidential mood, a cigar probably tilted at a relaxed angle, Sherman said:

> Wilson, I am a damned sight smarter man than Grant. I know a great deal more about war, military history, strategy, and grand tactics than he does. I know more about organization, supply, and administration, and about everything else than he does, but I'll tell you where he beats me and where he beats the world. He don't care a damn for what the enemy does out of his sight, but it scares me like hell! . . .

Sherman shook his head sadly. Compared to Grant, he couldn't deny his shortcomings:

. . . I am more nervous than he is. I am more likely
to change my orders or to counter-march my command
than he is. He uses such information as he has according
to his best judgment; he issues his orders and does his level
best to carry them out without much reference to what is
going on about him and, so far, experience seems to have
fully justified him.

In Gaylesville, at the time Sherman met with Wilson, Major
Connolly wrote his wife: "We may go to Mobile or Savannah." The air around the Yankee camps tingled with a
quickening excitement, for the men sensed, as Sherman recorded, that "at Gaylesville the pursuit of Hood by the army
under my command may be said to have ceased." Back in
Rome, Connolly wrote his wife on the 26th that "preparations
are being rapidly made for one of Sherman's peculiar movements." Connolly agreed with Sherman that there was no
sense in a Union army of seventy thousand chasing Hood's
forty thousand "up and down through Georgia," for it was

. . . like an elephant chasing a mouse; he won't let us
catch him, and unless we can catch him so as to whip him
soundly, his 40,000 are worth more to the Rebels, than
our 70,000 are to us, for it takes less to clothe, feed, and
pay them.

On November 1 Grant still seemed to resist the eager Sherman. From City Point he argued: "Do you not think it ad-
visable, now that Hood has gone so far north, to entirely ruir
him before starting on your proposed plan?" Sherman repliec
promptly that if he could hope to overhaul Hood "I woulc
turn against him with my whole force." No single army coulc
catch Hood now, but Thomas had a sufficient force to preven
Hood from "reaching any country in which we have an interest," and the best result would come from "defeating Jeff
Davis's cherished plan of making me leave Georgia by
manoeuvring."

The pressure on Grant to hold Sherman in check had grown intense. Halleck had devised an alternate plan, the President had wavered, and in this crisis, Carl Sandburg observed, Grant "did what Lincoln so often did. He raised objections almost as though to reassure both himself and Sherman that they were headed right and not moving too fast." Grant capitulated. He wired: "I say, then, go on as you proposed."

Sherman was to have his march to the sea even though Lincoln later would confess that he was "anxious, if not fearful" of the exploit. But now that the dream had become a reality, even Sherman must face the sobering reflection that if his march failed it "would be adjudged the wild adventure of a crazy fool."

3. "BEHIND US LAY ATLANTA"

INTO the preparations for the march went all of Sherman's zest for minutiæ. A special field-order, issued at Kingston on November 8, told the soldiers that "all the chances of war have been considered and provided for, as far as human sagacity can." Another order a day later divided the army into two wings, placing the XVth and XVIIth Corps under Howard and the XIVth and XXth Corps under Slocum. The "habitual order of march," Sherman directed, would be, wherever practicable, "by four roads, as nearly parallel as possible"; each corps would carry its own ammunition and provision trains and would "forage liberally on the country during the march." Under the command of "one or more discreet officers" each brigade would organize its own "good and sufficient foraging party," and whereas soldiers "must not enter the dwellings of the inhabitants, or commit any trespass" during a halt or when encamped, they would be permitted "to gather turnips, potatoes, and other vegetables, and to drive in stock in sight of camp."

Only to corps commanders was intrusted "the power to destroy mills, houses, cotton-gins, etc.," and in districts where the army was unmolested no destruction would be countenanced, but "should guerrillas or bushwhackers molest our march, or should the inhabitants burn bridges, obstruct roads, or otherwise manifest local hostility . . . a devastation more or less relentless" should be enforced. The cavalry would be permitted "to appropriate freely and without limit" horses, mules, and wagons, but Sherman advised discrimination between "the rich, who are usually hostile, and the poor and industrious, usually neutral or friendly." Negroes, where ablebodied, could be taken, and organized into pioneer battalions when feasible.

Sherman's mind fondled each detail. Artillery and wagon trains must be reduced to the barest serviceable minimum. One gun for each thousand men, drawn in batteries of four guns each, would be adequate. Each gun, caisson, and forge would be drawn by four teams of horses, and the army would carry about twenty-five hundred wagons with six mules to a wagon, and six hundred ambulances with two horses each. Wagon loads must be kept comparatively light at "about 2,500 pounds net," and each soldier would carry forty rounds of ammunition on his person, depending on the wagons to carry another two hundred rounds for each man and two hundred rounds "of assorted ammunition" for each gun. With eight hundred wagons to a corps these vehicles alone on a march would occupy at least five miles of road.

Around Sherman grew "a 'devil-may-care' feeling" that pervaded "officers and men" and made him conscious of "the full load of responsibility." Rations in possession of the troops numbered 1,200,000. "A good supply of beef-cattle to be driven along on the hoof" had been collected, and whereas corn and oats were down to a point that promised only a five-day supply of forage, Sherman reflected with satisfaction that the country was "well stocked with corn, which had been gathered and stored in cribs, seemingly for our use, by Governor Brown's militia."

Sherman planned to take, on his march to the sea, two hundred and eighteen regiments, all but thirty-four of which would be from the West. Ohio would give him fifty-two regiments, Illinois another fifty, Indiana twenty-seven, Iowa fifteen, Wisconsin thirteen, Michigan and Missouri each ten, Kentucky four, Minnesota three. His regiments from the East would number thirty-three, with New York supplying sixteen, Pennsylvania ten, New Jersey three, Massachusetts and Connecticut each two, and a company of "white Alabama Unionists" would ride with Kilpatrick's cavalry. From the old Northwest Territory, which Sherman knew and loved, one hundred and fifty-five of his regiments would come. Farm boys whose fathers had turned their eyes west to conquer the wilderness now proposed to march east again, and Major Connolly, writing home from Kingston on November 9, revealed the spirit that motivated them:

> . . . There is to me something romantic in the conception of this campaign, and I am really charmed with it. Nothing in military history compares with it except the invasion of Mexico by Cortez, the Spaniard, who, landing on its hostile shore, burned his ships, destroyed all means of retreat, and then turning to his army, told them they must rely on God and their own right arms; that they must conquer or die.

So it would be with Sherman's men—they must march to the sea or perish—and Connolly dreamed of the glorious day "when we reach the coast after having carried our flag from the Ohio to the Ocean." More than the excitement of the impending campaign stirred Connolly. From dawn to dusk on the previous day the polls had been opened in the North. Even though Connolly, as an Illinoisan, had been disfranchised, many soldiers had voted and the major reported with relish: "From the returns I have seen this morning I think Jeff Davis would have received as many votes in these camps as McClellan did."

In Washington, as November 8 passed quietly into history, the same jubilance was not shared in every quarter. "God save the Republic!" John Hay confessed to his diary; he would have nothing more to say "till the day after tomorrow." Lincoln spent the day alone, as though, Noah Brooks believed, "by common consent everybody had avoided the White House." In the evening the President wandered across the rain-soaked grounds to the War Department's telegraph office. In Boston an excited pro-Lincoln voter had shouted that "the Almighty must have stuffed the ballot boxes," and early returns from Philadelphia, from Baltimore, and from Boston were distinctly encouraging. Lincoln doubted the decisiveness of these pluralities. Nerves, strung taut, thrummed at every disturbance. Stanton snorted disgustedly as Lincoln whiled away the time telling humorous stories about himself and reading from the writings of Petroleum V. Nasby.

Toward midnight the strained look lessened, then vanished. The President had been re-elected! At a midnight supper Hay watched Lincoln "awkwardly and hospitably . . . shovelling out the fried oysters." Serenaders, a brass band, cheers, calls for a speech, greeted the President as he left the War Office at two in the morning. The war, as far as it could ever be decided at the ballot boxes, had been won, despite the proffered wager of ten thousand dollars by a sportsman banker earlier in the day "that if Lincoln is elected the war will last his term." The weary man in the dark cape splashed home to the White House. The only answer that could be given to the sportsman banker would have to come from Grant in Virginia and Sherman in Georgia.

The certainty of Lincoln's re-election should have kept Major Connolly's mood gay and lively when two days later he once more wrote his wife from Kingston, but in sober tones he warned: "After you receive *this*, you cannot expect to hear from me again for the next six or eight weeks," adding with a flash of pique that

> . . . A great many officers are resigning to avoid the coming campaign, and a great many others are trying to resign but cannot . . . Perhaps they have been away so long that their wives are urging them to come home, and the great boobies are consequently backing out and trooping home as fast as they can get away.

Connolly felt disgusted to observe

> . . . What a flutter this marching order is creating amongst our weak knee'd brethern in shoulder straps; up to the last moment they are tendering resignations and clamoring for leaves on account of sick families, sick wives, &c., but all their applications meet with flat, stern refusal.

On the 12th Connolly moved with his division through Kingston toward Cartersville. Cassville, now "a guerilla haunt," had been burned to the ground except for a solitary church spire. Connolly reached Cartersville at three in the afternoon to find Sherman "sitting on the hotel porch sending his last telegraphic message to the North." The last train already had departed from Atlanta for Chattanooga, now the telegraph wires were broken, and Connolly was "away down South in Dixie" to conquer or die! But Sherman would say, with boyish exhilaration: "Free and glorious I felt when the magic telegraph was cut!" No longer could a last-minute shift of opinion in Washington cancel the march to the sea. In a mood filled with sinister foreboding for the future, he would write to General "Little Phil" Sheridan:

> I am satisfied, and have been all the time, that the problem of war consists in the awful fact that the present class of men who rule the South must be killed outright rather than in the conquest of territory.

Connolly returned to Allatoona on Sunday, the 13th. The morning had turned cold and everyone acted out of humor. Along the roads he seemed only to see "sallow, poverty-stricken, snuff-dipping women"; the thriving little railroad village of Acworth had become a heap of ruins. "It is evident," Connolly wrote, "that our soldiers are determined to burn, plunder and destroy everything in their way on this march." At least, he rationalized, such ruthlessness proved that each soldier was "determined to strike with all his might against the rebellion, whether we get through or not." But in the face of this devastation he knew that capture by the Rebels probably would mean "a stout rope and a short shrift."

Determined that the military installations remaining in Atlanta must be destroyed before the break across Georgia to the sea, Sherman drove his troops back over the country through which they had chased Hood. Starting again at day-break, Connolly soon reached the line of entrenchments the Federals had built at Kenesaw. The mountain slumbered silently in the morning haze, and the Yankees, emerging from the woods to the open plains at the foot of Kenesaw, cheered wildly at the sight of the Union flag flying on its summit. But Connolly could only regard Kenesaw with

> . . . some of the same shy respect which I entertained for it last June, when we lay burrowing in rifle-pits at its foot, and its summit was crowned with Rebel artillery, which so often at mid-day and at mid-night thundered away at us, and encircled the mountain with wreaths of fire and smoke.

In the afternoon Connolly reached Marietta; the business section lay in ashes, burned the night before by Kilpatrick's cavalry. That night he slept across the Chattahoochee; on the morrow he would be back in Atlanta.

For Carrie Berry those early days of November, cold and cloudy and frequently rainy, were filled with "dred." On the 11th, when the last train puffed off to Chattanooga, the child wrote in her diary: "We are erbliged to stay here now." On the next day, while Sherman at Cartersville jubilantly cut the telegraph wires to the north, ten-year-old Carrie confessed that "we were fritened almost to death last night." The girl could not sleep "for fear they would set our house on fire," and rumors circulated that the Yankees "would set the last house on fire if they had to leave the place." On the 13th Carrie watched "nearly all day" as the Federals continued burning houses; another day repeated the pattern; and then the child could report that "we have a gard a little while after dinner and we feel a little more protected." But the portents all remained gloomy, and the smoldering ruins of houses wherever Carrie turned bore bitter testimony to the fate that the Yankees intended for Atlanta.

Sherman, back in the city, closeted himself with Colonel Poe, his chief of engineers, to discuss Poe's "special task of destruction." Whatever remained of the depot, the roundhouse, and the machine shops of the Georgia Railroad blazed and smoked. The fire stretched beyond the depot, catching a group of stores. As the afternoon advanced, the quartermasters stopped trying to issue clothing or load rations. Despite Sherman's intention that only the military installations of Atlanta be destroyed, the general feeling, Connolly noted, was that "the soldiers fought for it, and the soldiers won it, now let the soldiers enjoy it." The quartermasters and commissaries gave up any pretense of maintaining order. In effect, they said: "Boys, go in and take what you want before it burns up."

More than clothing and load rations fell into eager Yankee hands. Barrels of whiskey were rolled out and staved in. The sight of a blue-clad soldier reeling through streets and alleys, shouting and singing, arm flung over a comrade's shoulder, became common. With evening new fires broke out. Little Carrie Berry, sitting up all night with her parents and watching as the soldiers "were going around setting houses on fire where they were not watched," added bitterly: "They behaved very badly."

The fire crept into one of the railroad machine shops that the Rebels had used as an arsenal. Flame shot upward, an explosion rocked the city. Fragments of the bursting shells fell uncomfortably near the home of Judge Lyons, where Sherman had established his headquarters.

But the Yankees wouldn't give up their fun. "Drunken soldiers on foot and on horseback raced up and down the streets," Connolly reported, "while the buildings on either side were solid sheets of flames." Connolly pressed on through the crowds. Fires "wrapped" the city until he felt that the spectacle surpassed "all the pictures and verbal descriptions of hell." Gaping at the inferno Atlanta had become, drunk and sober alike shouted and danced and sang *Rally Around the Flag* while the flames spread into "costly edifices" and "pillar and roof and dome sank into one common ruin." A light as bright as midday dispelled the night for miles around. But Sherman must approve of the havoc, Connolly thought, "for he is somewhere near by, now, looking on at all this, and saying not one word to prevent it."

Watching the "grand and awful spectacle" of "this beautiful city, now in flames," Major George Ward Nichols, aide-de-camp to Sherman, wrote:

> . . . The heaven is one expanse of lurid fire; the air is filled with flying, burning cinders; buildings covering two hundred acres are in ruins or in flames; every instant there is the sharp detonation or the smothered booming sound of exploding shells and powder concealed in the buildings, and then the sparks and flame shoot away up into the black and red roof, scattering cinders far and wide.
>
> These are the machine-shops where have been forged and cast the Rebel cannon, shot and shell that have carried death to many a brave defender of our Nation's honor. . . . The city, which, next to Richmond, has furnished more material for prosecuting the war than any other in the South, exists no more. . . .

Part Five: "AND MAKE GEORGIA HOWL"

Grim-faced and bitter, the members of the fifty families remaining in Atlanta watched the shameful devastation.* The terror, the indignity of the past few days had produced a numbness, a cold rage that made the inhabitants almost afraid to speak. In the angle between Hunter Street, running east, and McDonough Street, running south, all the houses would be lost. Nothing could save the jail and calaboose now, or most of the business establishments, except possibly those on Alabama Street. With the exception of the Gate City, all of the hotels were in flames. Who could calculate the full damage? Four thousand or five thousand houses destroyed in a single night—would the one figure seem less disheartening than the other? City parks and city streets stood denuded of two-thirds of their trees; the carcasses of from two to three thousand animals littered fields and thoroughfares. The bleak eyes of Atlantans had grown used to such acts of pillage and indecency—the full flowering of Yankee chivalry—for had they not, as General Howard of the Georgia Militia would testify, seen these same blue-coated gallants turn loose their horses in the cemetery "to graze upon the grass and shrubbery," while "the ornaments of graves, such as marble lambs, miniature statuary, souvenirs of departed little ones, [were] broken and scattered abroad." General Howard said:

> The crowning act of all their wickedness and villainy was committed by our ungodly foe in removing the dead from the vaults in the cemetery, and robbing the coffins of the silver name plates and tippings, and depositing their own dead in the vaults.

St. Luke's, where the body of General Leonidas Polk had lain in state, burned with the Christian and African churches, but the city hall, the Second Baptist, the Second Presbyterian, Trinity and the Catholic churches, together with the dwellings

* General W. P. Howard's official report to Governor Brown detailing the full extent of the destruction of Atlanta, from which this account has been reconstructed, was published in the *Macon Telegraph* on December 10, 1864.

in the vicinity, were saved, General Howard reported, through the efforts of Father O'Riley,

> . . . who refused to give up his parsonage to the Yankees, who were looking out for fine homes for quarters, and there being a large number of Catholics in the Yankee army, who volunteered to protect their church and parsonage, and would not allow any houses adjacent to be fired that would endanger them. As a proof of their attachment to their church, and love for Father O'Riley, a soldier who attempted to fire Colonel Calhoun's house, the burning of which would have endangered the whole block, was shot and killed and his grave is now marked. So to Father O'Riley the country is indebted for the protection of the city hall, churches, etc.

But Father O'Riley could not save the female college, the machine shops, the rolling mills, the arsenals, the carsheds, the depots. "Amid the wild and terrific scene," wrote Edward A. Pollard, as "the Federal bands played 'John Brown's soul goes marching on,'" Sherman's army prepared to forsake "a . . . desolation such as had occurred in no modern picture of civilized war."

At seven o'clock the following morning Sherman rode down the Decatur Road, already "filled by the marching troops and wagons of the XIVth Corps." He mounted the hill close to the copse of woods where McPherson had fallen that bloody 22nd of July, and looked back over the Rebel works "upon the scenes of our past battles." An unforgettable memory took shape in his mind:

> Behind us lay Atlanta . . . the black smoke rising high in [the] air, and hanging like a pall over the ruined city. Away off in the distance, on the McDonough Road, was the rear of Howard's column, the gun-barrels glistening in the sun, the white-topped wagons stretching away to the south; and right before us the XIVth Corps, marching

steadily and rapidly, with a cheery look and swinging pace, that made light of the thousand miles that lay between us and Richmond. Some band, by accident, struck up the anthem of "John Brown's soul goes marching on"; the men caught up the strain, and never before have I heard the chorus of "Glory, glory, hallelujah!" done with more spirit, or in better harmony of time and place.

The clear sunlight, the bracing air made the day beautiful. Sherman worked his way past groups of soldiers, recognizing "an unusual feeling of exhiliration" that he described as a sense "of something to come, vague and undefined, still full of venture and intense interest." The men called:

"Uncle Billy, I guess Grant is waiting for us at Richmond!"

No, Sherman could have told them, their way was not direct to Richmond by Augusta and Charlotte, as so many believed. Savannah or Port Royal, South Carolina, was to be their objective, or, if an alternative were needed, Pensacola.

Major Connolly also traveled the Decatur Road. "How many prayers for our success went up from Northern homes this morning?" he ruminated. "We must succeed." The bands playing, flags flying, men cheering stimulated his resolution: "We'll march straight through and shake the rebellious old State from center to circumference." He passed the ground where McPherson had fallen, fields "studded with the graves of our gallant comrades, and none lie there more thickly than the men of Illinois." Did he, like Sherman, turn back for a last look before he turned east and lost view of Atlanta behind a screen of trees? Perhaps he remembered the closing sentence written in his diary the night before:

"Gate City of the South, farewell!"

4. "ALL SHADES AND SIZES"

NIGHT came. Near Lithonia, a village of about three hundred inhabitants, the Federals encamped at the end of the first day's march. Distantly the bald granite massiveness of Stone Mountain rose against the sky, and the "horizon was lurid with the bonfires of rail-ties." All through the night the men could be seen moving in groups, heating the middle of the rails over the blazing cross-ties, then bending the malleable iron around a telegraph pole or tree trunk. "I attached much importance to this destruction of the railroad," Sherman confessed, "gave it my personal attention, and made reiterated orders to others on the subject."

The destruction of the railroads—the first night at Lithonia, the second at Conyers—formed part of an emerging pattern that would become commonplace in the days following. At every encampment the Negroes appeared. To Connolly they seemed to arrive in "all shades and sizes," happy if they could be permitted to march along with the Yankees. Sherman could think of nothing he desired less. Feeding his own men was enough of a problem, but still the Negroes came, "simply frantic with joy," clustering around the general's horse, shouting and praying, and like one "poor girl" whom Sherman recalled:

> . . . in the very ecstasy of the Methodist "shout," hugging the banner of one of the regiments, and jumping up to the "feet of Jesus."

Exactly how to handle the Negroes weighed on Sherman's mind. Crossing the Ulcofauhachee River, the Federals bivouacked about four miles east of Covington, and Sherman walked up to a plantation house. The Negroes came in a swarm to meet him, among them "an old, gray-haired man, of as fine a head as I ever saw."

Did the old man understand "about the war and its progress"?

"Yes, suh!" the old man said; he had been looking for "the angel of the Lord" since "he was knee-high."

Did all the Negroes understand that "slavery was the cause" of the war and "that our success was to be his freedom"?

Yes, suh, that they all knew.

Sherman drew a breath. He must explain to this old man that he wanted the slaves to remain where they were, rather than load him down "with useless mouths." A few young, hearty men could be employed as pioneers, but if the "old and young, feeble and helpless" followed along "it would simply . . . cripple us in our task." Sherman would write:

> . . . I believe that old man spread this message to the slaves, which was carried from mouth to mouth, to the very end of the journey, and that in part saved us from the great danger we incurred of swelling our numbers so that famine would have attended our progress.

While Sherman talked to the old Negro, Connolly encamped on a plantation belonging to a Mr. Zachry. The Negroes crept down to the Federal campfires. Old Zachry, they whispered, had a son who was a colonel with Lee's army in Virginia, and "the old sinner" had hidden away in his house "a Federal flag . . . captured and sent home from Virginia a year ago." Yankee tempers flared. Zachry and his wife denied having the flag, the house was searched without finding it, "but one of their house servants told me most positively tonight that it *is* in the house." Zachry's gin, filled with cotton, was burned as a warning. In the morning Connolly faced Zachry with an ultimatum. Either "the old rascal" could surrender the flag or see his plantation destroyed.

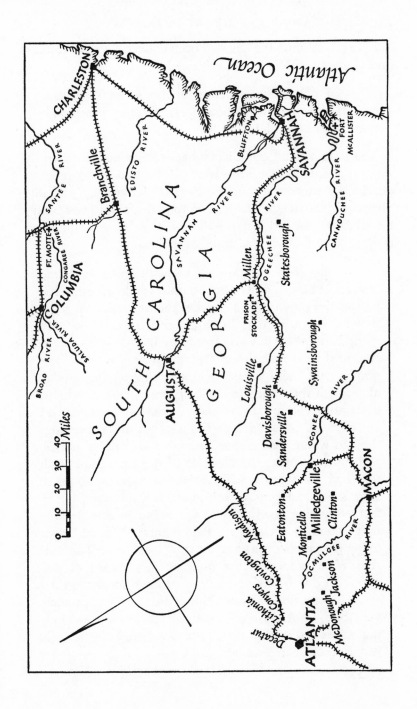

Within ten minutes the flag had been delivered to the Yankees and Connolly commented dryly:

> . . . I don't know whether his house was burned or not. I know he owns about forty Negroes less tonight than he did last night.

The land around the Ulcofauhachee was not tenanted by wealthy planters. The farms were all "in hundred acre lots," although their owners called them "plantations." Despite Sherman's conviction that here in the Ulcofauhachee country his talk with the old Negro had solved the problem of slaves trailing after the army, Connolly reported:

> . . . the Negroes stare at us with open eyes and mouths, but generally, before the whole column has passed they pack up their bundles and march along, going they know not whither, but apparently satisfied they are going somewhere toward freedom; but these wretched creatures, or a majority of them, don't know what freedom is. Ask them where they are going as they trudge along with their bundles on their heads, and the almost invariable reply is: "Don't know Massa; gwine along wid you all." . . . Foraging parties start out in the morning; they go where they please, seize wagons, mules, horses, and harness; make the Negroes of the plantation hitch up, load the wagons with sweet potatoes, flour, meal, hogs, sheep, chickens, turkeys, barrels of molasses, and in fact everything good to eat, and sometimes considerable that's good to drink. . . . Passed through Sand Town today [November 19th] about 2 o'clock. . . . The citizens were not expecting us, but they heard of our approach day before yesterday and have spent the time since in carrying off and hiding in the swamps their valuables, but the Negroes told the soldiers of these hiding places and most of these hidden valuables found their way into our camp tonight. . . .

The camaraderie forming between the slaves and the Yankees, regardless of its motivation, promised a climax for
Connolly that no one then could have foreseen.

A soldier passing Sherman "with a ham on his musket,
a jug of sorghum-molasses under his arm, and a big piece of
honey in his hand, from which he was eating," attracted the
general's eye and said *sotto voce* to a comrade, quoting Sherman's order: "Forage liberally on the country." Sherman's
red hair matched his temper. The soldier caught it. But in a
more judicious mood the general would remember:

> The skill and the success of the men in collecting
> forage was one of the features of the march. . . . Often
> would I pass these foraging-parties at the roadside, wait-
> ing for their wagons to come up, and was amused by
> their strange collections—mules, horses, even cattle,
> packed with old saddles and loaded with hams, bacon,
> bags of cornmeal, and poultry of every character and
> description. . . . there seemed to be a charm about
> [foraging] that attracted the soldiers, and it was a privi-
> lege to be detailed on such a party. . . . No doubt
> many acts of pillage, robbery, and violence, were commit-
> ted by these parties of foragers, usually called "bum-
> mers"; . . . but . . . I never heard of any cases of
> murder and rape; * and no army could have carried
> along sufficient food and forage for a march of three
> hundred miles. . . . The country was sparsely settled,
> with no magistrates or civil authorities who could respond
> to requisitions, as is done in all the wars of Europe; so
> that this system of foraging was simply indispensible to
> our success. . . .

* Lloyd Lewis believed that Sherman "knew of but two cases of rape among
his soldiers in 1864–65," and added that "many Southern scholars, examining
the evidence one or two generations later," confirmed the opinion that this crime
was "nearly unknown." The *Macon Telegraph* of December 7, 1864, reported
widespread despoilation of Southern womanhood as "the cesspools of Northern
infamy and corruption have been dredged to their vilest dregs," but propaganda
frequently is most effective when filled with the ring of poetry.

The quartermasters soon developed remarkable skill in gathering forage as the army pushed ahead. While the men marched, they would shift loads so that they always seemed to have from six to ten empty wagons. Then, riding well ahead, Sherman said, they

> . . . would secure possession of certain stacks of fodder near the road, or cribs of corn, leave some men in charge, then open fences and a road back for a couple of miles, return to their trains, divert the empty wagons out of column, and conduct them rapidly to their forage, load up and regain their place in column without losing distance. . . .

On November 22nd, driving toward Milledgeville through a raw, cold wind that scattered the branches of the wild-plum bushes, Sherman approached a plantation that aroused his curiosity. As the general dismounted, the usual assortment of underclothing, maps, a flask of whiskey, and a bunch of cigars were handed to his orderly. Then:

> . . . Taking a drink and lighting a cigar, I walked to a row of Negro huts close by, entered one, and found a soldier or two warming themselves by a wood-fire. . . . I was talking to the old Negro woman, when some one came and explained to me that, if I would come farther down the road, I could find a better place. So I started on foot, and found on the main road a good double-hewed-log house. . . .

Here the fireplace soon flared and Sherman, looking around, spied a small box, like a candle-box, marked "Howell Cobb." Was this the Howell Cobb who served as a general in the Confederate army and who had been Secretary of the Treasury under Buchanan? When the proof became incontestable that Sherman lodged on Cobb's plantation, one brusque command was given: "Spare nothing." The 23rd Missouri carried out the devastation with a thoroughness that may have been inspired by Cobb's address, published in a Macon paper, calling on all Georgians to "rise and defend their liberties." Nichols, sniffing at "the wretched condition of his Negroes and their quarters," remembering that "this plantation was the property of Cobb's wife, who was a Lamar," found the granaries filled with corn and wheat, and a "large supply of sirup made from sorghum" stored in an outhouse, which were given, in part, to "the poor decrepit Negroes which this humane, liberty-loving general left to die." With the approach of the Yankees, Nichols declared:

> . . . Cobb . . . removed all the able-bodied mules, horses, cows, and slaves. He left here some fifty old men —cripples—and women and children, with nothing scarcely covering their nakedness, with little or no food, and without means of procuring it. We found them cowering over the fireplaces of their miserable huts, where the wind hurled through the crevices between the logs, frightened at the approach of the Yankees, who, they had been told, would kill them. A more forlorn, neglected set of human beings I never saw.

In the blazing light of Cobb's burning plantation Connolly reported that an old Negro came to the door of the log house and asked to see Sherman. One glance appeared to satisfy the old fellow, for he went away very much pleased with himself and muttering happily:

"He's got the Linkum head, the Linkum head, he's got the Linkum head."

On the 23rd of November, Milledgeville was occupied. After walking the streets of Joe Brown's citadel, Connolly wrote in his diary:

> . . . My boyish desire is gratified. . . . As one rides along its sandy streets, even at this season of the year, the faint perfume from every variety of tree and shrub, bud, blossom and flower fills the air with delicious fragrance.

231

The exterior of the residences bespeak refinement within, and everything about the city serves to impress one with the idea that he is in an old, aristocratic city, where the worth of a man is computed in dollars and cents. . . . The capitol . . . overlooking the Oconee River . . . is built of reddish looking sandstone and is a large square building, with rather a superabundance of fancy cornice outside. . . . The offices and State library are on the first floor, the legislative halls on the second floor, and also the committee rooms. Each chamber has life size oil paintings of the prominent old men of Georgia hung around its walls in plain gilt frames. I should have thought "Oglethorpe" would have appeared in this State picture gallery, but he does not. General Jackson does, though, tricked out in a line officer's coat with a general's epaulettes on his shoulders, a line officer's sash around his waist, and a sort of cross between a Turkish scimitar and an artillery sabre by his side. . . .

Connolly watched, outraged, as soldiers and officers plundered the State Library. Law books worth thousands of dollars were carried off, but Connolly wouldn't touch a volume. "I should feel ashamed of myself every time I saw one of them in my book case at home," he confessed. He did not object to stealing "horses, mules, niggers and all such *little things*," but the theft and destruction of public libraries sickened him. "Let them alone," he thought, "to enlarge and increase for the benefit of the loyal generations that are to people this county long after we shall have fought our last battle and gone into our eternal camp." In the library Connolly found the musty records of the Colony of Georgia, and read through them with such fascination "that I used up nearly the whole day." He decided anew: "Sherman will, some day, regret that he permitted this library to be destroyed."

At that moment, strolling the streets of Milledgeville with their neatly painted signboards, and noticing the churches that looked more like public offices, Sherman felt pleased with himself. Newspapers told of "the consternation which had filled the Southern mind at our temerity," and he sneered at the flight of "brave and patriotic" Governor Brown and his legislature. Brown had stripped the Governor's Mansion of "even the cabbages and vegetables from his kitchen and cellar." A group of Yankee officers gathered in the vacant halls of the Representatives, elected a Speaker, and constituted themselves the "Legislature of the State of Georgia." The gavel fell. One item of business concerned this rump session, an ordinance to repeal secession. The proposed legislation, Sherman said, was "well debated" and secession nullified "by a fair vote!" In the spirit of the new order that had come to Georgia, Connolly unrolled

. . . the flag we took from old Zachry . . . made a staff for it, and raised it in front of our headquarters, where it is still flying. Little did the old sinner think, when he first received this trophy from his Rebel son, that Yankee hands would ever unfurl it in triumph over the capital of his State.

5. "LET EVERY MAN FLY TO ARMS!"

From Corinth, Mississippi, Beauregard called on the people of Georgia: "Be resolute!" Old "Bory" counseled: "Trust in an overruling Providence, and success will soon crown your efforts." Meanwhile, Beauregard said: "I hasten to join you in the defense of your homes and firesides."

Senator Benjamin H. Hill pleaded from Richmond: "Georgians, be firm!" The hour had come, Hill exhorted his constituents, to "act promptly, and fear not!" Now:

Every citizen with his gun, and every Negro with his spade and axe, can do the work of a soldier. You can destroy the enemy by retarding his march.

At the foot of Hill's appeal, Secretary of War Seddon wrote stanchly: "I most cordially approve the above." Then from Richmond next day [November 19th] came an even more explicit directive:

To the People of Georgia:

We have had a special conference with President Davis and the Secretary of War, and are able to assure you that they have done and are still doing all that can be done to meet the emergency that presses upon you. Let every man fly to arms! Remove your Negroes, horses, cattle, and provisions from Sherman's army, and burn what you cannot carry. Burn all bridges, and block up the roads in his route. Assail the invader in front, flank, and rear, by night and by day. Let him have no rest.

Julian Hartridge,	Mark Blauford,
J. H. Reynolds,	General N. Lester,
John T. Shoemaker,	Joseph M. Smith,
	Members of Congress.

From these proclamations, and, Sherman said, "from the tone of the Southern press of that day," the outside world "must have supposed us ruined and lost." Within Southern homes, however, anxiety could not be disguised. Seamed, worried faces watched every distant cloud of dust, wondering where Sherman had struck today, where he might strike tomorrow.

As far away as Montgomery, Alabama, to which Sallie Clayton had escaped during the evacuation of Atlanta, the fear that one of Sherman's detachments might come almost matched the terror of his actual presence. A kind of dull, unreasoning dread haunted the night shadows. Sallie Clayton remembered how, shortly after she reached her uncle's plantation at Montgomery, the fear arose that they had come "very near having a visit from Federal troops." Sallie awakened one night to hear low voices outside the window. Her uncle said tensely that he had received "a message from the overseer of the Pickett plantation adjoining theirs, to take care of himself." What could such a communication mean except that the Yankees approached? Sallie dressed quickly. From outside a loud sound of tramping feet shook her nerve. "We thought," she recalled, "our guests had arrived before anyone could hasten out to meet them." And yet there was something strange in the incident, for:

> The sound came from the rear of the house, whereas our visitors were expected to come up the front way. On looking through a back window we saw in the beautiful moonlight the plantation hands all marching in a double column directly to the house, and . . . the sight did not rouse in us much more courage and pleasure than if they had been bluecoats. However, when we went downstairs we found they had gathered up there from sheer fright. With a common bond of sympathy we stood in the moonlight, at the head of an avenue of [trees] leading up to the front of the house, awaiting developments.

A call, "like a command to halt," started every "white and black" running "as fast as our feet could carry us for the woods that lay some distance behind the servants' quarters." Hearts pounded. Fear gave a dry taste to many mouths. Then, with chagrin, Sallie and the Negroes realized that what they had heard "was the men on the next plantation calling to their mules." But they had thought it was that devil Sherman, and throughout the remainder of 1864 the dread never disappeared that next time it could be Sherman!

But little ten-year-old Carrie Berry didn't care where Sherman went so long as he never returned to Atlanta. She had been "fritened" enough. The girl's diary for the closing days of November revealed her misery:

Tues. Nov. 22. It is just a week to day since the Federals were burning. Papa and Mama say that they feel very poor. We have not got anything but our little house. It is still very cold.

Wed. Nov. 23. It has ben more pleasant to day. I went over with Ella to the city hall to get some hickory nuts but we did not get many. . . .

Thurs. Nov. 24. . . . We all feel very lonesome.

Fri. Nov. 25. We have ben very lonesome to day, Papa being gone. The Country people are picking up everything. . . .

So the pendulum of Southern agony swung between those who felt the crushing weight of Sherman's heel and those who waited for its blow to fall. At the Executive Mansion in Richmond a flood of suggestions poured in on Davis, advising the President how to cope with Sherman. A "Georgian" berated Davis for his public attack on Joe Johnston, a "Carolinian" thought Forrest should replace Hood, and from Mobile came a letter asking the President:

Do you not believe in prayer? In offering to God the Father our thanks? And to invoke His aid in our great trouble?

It seems to me that if you would order another day of "Fasting & Prayer" that there would be good results therefrom.

I know that we can pray without an order from you: —but have you *marked* the results after our National prayer days? We have always been blessed with victories and success immediately after.

> I am Sir your most
> Obedient Servant
> James Malone.

But a national prayer day scarcely would have helped Dolly Sumner Lunt as she awaited the approach of Sherman and his army. Alone on the plantation with her slaves and Sadai, her nine-year-old daughter, the woman went outdoors one November night and saw "large fires like burning buildings." Distracted, Dolly Lunt thought: "Am I not in the hands of a merciful God who has promised to take care of the widow and orphan?"

In the morning the Yankees still had not arrived, and the plantation bustled with schemes to outwit Sherman's "bummers." Mules were taken to the woods, forty fattening hogs turned loose in a remote swamp, part of the meat from the smokehouse hidden "under some fodder." A barrel of salt, "which had cost me two hundred dollars," was taken into the yard of the slave quarters and covered with "leached ashes" to resemble the kind of tub used in the old-fashioned method of making lye for soap. The Yankees that night were reported at a nearby plantation, and, the Negroes said, were "taking all the stock in the country."

Dolly Lunt's nervousness increased. That night she "slept in my clothes," and after breakfast walked with Sadai to a neighbor's home, where she learned that "the Yankees went to James Perry's the night before, plundered his house, and drove off all his stock." As the group stood by the roadside an advance detachment of bluecoats appeared over a hilltop. Jim Perry "raised his gun, swearing he would kill them, anyhow."

Dolly Lunt begged: "No, don't!" But she didn't wait to see whether Jim carried out his threat. Prodding Sadai along in front, the woman ran for home. Behind her she could hear the Yankees crying "Halt! Halt!" and "their guns went off in quick succession." The thought stabbed Dolly Lunt's heart: "Oh God, the time of trial has come!" She reached her plantation moments before the invaders "came filing up":

> . . . I hastened back to my frightened servants and told them that they had better hide, and then went back to the gate to claim protection and a guard. But like

demons they rush in! My yards are full. To my smokehouse, my dairy, pantry, kitchen and cellar, like famished
wolves they come, breaking locks and whatever is in
their way. The thousand pounds of meat in my smokehouse is gone in a twinkling, my flour, my meat, my lard,
butter, eggs, pickles of various kinds—both in vinegar
and brine—wine, jars and jugs are all gone. My eighteen
fat turkeys, my hens, chickens, and fowls, my young pigs,
are shot down in my yard and hunted as if they were
Rebels themselves. . . .

Dolly Lunt appealed to the guard for help. "I cannot help
you, Madam," he said. "It is orders." In misery, Mrs. Lunt
watched old Dutch, her buggy horse, and old Mary, her brood
mare, driven off. "There go my mules," she lamented, "my
sheep, and worse than all, my boys!" One slave jumped into
bed declaring he was sick, another, a lame boy, crawled under
the floor, but the Yankees found them both, cursed them
roundly, and declared that "Jeff Davis wanted to put them in
his army, but that they should not fight for him but for the
Union." Now Mrs. Lunt's ire surged:

> . . . No! Indeed no! They are not friends to the slaves.
> We have never made the poor cowardly Negro fight, and
> it is strange, passing strange, that the all-powerful Yankee
> nation with the whole world to back them, their ports
> open, their armies filled with soldiers from all nations,
> should at last take the poor Negro to help them out
> against this little Confederacy which was to have been
> brought back into the Union in sixty days' time!

Watching the slaves driven away, Mrs. Lunt could only
think: "My poor boys! My poor boys!" Her heart was wrung.
The cabins of the Negroes seemed to suffer no less than the
plantation house, for the slave quarters, Mrs. Lunt testified,
were

. . . rifled of every valuable, the soldiers swearing that their Sunday clothes were the white people's, and that they never had money to get such things as they had. Poor Frank's [a slave's] chest was broken open, his money and tobacco taken. He has always been a money-making, and saving boy; not infrequently has his crop brought him five hundred dollars and more. . . .

Bitterly, Dolly Lunt turned back to her own losses: "Ovens, skillets, coffee-mills, of which we had three, coffee-pots—not one have I left." Even the sifters all vanished!

Sherman "himself" and the greater portion of his army passed the Lunt plantation that day. "As the sad moments rolled on," Dolly Lunt said, the Federals swept

. . . not only in front of my house, but behind; they tore down my garden palings, made a road through my back yard and lot field, driving their stock and riding through, tearing down my fences and desolating my home—wantonly doing it when there was no necessity for it.

Such a day, if I live to the age of Methuselah, may God spare me from ever seeing again!

Beside the woman little Sadai sobbed. Even Mary, the child's favorite doll, had been taken!

The march by now had toughened Sherman, or so it would seem to some of those closest to him. "In the beginning," he would admit, he had held to "the old West Point notion that pillage was a capital crime," to be punished by shooting, but "the Rebels wanted us to detach a division here, a brigade there, to protect their families while they were fighting," and to Sherman "this was a one-sided game of war" and "minor things" were soon ignored as he "went in to subdue . . . the Rebels who had forced us into the war, and who deserved all they got and *more*." Alabama-born Henry Hitchcock, riding by Sherman's side, came to agree with the general that war must be made "so terrible" that when peace came "it will *last*."

6. "THE BEST MOVE IN MY CAREER AS A SOLDIER"

SAM HOOD never lost hope that the great moment would come. Stung to the quick by the public doubt of his ability, the big Texan-by-adoption yearned to redeem the loss of Atlanta. Squinting over his military maps, Sam wondered about Schofield's Army of the Cumberland. So Sherman thought that by sending Schofield to reinforce Thomas at Nashville while Sherman dashed for the sea he could doom the Confederacy? Sam's eyes narrowed and he cursed the twinge in his leg. If he could catch Schofield and defeat him before a juncture with Thomas, if then he could fall on Thomas and destroy him, why by every glorious bar and star in the Confederate flag, he would have twisted Sherman's tail! By the 21st of November, as Sherman swung down on Milledgeville, Hood "found my army in full motion." His hope was to beat Schofield's army to Duck River, but, he must add sadly: "The Federals became alarmed and by forced marches reached Columbia [Tennessee] just in time to prevent our troops cutting them off."

Sam was far from discouraged. If he shifted the main body of his army to Spring Hill, twelve miles directly in the enemy's rear, the situation "presented an occasion for one of those beautiful moves [that is, to attack and capture Schofield's army] for which I had often desired an opportunity." On the 29th of November, Hood brought his army to within "about two miles and in full view of the pike from Columbia to Spring Hill and Franklin," where he could see "the enemy's wagons and men passing at double-quick along the Franklin Pike." Cheatham commanded the leading corps; fiery Cheatham, hero of Kenesaw, who, placed across the pike at Spring Hill with Pat Cleburne assisting him, should be able to raise holy hell! Cheatham's corps and Cleburne's division moved off;

within half an hour "skirmishing began," and through a staff officer Hood urged Cheatham "to lose no time in gaining possession of the pike at Spring Hill." As time sped on something seemed queer to Hood, for "there was no continued roar of musketry." A second messenger returned with the news that Cheatham had not yet taken possession of the pike.

Twilight closed in. Cheatham appeared in person. Sam Hood's tightening nerves had to find release somewhere. Turning to Cheatham, he blurted:

"General, why in the name of God have you not taken possession of that pike?"

Cheatham answered tersely that "the line looked a little too long for him," and Hood could hardly believe his hearing, never believing that "this brave old soldier, who had given proof of such courage and ability upon so many hard-fought fields, would ever make such a report." With darkness Stewart's corps went into bivouac, "near but not across the pike."

The Federal army marched by that night, as Hood would report, "almost under the light of the campfires of the main body of our army," and Captain Thomas E. Milchrist of Schofield's army, remembering how he passed through Spring Hill within sight of the Confederates, could only marvel that he did not "diet in Libby or Andersonville before I saw old friends again." Bitterly, Hood felt:

> The best move in my career as a soldier I was thus destined to behold come to naught. I thereupon decided, before the enemy would be able to reach his stronghold at Nashville, to make another and final effort to overtake and rout him and drive him into the Harpeth River at Franklin since I could no longer hope to get between him and Nashville.

On November 30th Hood's graybacks started at dawn to catch Schofield at Franklin. On a ridge over which the turnpike passed, about three miles from the town, the Federals were discovered, but as soon as Hood's boys began to deploy, the Yankees edged off into the environs of Franklin. By three o'clock the bluecoats were found behind hastily prepared entrenchments; Hood gave his own men explicit orders: "Drive the enemy into the river *at all hazards.*" Pat Cleburne felt exalted.

"General," he told Sam Hood, surveying the open ground in front of Schofield's army, "I have more hope in the final success of our cause than I have had at any time."

"God grant it!" Hood replied.

Forty minutes later Cleburne "lay lifeless upon the breastworks of the foe." Pat's death was a terrible omen. The Federal lines were broken at many points, Federal guns captured and turned on the Yankees, but, Hood said, "just at this critical moment a brigade of the enemy gallantly charged and restored the Federal line, capturing at the same time about 1,000 of our troops within the entrenchments." The fighting grew savage and a Union captain would remember seeing men with "their thumbs chewed to a pulp," because, wounded, "their agony had been so great that they had stuck their thumbs in their mouths and bit on them to keep from bleating like calves." At nine o'clock the battle ended. The Yankees withdrew in order and again Sam Hood had failed. His enormous losses at Franklin left him "with an effective force of only 23,000." His heart grew heavy, his confidence wavered, and he wrote:

> . . . The only remaining chance of success in the compaign was to entrench around Nashville and await Thomas' attack which, if handsomely repulsed, might afford us an opportunity to follow up our advantage on the spot and enter the city on the heels of the enemy.
>
> In accordance with these convictions I ordered the army to move forward on the first of December in the direction of Nashville. On the morning of the second the line of battle was formed.

If Hood felt depressed by the situation, so too did Grant and Sherman, as the days dragged on and Thomas made no move to come after the Confederates. From City Point on the 3rd of December, Grant wrote Sherman, almost peevishly: "Thomas has got back into the defenses of Nashville," when he controlled all the roads except the main one to Chattanooga and when "in my opinion, Thomas far outnumbers Hood in infantry." Grant's annoyance continued, and three days later he would again write Sherman: "I have said all I can to force him [Thomas] to attack, without giving the positive order until today. Today, however, I could stand it no longer, and gave the order without reserve."

Sherman must bear the responsibility for Thomas, and if Thomas failed, the fault would be Sherman's for having abandoned Hood to chase across central Georgia. Now Sherman wrote Grant that: "I myself am somewhat astonished by the attitude of things in Tennessee." He had waited in Kingston until Thomas had promised that "he would ruin Hood if he dared to advance from Florence," and, Sherman confided to Grant: "Why he did not turn on him at Franklin, after checking and discomfiting him, surpasses my understanding." Thomas was "slow in mind and action," but "judicious and brave" and since "the troops feel great confidence in him" Sherman still hoped Thomas would "out-manoeuvre and destroy Hood."

Grant thought of going to Nashville in person to prod Thomas into action, then decided to send Johnny Logan to supersede Thomas. On the 16th of December Thomas moved —and "thus escaped," Sherman believed, "so terrible a fate."

On the day of the battle for Nashville, Sam Watkins of the 1st Tennessee would remember how, after Franklin, "not one single general out of Cheatham's division was left." Sam said that nearly all captains and colonels also were gone, so that "companies mingled with companies, regiments with regiments and brigades with brigades." A few rawboned horses "stood shivering under the ice-covered trees, nibbling the

short, scanty grass." Watkins never had seen an army "so con-
fused and demoralized"; every soldier "mistrusted General
Hood's judgment." Sam, who had loved Joe Johnston, passed
Hood:

> . . . I remember . . . how feeble and decrepit he
> looked, with an arm in a sling and a crutch in the other
> hand, trying to guide and control his horse. I prayed in my
> heart that day for General Hood. Poor fellow!

But the end was near for Hood's great hope. Thomas's boys
charged, coming up over their breastworks, piercing the Confederate line, pressing bitterly as it gave way, battering straight
through, while Hood "seated on my horse not far in rear
when the breach was effected" saw "for the first and only time
a Confederate army abandon the field in confusion." Sam
Hood could not understand the debacle, but Sam Watkins
could:

> . . . We could see the Federals advancing. I heard,
> "Surrender, surrender!" I picked up my gun and ran.
> The whole army had broken and were running in every
> direction. Such a scene I never saw. The woods every-
> where were full of running soldiers. Our officers were
> crying, "Halt! Halt!" and trying to rally and reform their
> broken ranks. The Federals would dash their cavalry in
> among us, and even their cannon joined in the charge.
> Wagon trains, cannon, artillery, cavalry and infantry
> were all blended in inextricable confusion. Broken-down
> and jaded horses and mules refused to pull, and the
> badly scared drivers looked like their eyes would pop out
> of their heads from fright. The officers soon became af-
> fected with the demoralization of their troops and rode on
> in dogged indifference. Generals Cheatham and W. W.
> Loring tried to form a line at Brentwood, but it was like
> trying to stop Duck River with a fish net. I saw a wagon
> abandoned, and unhitched one of the horses and rode to

Franklin, General Hood's headquarters. He was much agitated and affected, pulling his hair and crying as though his heart would break. The citizens seemed to shrink and hide as we approached them. The once proud Army of Tennessee had degenerated into a mob. Our country was gone, our cause lost.

So the dream of redemption ended in shattering disillusionment for Sam Hood. Cassville, Kenesaw, Atlanta, Allatoona, Spring Hill, Franklin, Nashville—each belonged to the same pattern: the same damned bad luck! How each must have hurt the proud general who hated his cork leg and felt every change of temperature in his injured limbs! In time he would see himself as right, and would write Jefferson Davis with an old soldier's gallantry:

> Before leaving for Texas allow me to say that I more than appreciate all of your kindness to me. Please never allow anyone to cause you to think for one moment, that I did not know you were ever more than ready to assume all responsibility naturally belonging to you. I know Sir you were in no way responsible for my operations whilst commanding the Army of Tenn. Believe me Sir ever your sincere friend. And I pray God, may ever bless and protect you

But his postscript would be more revealing:

> I am more content & satisfied with my own work whilst in command of the army of Tenn, than all my military career in life.
>
> Your friend
J. B. H.

But this was the afterthought, written to the President on March 31, 1865. Tonight, at Franklin, only the failure, only the disillusionment existed for Sam Hood as he cried "as though his heart would break." He had gambled and lost. He was through.

7. "A SOLDIER'S LIFE IS ALWAYS GAY"

THE tollkeeper of the bridge across the Oconee at Milledgeville—"a fat, dirty, lazy looking citizen"—assured Connolly that as a Mason he "allers bin for the Union and wus yit," but this avowal of loyalty could not save his bridge. A day's march after Milledgeville saw Sherman's troops "encamped fifteen miles nearer the Atlantic." The Federal troops now entered the Georgia pines, where "grasshoppers couldn't live." The trees grew so close that "a man can scarcely walk through them," and the pine needles gave the ground the softness of "a carpet well stuffed with straw." Connolly found that danger lurked in these pines:

> . . . Citizens say that strangers traveling through these woods will get lost as readily as on a prairie if they go far from the road, and I can readily believe it, for we passed over many miles today in which every tree and spot looked exactly like every other tree and spot. Notwithstanding the extreme barrenness of these "piney woods," we now and then passed a miserable looking little cabin today, about which we generally found two or three sickly, sallow women and from five to fifteen children, all looking like persons I have read of called "dirt eaters"; I guess they *are* dirt eaters, and I think they must live on it, for I don't see place for anything but children to grow in these "woods." We are now going toward the Ogeechee, and citizens tell us we will find very poor country all the way from the Oconee to the Ogeechee. Our foragers came into camp tonight pretty well loaded, and I can't imagine where they found so much stuff through this country. I suppose the Negroes assisted them. . . .

"Where can all the Rebels be?" Connolly wondered. The Federals rode "rough shod over Georgia," burning houses,

barns, fences, cotton, "and everything else," and yet "none of
the Southern braves show themselves to punish us for our
vandalism." Were the Rebels preparing a trap? But if they
were, Connolly merely shrugged his shoulders, confiding to
his diary:

> . . . We are living finely, and the whole army would
> have no objection to marching around through the State
> for the next six months. Indeed, the whole trip thus far
> has been a holiday excursion, but a very expensive one to
> the Rebels.

On Saturday, November 26, Sherman's forces reached
Sandersville. Wheeler's cavalry occupied the town when the
Union troops reached there, but Sherman timed the marching
of his two columns so well that at almost the same moment
one column entered from the west and one from the southwest. "The men," Connolly recorded, "marched right into
town loading and firing as they advanced; bands playing,
flags waving, and Mr. Wheeler and his Rebels, of course,
running almost without returning a shot." Rebel papers from
Augusta, falling into Yankee hands, aroused the ire of Sherman's men. The Southern press called on the citizens to fell
timbers across the roads, destroy forage and provisions, and
do "everything possible to harass us and retard our march."
Connolly thought angrily:

> . . . Let them do it if they dare. We'll burn every
> house, barn, church, and everything else we come to;
> we'll leave their families houseless and without food; their
> towns will *all* be destroyed, and nothing but the most
> complete desolation will be found in our track. This army
> will not be trifled with. . . . If citizens raise their hands
> against us, neither youth nor age, nor sex will be re-
> spected. Everything must be destroyed. . . . We have
> gone so far now in our triumphal march that we will not
> be balked. It is a question of life or death with us, and all

considerations of mercy and humanity must bow before the inexorable demands of self-preservation. . . .

Still Connolly could not deny that the presence of Wheeler's cavalry brought a growing tension and fear. On the 27th, Sherman's army crossed the Ogeechee into a country where the land was more cultivated and the plantations larger. Persimmons grew abundantly along the roadside, and as the orderlies rode along they gathered the fruit in their handkerchiefs. Connolly suddenly reflected: "I haven't seen a particle of hay." Corn leaves, "stripped from the stalk while green, and carefully cured in the sun," provided the only winter feed for horses and cattle. Georgians called these dried leaves "blades," but Connolly declared: "I don't think there is very much nutriment in them." Beyond the Ogeechee the road was filled with "cavalry tracks going eastward," and Connolly, "as full of curiosity as a woman," rode along with the skirmish line:

> . . . watching every tree and stump, listening very intently, and moving as quietly as a cat in the sandy road, expecting every moment to hear the crack of a rifle from some concealed Rebel; at such a moment the excitement is so intense that all thoughts of personal safety are forgotten, the senses of sight and hearing are extraordinarily acute, but they take no notice of anything passing, being intent alone on discovering the enemy before he discovers you; we moved up until we could hear the sound of rushing water—no other sound could be heard; if at this moment my horse had neighed I should have been startled as from a dream, but "Frank" was quiet, and moved steadily with his ears erect as if he too were looking for the graybacks; a little turn in the road brings us in sight of "Fenn's Bridge," a long frame structure spanning the "Ogeechee"—not a plank disturbed, not a Rebel in sight. . . .

Joseph Wheeler—his men called him "Fighting Joe" and "Little Joe"—had been itching for a nip at the rear of Sherman's army since reaching Griffin, Georgia, on the 16th of November. Studying scouting reports, Wheeler believed that the Federals were turning their main column on Macon. In a tone of urgency, he wired Beauregard, Bragg, and Hood: "I have no orders regarding the holding of any city should enemy besiege or assault. Please give me wishes and intention of Government, or send some one who knows the course they desired pursued." With less than two thousand cavalrymen, Wheeler set himself to five tasks. He would impede and harass "enemy's columns when practicable"; he would attack "and defeat" exposed detachments; he would hamper the Federal foragers "from extending into and despoiling the country, except near their main columns"; he would keep everyone "fully informed of Sherman's movements"; and he would "defend all cities along the line of railroad, depots of stores, arsenals, government and other important works, etc."

From General Richard Taylor at Selma, Alabama, came the advice, "should enemy move east," to telegraph "Hardee and Richmond direct." Beauregard's counsel was simply to "employ your cavalry to best advantage," but Hood warned: "It is very important that you should not allow any portion of your mounted forces to be shut up in a besieged city." So convinced had Wheeler become that Sherman intended to overrun Macon that he ordered the militia and reserves to concentrate there and to "prepare the fortifications and city for vigorous defence." Wheeler reached Macon at midnight on the 19th, claiming that "by fighting superior force" he had "defended and saved the town of Forsyth," and later that he had captured some forty of the enemy during a skirmish en route to Macon. Wheeler soon expanded his claims of victory —first near Clinton, where he "led in person" an attack; then at Griswoldville, where he "drove the Federal force out . . . capturing a number of prisoners"; and again at Dublin and Blackman's Ferry on the Oconee, where he "swam the river," and by a "rapid march," checked "and drove back a column then attempting to cross at Ball's Ferry." Wheeler, who apparently never slept, marched all night, and with the daylight on the 25th confronted "the enemy's main army" after it had crossed the Oconee at Milledgeville. Now:

> After disposing troops to watch all roads by which Sherman could approach the Savannah Railroad or city of Augusta, General Wheeler marched through Sandersville on the afternoon of the 25th, and was soon met by Sherman's main force, which made a furious charge with cavalry, supported by infantry, upon our small command. Wheeler had anticipated this, and placing his troops in position, countercharged the enemy, driving them pell-mell for two miles, killing and wounding a large number in the running mêlée, capturing thirty prisoners and a valuable headquarters wagon. At night we encamped near the enemy, and on the morning of the 26th, by warm fighting, Wheeler resisted the advance of Sherman's massive lines, gradually yielding ground until he was finally driven through and beyond Sandersville.

Sherman dismissed with a shrug the skirmish with Wheeler's cavalry, but the sight of the Rebel cavalry burning stacks of fodder in a field set Sherman's eyes blazing and brought terse orders "to burn some occupied dwellings close by." Then, entering Sandersville, Sherman said:

> . . . I told certain citizens (who would be sure to spread the report) that, if the enemy attempted to carry out their threat to burn their food, corn, and fodder, in our route, I would most undoubtedly execute to the letter the general orders of devastation made at the outset of the campaign. With this exception, and one or two minor cases near Savannah, the people did not destroy food, for they saw clearly that it would be ruin to themselves.

Connolly believed that most of the stories of hard fighting a cavalryman told were "cut after Baron Munchausen's style." Kilpatrick, in Connolly's opinion, looked "more like a monkey than a man on horseback" and was "the most vain, conceited, egotistical popinjay I ever saw." But for once Connolly worried. Kilpatrick had left the army at the Oconee to make a raid toward Augusta and Millen. Serious trouble could have overtaken him. A brigade was sent to support Kilpatrick. Without breakfast:

. . . The brigade was in motion before sunrise, and after marching about five miles they began to hear the sounds of skirmishing ahead; selecting a good position they immediately formed a line, and in about ten minutes Kilpatrick's jaded cavalry hove in sight, skirmishing with Wheeler and retiring before him; but when they saw the line of blue coated infantry drawn up in line across the road, and extending off into the woods on either side, they knew that they were saved, and sent up such shouts as never before were heard in these "Piney Woods" which our infantry responded to with right good will. Mr. Wheeler, taking the hint from this shouting, prudently refrained from pursuing any farther, and quietly withdrew; while Kilpatrick . . . reports that he has been near to Waynesboro, has burned a R.R. bridge on the road between Waynesboro and Augusta; has destroyed two or three miles of R.R. between Waynesboro and Millen but didn't reach the prison pen at Millen as Wheeler, with some Georgia militia, got after him; he says . . . there is plenty of forage in the country ahead of us, but that Wheeler's men will destroy it all, and fall timber in the roads ahead of us. If they do this they will seriously annoy us, but as the enemy are still under the impression that Sherman first intends to take Augusta, before moving on Savannah, they may do most of their timber-chopping on

251

the roads leading to Augusta, leaving the roads to Savannah comparatively clear. . . .

A group of refugee Negroes encamped near headquarters staged a "Plantation Dance" that night. It was a sight that one really had to see to believe, Connolly thought.

> . . . The dress, general appearance, action, laughter, music and dancing of the plantation Negro is far more grotesque and mirth-provoking than the broadest caricatures of "Christy's Minstrels." They require neither fiddle nor banjo to make music for their ordinary plantation dances, and the dancers need no prompter, but kick, and caper and shuffle in the most complicated and grotesque manner their respective fancies can invent, while all who are not actually engaged as dancers stand in a ring . . . clapping their hands, stamping their feet, swinging their bodies, and singing as loud and as fast and furious as they can, a sort of barbaric chant, unlike anything I ever heard from the lips of white mortals; I observed, however, that there is a tone of melancholy . . . pervading all their rude music, which was plainly discernible even when the mirth of the dancers and singers had apparently reached its highest pitch. There is more fact than fiction in the saying that a "Soldier's life is always gay," for here we are in the midst of a hostile country, engaged in a campaign which probably the whole world, at this moment, is predicting will end in our complete destruction, and yet I have spent the evening laughing at the oddities of these Negroes until my head and sides are aching.

Another witness to the fact that a "Soldier's life is always gay" was Major George Ward Nichols. Nichols was amused by the camp pets he saw everywhere along the march—dogs and cats, a small donkey and a raccoon—but, he found, "the favorite pet of the camp . . . is the hero of the barnyard." There existed a good reason why every regiment and company, every teamster or Negro at headquarters, possessed a rooster of "one kind or another":

> . . . When the column is moving, these haughty gamecocks are seen mounted upon the breech of a cannon, tied to the pack saddle of a mule, among pots and pans, or carried lovingly in the arms of a mounted orderly; crowing with all his might from the interior of a wagon, or making the woods re-echo with his triumphant notes as he rides perched upon the knapsack of a soldier. These cocks represent every known breed, Polish and Spanish, Dorkings, Shanghais, and Bantams—high-blooded specimens traveling with those of their species who may not boast of noble lineage. They must all fight, however, or be killed and eaten. Hardly has the army gone into camp before these feathery combats begin. The cocks use only the spurs with which Nature furnishes them; for the soldiers have not yet reached the refinement of applying artificial gaffs, and so but little harm is done. The game-cocks which have come out of repeated conflicts victorious are honored with such names as "Bill Sherman," "Johnny Logan," etc.; while the defeated and bepecked victim is saluted with derisive appellations, such as "Jeff. Davis," "Beauregard," or "Bob Lee."

Cock-fighting, Nichols admitted, was not "one of the most refined or elevating of pastimes," but it furnished "a certain kind of fun" and was not "carried to the point of cruelty." Along the roadside one day Nichols encountered a pungent old man, "his face . . . grave as a Quaker's," who held "his auditors in a roar of merriment" while he philosophized upon the war:

> They say you are retreating, but it is the strangest sort of retreat I ever saw. Why, dog bite them, the newspapers have been lying in this way all along. They allers are whipping the Federal armies, and they allers fall back

after the battle is over. It was that ar' idee that first opened my eyes. Our army was always whipping the Feds, and we allers fell back. I allers told 'em it was a damned humbug, and now by Jesus I know it, for here you are right on [my] place; hogs, potatoes, corn, and fences all gone. I don't find any fault. I expected it all.

Jeff Davis and the rest talk about splitting the Union. Why if South Carolina had gone out by herself, she would have been split in four pieces by this time. Splitting the Union! Why [with a round oath] the State of Georgia is being split right through from end to end. It is these rich fellows who are making this war, and keeping their precious bodies out of harm's way. There's John Franklin went through here the other day, running away from your army. I could have played dominoes on his coat-tails. There's my poor brother sick with small-pox at Macon, working for eleven dollars a month, and hasn't got a cent of the damned stuff for a year. 'Leven dollars a month and eleven thousand bullets a minute. I don't believe in it, sir!

The philosopher's wife came from Canada, and he might have gone there except that he had been "allers afraid of the ice and cold," but now Georgia had become "too cussed hot." The Confederates were idiots tearing up trees and burning bridges; "a natural born fool cut in two had more sense in either end than any of them." Georgia had been brought to a sad condition and it would require "the help of Divine Providence, a heap of rain, and a deal of elbow-grease, to fix things up again."

Despite the excitement of cock-fighting or the amusement supplied by a roadside philosopher, Nichols could not escape "the most pathetic scenes" that occurred "daily and hourly" along the line of Sherman's march. By the thousands, Negro women would join the Federal columns:

> . . . some carrying household goods, and many of them carrying children in their arms, while older boys

and girls plod by their side. All these women and children are ordered back, heartrending though it may be to refuse them liberty. One begs that she may go to see her husband and children at Savannah. Long years ago she was forced from them and sold. Another has heard that her boy was in Macon, and she is "done gone with grief goin' on four years."

But the majority accept the advent of the Yankees as the fulfillment of the millennial prophecies. The "day of jubilee," the hope and prayer of a lifetime, has come. They cannot be made to understand that they must remain behind, and they are satisfied only when General Sherman tells them, as he does every day, that we shall come back for them some time, and that they must be patient until the proper hour of deliverance arrives.

But even under Sherman's reassurances that the Yankees would return, many Negroes refused to be turned back. Nichols remembered a woman with a child in her arms, who was "working her way along among the teams and crowds of cattle and horsemen," when an officer called:

"Where are you going, aunty?"

"I'se gwine whar you'se gwine, massa," the woman replied in a tone intended to end the dispute.

An officer of the 70th Indiana regiment told his wife how touching it was to see

> . . . the vast numbers of colored women following after us with babies in their arms, and little ones like our Anna clinging to their tattered skirts. One poor creature, while nobody was looking, hid two boys, five years old, in a wagon, intending, I suppose, that they should see the land of freedom if she couldn't. . . .

J. B. Conyngham would describe a mule with "a black head with large staring eyes peeping out of a sack" on one side "and a ham and turkey balancing it on the other."

Conyngham declared that the practice of miscegenation grew commonplace. Men long weeks away from home crept off into the woodland darkness when the army encamped, and found many a Negro girl willing to be loved. Some were just farm boys, as green to love-making as they once had been to battle, who felt that these nocturnal adventures were all part of the lark the war seemed to have become; they grew bolder with experience, and Negresses who proved compliant were found living "luxurious lives, stowed away in baggage wagons." Conyngham swore that it would have been "vexatious to the Grand Turk or to Brigham Young" if either could have seen

> . . . how many of the dark houris were in the employment of officers' servants and teamsters. I have seen officers themselves very attentive to the wants of pretty octoroon girls, and provide them with horses to ride.

8. "THIS NIGGER WILL HAVE NO SLEEP THIS NIGHT!"

ON THE 3rd of December, riding with the XVIIth Corps, Sherman entered Millen. Howard and the XVth Corps moved south of the Ogeechee opposite Scarboro; Slocum and the XXth Corps had reached Buckhead Church, four miles north of Millen; and Davis and the XIVth Corps, traveling the Augusta Road with Kilpatrick's cavalry, paused at Lumpkin's Station, ten miles north of Millen. Sherman could not disguise his high spirits. With little or no loss, he had covered two-thirds of the distance from Atlanta to the sea! Sherman bowed over the reports that reached him at Millen. Braxton Bragg was in Augusta and Wade Hampton had been rushed from Richmond "to organize a large cavalry force with which to resist our progress." Hardee rested somewhere ahead, "between us and Savannah," with McLaw's division and other "irregular troops" that could not exceed ten thousand men. Sherman had the lot of 'em buffaloed! "Until yesterday," Major George Ward Nichols reported, "it was General Sherman's intention to move on Augusta," but now that "the curtain had been withdrawn" the South soon would learn that the Federals were driving straight for Savannah. It was Sherman's flank movements that had bewildered the Confederates, Nichols believed, for

> . . . first, the right wing, with Kilpatrick's cavalry, moved upon Macon, in the early part of the campaign; next, after disappearing from that flank, to the great amazement of the Rebels, the same troops marched across our rear and suddenly appeared upon our left flank, supported by Davis, and demonstrating savagely upon Augusta; and now Howard is performing the same office on our right. This style of manoeuvring has not been practiced on account of any apprehension that we can not run over and demolish any Rebel force in Georgia, for all the troops of the enemy in the state could not stand for a moment against this army on any battle-field; but because General Sherman neither wishes to sacrifice life needlessly nor be detained. A very small force of infantry or cavalry in position at a river-crossing could delay a marching column half a day, or longer; our flanking column prevents this. Besides, our soldiers have tired of chickens, sweet potatoes, sorghum, etc., and have been promised oysters at the sea-side, oysters roasted, oysters fried, oysters stewed, oysters on the half shell, oysters in abundance, without money and without price. In short, the soldiers themselves don't wish to be delayed!

The depot at Millen, "a wooden structure of exceedingly graceful proportions," was burned at Sherman's orders, and to Nichols the spectacle was so brilliant with "the exquisite architecture traced to lines of fire," that even "the rank and file observed and made comments . . . a circumstance that may be counted unusual, for the taste for conflagrations has been so cultivated of late in the army that any small affair of that kind attracts very little attention." Another sight in Millen, Nichols declared, "fevered the blood of our brave boys," and "hideous" was the only word he could apply to the prison-pen the Confederates had constructed there. In a space of ground about three hundred feet square, enclosed in a stockade and without any covering whatever, Nichols said:

> . . . was the hole where thousands of our brave soldiers have been confined for months past, exposed to heavy dews, biting frosts, and pelting rains, without so much as a board or tent to protect them after the Rebels had stolen their clothing. Some of them had adopted the wretched alternative of digging holes in the ground, in which they crept at times. What wonder that we found evidence that seven hundred and fifty men had died there! From what misery did death release them? I could realize it all when I saw this den, as I never could before, even when listening to the stories of prisoners who had fled, escaping the villains who rushed after them in hot pursuit, and foiling the blood-hounds which had been put on their track.

With grim satisfaction, Nichols reported coming upon a dooryard where "lay the bodies of several blood-hounds." Wherever the Union army passed, "every thing in the shape of a dog has been killed," for soldiers and officers alike were determined that "no more flying fugitives, white men or Negroes, shall be followed by hounds that come within reach of their powder and ball."

Another witness to the miserable conditions of the prison pen at Millen was G. S. Bradley, Chaplain of the 22nd Wisconsin. The huts where the Yankees had been confined, Bradley declared, were "hardly fit for our swine to live in," and the men from Sherman's army who visited the spot went away "muttering louder curses on Jeff. Davis and all his murderous crew." Bradley noticed especially that

> . . . Near the entrance way was a small building, or rather the roof to one, set on posts, under which our soldiers were punished, I conclude, as stocks for the feet were lying near. I counted holes enough for seven persons, and they appeared to be well worn. Also noticed a lot for the neck. I never knew before that our soldiers had to undergo this barbarous method of torture, but there was no mistaking the fact now.

Grimly Bradley's eyes followed the "dead line" around the inside of the stockade, "beyond which it was death for any man to pass." Forty sentry boxes had guarded the prison.

After a day's pause in Millen, Sherman drove on to Ogeechee Church, about fifty miles from Savannah and those promised oysters. Fresh earthworks, thrown up by McLaw's division, protected Ogeechee Church, but McLaw realized that both his flanks were being turned and "prudently retreated to Savannah without a fight." Sherman felt that weather, roads, "every thing" seemed to favor him. Never, he would write:

> . . . do I recall a more agreeable sensation than the sight of our camps by night, lit up by the fires of fragrant pine-knots. The trains were all in good order, and the men seemed to march their fifteen miles a day as though it were nothing. No enemy opposed us, and we could only occasionally hear the faint reverberation of a gun to our left rear, where we knew that General Kilpatrick was skirmishing with Wheeler's cavalry, which persistently followed him. . . .

Major Connolly marched with Davis's XIVth Corps hard on the heels of Kilpatrick's cavalry. Sherman's objective was to employ these troops and horsemen to drive Wheeler across Briar Creek, five miles north of Waynesboro, and keep up "the idea that we are moving on Augusta." Pushing on toward Waynesboro on the 4th of December, past Georgia fields of "poor, pale looking sand" suitable only for raising melons and peanuts, Connolly would remark that "this has been a regular field day," with "lots of fun" chasing Wheeler and his cavalry. Kilpatrick was "full of fun and frolic" and "elated at the idea of whipping" his old West Point classmate, for even during his student days at the Academy, Kilpatrick avowed, "Little Joe" Wheeler had been "a great sloven." Connolly found that a cavalry fight was

> . . . just about as much fun as a fox hunt; but, of course, in the midst of the fun somebody is getting hurt all the time. But it is by no means the serious work that infantry fighting is. Wheeler himself had to run at an ingloriously rapid rate through the streets of Waynesboro today. That must have been very humiliating to this proud cavalier. We entered Waynesboro about noon and pushed on after the flying Rebels to Briar Creek, twenty-two miles from Augusta. I presume the Augustans were frightened again today when they heard we were coming so close to their city.

On the next day, marching from sunrise to sunset, the XIVth Corps reached Jacksonboro, a distance of nineteen miles. Connolly wondered how Wheeler felt this morning when he discovered that "instead of being in our front, as he supposed himself, he is in our rear, and far in our rear, too—so far that it will now be impossible for him to get in our front until we are battering away at Savannah." But in this thought alone could Connolly find comfort after a day's tramping past pine woods where "the few women and children we have seen look utterly ignorant and stupid." On the sixth, following a line parallel to the Savannah River, the XIVth Corps covered another twelve miles. Reports brought in by cavalry scouts revealed that the Confederates expected the XIVth Corps to cross the river and strike for Charleston, but, Connolly commented sardonically, "South Carolina is reserved for a future day." Or was it? At intervals "heavy cannonading, apparently very distant, and in the direction of the coast" could be heard. Was Charleston even then under bombardment? There was no way of knowing. Another day's march through the pines and the Jack oaks of the low, level country brought the XIVth Corps to Mill Creek, where Davis decided to camp for the night rather than risk a crossing over the dark and treacherously deep water. But now Connolly would learn that a soldier's life is not always gay, for:

> . . . just about dark, the cavalry in our rear came
> · rushing past us pell-mell, and the sounds of musketry in-
> formed us that the Rebels in some force were following
> our rear closely, so our headquarters were taken down
> again, preparations for supper suspended, wagons re-
> loaded, and the troops disposed in proper order to resist
> an attack; our lines were opened and Kilpatrick's fright-
> ened cavalry permitted to come through and take shelter
> behind us; about this time came orders that we must
> cross Mill Creek and move on to the vicinity of "Sister's
> Ferry" some seven miles beyond, if it should take us all
> night. This was hard, for we were all tired and hungry,
> but there was no time to rest, so about 9 o'clock we got
> started out again, and after marching all night we
> reached "Sister's Ferry" at 4 o'clock next morning. I
> think this was the hardest night march I ever made. Just
> before the troops began to cross the "Mill Creek" ravine,
> word came to the General that the enemy was in our
> front just on the opposite side of the ravine, and I went
> ahead to see about it. . . . I cautiously groped my way
> through the dark ravine, but I found no enemy. . . . I
> was exceedingly sleepy, and laid down on a brush pile by
> the road side where I slept an hour, until the General
> came up with the rear brigade, when we all started
> ahead; I slept on my horse as we rode along, and at every

halt I dismounted and laid down beside my horse to snatch a little sleep, being afraid, all the time, that by some unfortunate mischance, the column might move on and leave me.

Again through the day and night the distant cannonading could be heard. With "everybody tired, sleepy and worn out," the XIVth Corps moved off the morning of the 8th. Connolly, who had "tumbled down on the ground by a burning stump at the road side about five o'clock," stole an hour's sleep, then "got a tin cup full of coffee for breakfast, gave my horse some corn, and by half past six was on the road for the day." About a month of this kind of soldiering would finish him, he thought. Wheeler's cavalry threatened the Federal column constantly, and Rebel gunboats on the Savannah shelled the road. At Ebenezar Creek another night crossing was ordered. Davis waited until after midnight to begin the movement "in the utmost silence, not a bugle being sounded nor a loud command being given." With the enemy in the rear, "undoubtedly listening for every sound that would indicate a movement on our part," the Federals must pass through a mile of dismal cypress swamp over a narrow causeway barely wide enough for a single wagon. Connolly squirmed. An enemy artillery piece placed in the road "could have killed or wounded three-fourths of the men in the division, and we should have been utterly helpless to defend against it." Why had the Confederates overlooked this chance? Connolly could give only one answer: "I don't believe they thought we would be foolish enough to *try* to cross here." But it was not the threat of the enemy that set Connolly boiling at Ebenezar Creek:

When the head of the column reached the "Ebenezar Causeway" I went ahead with one of Genl. Davis' aids who had come back to point out our ground for camping, and as I reached the bridge, I found there Major Lee, Provost Marshall of the Corps, engaged, by Genl. Davis' order, in turning off the road, into the swamp, all the fugitive Negroes that came along. When we should cross I knew it was the intention that the bridge should be burned, and I inquired if the Negroes were not to be permitted to cross; I was told that Genl. Davis had ordered that they should not. This *I* knew, and Genl. Davis knew, must result in all the Negroes being captured or perhaps brutally shot down by the Rebel cavalry tomorrow morning. The idea of five or six hundred black women, children and old men being thus returned to slavery by such an infernal copperhead as [Union General] Jeff. C. Davis was entirely too much for my Democracy; I suppose loss of sleep, and fatigue made me somewhat out of humor too, and I told his staff officers what I thought of such an inhuman, barbarous proceeding in language which may possibly result in a reprimand from his serene Highness, for I know his toadies will repeat it to him, but I don't care a fig; I am determined to expose this act of his publicly, and . . . I expect this will cost me my Brevet as Lieut. Colonel, but let it go, I wouldn't barter my convictions of right, nor seal my mouth for any promotion. . . .

Connolly's bad temper lingered. The night marching had begun to make him "feel old," and his estimate of army service was that of "a perfect dog's life." He'd gladly quit it were it not for the fact that "the young man, who in these eventful times is found at home, is but a drone in the hive." Now, as Connolly resumed the march, the trees were overhung "with the long streamers of dingy grey Spanish moss," so that one almost fancied "they were thus adorned for some fairy festival long ago, all traces of which have now disappeared except the soft yielding carpet of pine leaves, and the faded drapery overhead." That night, as the XIVth Corps encamped within eighteen miles of Savannah, rumors placed the right wing of the army within four miles of the city. Connolly thought: "I saw one city (Atlanta) destroyed, and that was enough for me. I want Savannah to fall, but not in ruins."

Meanwhile Sherman rode with the XVIIth Corps. A torpedo, planted in the road by the Rebels, had literally blown "off all the flesh" from the leg of "a handsome young officer" and killed his horse. Sherman found the officer standing in the corner of a fence, waiting for a surgeon to amputate his leg. The torpedo had been an eight-inch shell equipped with friction matches so that it would explode when trodden upon. Sherman's anger blazed. "This was not war, but murder!" Immediately Sherman ordered

> . . . a lot of Rebel prisoners to be brought from the provost-guard, armed with picks and spades, and made them march in close order along the road, so as to explode their own torpedoes, or to discover and dig them up. They begged hard, but I reiterated the order, and could hardly help laughing at their stepping so gingerly along the road, but they found no more torpedoes till near Fort McAllister. . . .

On the night of the 8th Sherman reached Pooler's Station, eight miles from Savannah. For two days he waited for the several corps to close in on the defenses of the city. The XIVth Corps, on the left, touched the river; the XXth and the XVIIth were next; and the XVth on the extreme right formed the pattern for "completely investing" Savannah. For Sherman, the march to the sea almost ended at Pooler's Station. Exploring a cut about four feet deep, through which a side-track of the railroad passed, the general suddenly noticed

> . . . about eight hundred yards off . . . a rebel parapet and battery. I could see the cannoneers preparing to fire, and cautioned the officers near me to scatter, as we would likely attract a shot. Very soon I saw the white puff of smoke, and, watching close, caught sight of the ball as it rose in flight, and, finding it coming pretty straight, I stepped a short distance to one side. . . .

But a Negro, crossing the track at right angles, was not so lucky. The first ricochet of the thirty-two-pound round shot "caught the Negro under the right jaw, and literally carried away his head, scattering blood and brains about."

The taking of Fort McAllister became the key to the capture of Savannah. Mower's division of the XVIIth Corps, crossing the canal to the right of the Louisville Road, found a continuous line of parapet, and Sherman reflected sadly: "it looked as though another siege was inevitable." The Union fleet supposedly waited with supplies and clothing in Ossabaw Sound. One of Howard's best scouts had drifted in a canoe past Fort McAllister some nights previously to convey knowledge of Sherman's approach. Kilpatrick's cavalry, transferred to the south bank of the Ogeechee, likewise had been instructed to open communication with the fleet, and, unknown to Sherman, had done so at Kilkenny Bluff [St. Catharine's Sound].

Sherman strained at the Confederate leash holding him out of Savannah. Slocum's task was to press the siege, while Howard's engineers rebuilt King's Bridge, fourteen and a half miles southwest from Savannah. On the night of the 12th Sherman rode over to see how Howard's boys were progressing, and that night the bridge was repaired. General William B. Hazen, who commanded the old division with which Sherman had fought at Shiloh and Vicksburg, received straightforward orders: "To march rapidly down the right bank of the Ogeechee, and without hesitation to assault and carry Fort McAllister by storm." With Hazen "fairly off," Sherman rode down the left bank of the Ogeechee ten miles to a rice plantation where Howard had established a signal station "to overlook the lower river, and to watch for any vessel of the blockading squadron, which the Negroes reported to be expecting us."

From the signal station Fort McAllister, "Rebel flag flying," could be seen across the three miles of salt marsh. Sherman climbed to the roof of a shed attached to the rice mill.

The tense vigil dragged on. Then, about two o'clock in the afternoon, the fort came alive. One or two guns, turned inland, opened fire, and from the woods close to McAllister came the sound of musket-skirmishing. A signal message from Hazen said that "he was making his preparations, and would soon attempt the assault," but when the sun began "rapidly declining," Sherman admitted, "I was dreadfully impatient." Now a new tension developed, for "a faint cloud of smoke, and an object gliding" appeared "along the horizon above the tops of the sedge toward the sea." Little by little the "object gliding" grew into the smokestack of a steamer flying the Union flag. Signal messages passed quickly between the vessel and the general on the roof of the mill shed:

"Who are you?"

"General Sherman."

"Is Fort McAllister taken?"

"Not yet, but it will be in a minute!"

An hour's sunlight remained. From the platform on the ridgepole of the rice mill, the signal men shouted down that Hazen "was all ready." Sherman's reply was: "Go ahead." Almost at once Hazen's division came out of "the dark fringe of woods" around the fort, "the lines dressed as on parade, with colors flying, and moving forward with a quick, steady pace." The big guns of McAllister belched forth "dense clouds of smoke."

Beside Sherman on the rooftop of the mill shed stood George Ward Nichols. But Sherman could not stand still. He "walked nervously to and fro," Nichols said, "turning quickly now and then from viewing the scene of conflict to observe the sun sinking slowly behind the tree-tops." To Nichols "the fort seemed alive with flame," with:

> . . . quick, thick jets of fire shooting out from all its sides, while the white smoke first covered the place and then rolled away over the glacis. The line of blue moved steadily on; too slowly, as it seemed to us, for we ex-

claimed, "Why don't they dash forward?" But their measured step was unfaltering. Now the flag goes down, but the line does not halt. A moment longer, and the banner gleams again in the front. We, the lookers-on, clutch one another's arms convulsively, and scarcely breathed in the eager intensity of our gaze. Sherman stood watching with anxious air, awaiting the decisive moment. Then the enemy's fire redoubled in rapidity and violence. The darting streams of fire alone told the position of the fort. The line of blue entered the enshrouding folds of smoke. The flag was at last dimly seen, and then it went out of sight altogether.

"They have been repulsed!" said one of the group of officers who watched the fight.

"No, by Heaven," said another. "There is not a man in retreat—not a straggler in all the glorious line!"

The firing ceased. The wind lifted the smoke. Crowds of men were visible on the parapets, fiercely fighting—but our flag was planted there.

The musket shots grew fewer and more scattered, then broke off as the Yankees swarmed into the bomb-proofs and parapets of McAllister. On the shed roof the officers "grasped each the other's hand, embraced . . . and some of us found the water in our eyes." Sherman's elation bubbled over. To the group he exclaimed:

"This nigger will have no sleep this night!"

With a volunteer crew and a borrowed skiff, the general set off to communicate with the fleet. But he stopped first at the McAllister plantation to eat supper with General Hazen. In a jubilant note to Stanton, written "On Board *Dandelion*, Ossabaw Sound," Sherman declared: "I regard Savannah as already *gained*."

9. "I BEG TO PRESENT YOU AS A CHRIST-MAS-GIFT"

ON THE 14th of December, encamped across the Louisville Road almost within sight of Savannah, Connolly found that the order from Sherman announcing the fall of Fort McAllister set "the men . . . cheering and yelling like Indians all day." Everybody felt jolly, with the "bands all playing, batteries all firing, flags all flying, and everybody voting everybody else in this army a hero." But Connolly was sick of the rice country. There was "as much difference between niggers on rice plantations and up-country ones," he said, "as there is between Negroes and baboons." On one plantation he saw "150 niggers, principally women and children, and nearly every one of them sick." Except for the rice, stacked up in straw, there was "not a mouthful for them to eat." Rice plantation Negroes, "scarcely a single remove from brutes," soon wore out their lives. But no wonder, he thought: "the Negroes are treated with just the same brutality as our army mules." What if one of them died? Profits were large, and "another can easily be bought." Wherever Connolly turned the problems of the Negroes confronted him:

Our horses and mules are living on rice straw, and the Lord only knows how the ten or twelve thousand fugitive Negroes within our lines are living, but they appear to be cheerful and happy, grinning and bowing to everybody; they are encamped all around . . . in squads of ten to a hundred; their little fires form a complete circle around our Head Quarters at night; I believe they have taken a fancy to our Head Quarters, for they come to us with their little complaints; get all waste victuals from our mess, and make their little camps as close to us as they dare; indeed the General lets them camp closer to our Head Quarters than he would like to have the soldiers;

they appear to shun Davis' Head Quarters though—they find no sympathy there.

The thought of Davis revived memories of the affair at "Ebenezar Causeway." Quietly Connolly reached a decision:

. . . I wrote out a rough draft of a letter today relative to Genl. Davis' treatment of the Negroes at Ebenezar Creek. I want the matter to get before the military committee of the Senate; it may give them some light in regard to the propriety of confirming him as a Brevet Major General. I am not certain yet who I had better send it to.

Sherman's impatience soon pricked his balloon-like exuberance over the capture of Fort McAllister. A meeting with Admiral Dahlgren on the *Harvest Moon* in Wassaw Sound completed the details by which the river could be cleared of torpedoes, and rations and guns of heavy caliber transported from Port Royal. The low country back of Savannah, "intersected with innumerable salt-water creeks, swamps, and ricefields," posed a problem that Sherman feared more than Hardee's troops inside the city, for if the winter rains set in, impassable roads would bog down the Union army. To Slocum and Howard fell the task of placing the siege guns in position to bombard Savannah, "and to prepare for the general assault." A wharf and depot at King's Bridge was ordered built, and the roads "leading thereto" corduroyed. Hardee occupied not only the city, but also the numerous forts guarding the approaches from the sea. But Hardee "could not have a garrison strong enough for all these purposes," and Sherman was determined "to break his line before he could receive reinforcements from Virginia or Augusta."

Then the army, after two months of being shut off from the world, received mail. Two of the letters for Sherman were from Grant in City Point. In the first, dated December 3, Grant said that "the little information gleaned from the

Southern press" indicated "no great obstacle to your progress," but he would refrain from rejoicing "until bottom
has been struck." Since Sherman had left Atlanta, Grant reported, "no very great progress has been made here"; Bragg
had gone to Wilmington, and Admiral Porter and Ben Butler
prepared to blow up Fort Fisher ("which, while hoping for the
best, I do not believe a particle in"). Grant wrote: "I do not
intend to give you any thing like directions for future action
. . . and will get your views after you have established yourself on the sea-coast." Almost boyishly, Grant concluded:

> After all becomes quiet, and roads become so bad up
> here that there is likely to be a week or two when nothing
> can be done, I will run down the coast to see you. If you
> desire it, I will ask Mrs. Sherman to go with me.

The second letter, dated December 6, stated Grant's conviction that "the most important operation toward closing out
the rebellion will be to close out Lee and his army," and included a paragraph that Sherman confessed "gave me great
uneasiness":

> My idea now is that you establish a base on the sea-
> coast, fortify and leave in it all your artillery and cavalry,
> and enough infantry to protect them, and at the same
> time so threaten the interior that the militia of the South
> will have to be kept at home. With the balance of your
> command come here by water with all dispatch. Select
> yourself the officer to leave in charge, but you I want in
> person. Unless you see objections to this plan which I can-
> not see, use every vessel going to you for purposes of trans-
> portation.

Sherman could see nothing but objections. Tactfully he responded: "I have initiated measures looking principally to
coming to you with fifty or sixty thousand infantry, and inci-
dentally to capture Savannah, if time will allow." The morale
of his army was fine; would it be the same after the voyage to

Virginia? "I had expected," Sherman wrote, "after reducing Savannah, instantly to march to Columbia, South Carolina; thence to Raleigh, and thence to report to you." Would the land route really take so much longer? Next day, December 18, Sherman dispatched an ultimatum to Hardee, asking for the unconditional surrender of Savannah:

> Should you entertain the proposition, I am prepared to grant liberal terms to the inhabitants and garrison; but should I be forced to resort to assault, or the slower or surer process of starvation, I shall then feel justified in resorting to the harshest measures, and shall make little effort to restrain my army—burning to avenge the national wrong which they attach to Savannah and other large cities which have been so prominent in dragging our country into civil war. . . .

Hardee replied that he neither believed Sherman controlled "every avenue by which the people and garrison can be supplied" nor that he had "received guns that can cast heavy and destructive shot into the heart of the city." Hardee refused to surrender, adding sinisterly: "I have hitherto conducted the military operations intrusted to my direction in strict accordance with the rules of civilized warfare, and I should deeply regret the adoption of any course by you that may force me to deviate from them in the future."

Hardee's bark proved more ferocious than his bite. On the morning of the 21st, when the skirmishers of the XXth Corps reached for the enemy's lines, they were empty. Quietly during the night, Hardee had slipped across the river on a pontoon bridge, "carrying off his men and light artillery, blowing up his iron-clads and navy-yard, but leaving us [Sherman said] the heavy guns, stores, cotton, railway-cars, steamboats, and an immense amount of public and private property." Next morning Sherman rode into Savannah, established his headquarters in the comfortable private residence of Charles

Green, and dispatched a telegram that soon would be quoted in city and hamlet throughout the North:

> Savannah, Georgia, *December* 22, 1864.
> *To His Excellency President* LINCOLN, *Washington, D.C.:*
> I beg to present you as a Christmas-gift the city of Savannah, with one hundred and fifty heavy guns and plenty of ammunition, also about twenty-five thousand bales of cotton.
>
> W. T. Sherman, *Major-General.*

James Austin Connolly marched into Savannah with the XXth Corps. Almost with electric speed, the word ran around the entire lines: "Savannah is evacuated." Soldiers who had wanted to sleep rolled out of their tents, "some dressed, and some *en deshabille*," shouting and hurrahing "from the bottom of their lungs." In a letter he asked his wife: "Are you busy celebrating the Union triumphs?" Wherever Connolly turned, he heard rumors that Jeff Davis was dead, and he could only comment: "If that is so, God has been good to him."

Affairs were taking a distinct turn for the better for Connolly. He regarded the war as ended, for Lee needed one more "good drubbing," and "either Grant or Sherman or both together will do it." The fugitive Negroes over which he had worried were marched to King's Bridge whence they would be shipped to Hilton Head, South Carolina. "It was a strange spectacle," he wrote, "to see those Negroes of all ages, sizes, and both sexes, with their bundles on their heads and in their hands trudging along, they knew not whither, but willing to blindly follow the direction given them by our officers." At least five thousand fugitives, he believed, had marched by his headquarters.

Connolly's report on the incident at "Ebenezar Causeway," finally addressed to the Congressman from his Illinois district, had been published, in substance, in the *New York Tribune* and had been forwarded to Secretary of War Stanton. Connolly had stirred up a hornet's nest. Halleck, who loved gossip, warned Sherman: ". . . a certain class having now great influence with the President . . . are . . . disposed to make a point against you . . . in regard to 'Inevitable Sambo.' " In annoyance, Sherman told Halleck that the matter was "humbug," that "Jeff C. Davis . . . took up his pontoon bridge, not because he wanted to leave them [the Negroes], but because he wanted his bridge," and with understandable relief Connolly wrote his wife:

> . . . My name is not connected with [the report] here, and I don't want it to be, unless the matter comes before the military committee of the Senate, and then I don't care, for I know all the officers whose names I have mentioned will corroborate my statements of fact.

Stanton appeared in Savannah. Sherman, unaware of how high the Abolitionists and the Radicals were riding in the North, would confess in his *Memoirs:*

> . . . The Negro question was beginning to loom up among the political eventualities of the day, and many foresaw that not only would the slaves secure their freedom, but that they would also have votes. I did not dream of such a result then . . . and did not suppose that the former slaves would be suddenly, without preparation, manufactured into voters, equal to all others, politically and socially. . . .

Stanton, courting favor with the Radicals, guardedly now but openly within a few months, asked for a meeting with the Negroes. Sherman arranged for "the most intelligent of the Negroes, mostly Baptist and Methodist preachers . . . to meet the Secretary of War," and George Ward Nichols commented:

> . . . With all due respect for the clerical profession, I doubt if twenty white ministers of the Gospel could have

been called out of one of our Northern cities (certainly not in the South) who could represent so much common sense and intelligence as these men. Nor would an average score of [white] clergymen present an array of nobler heads. In an artistic sense, the Negroes would certainly have the advantage of color.

It was a "singular interview," Nichols said. Stanton sat at a table, asking questions, noting the replies, and "now and then putting down his pen and adjusting his spectacles in a surprised way." Sherman stood "near the fireplace," occasionally walked "to and fro," or made "some pregnant suggestion." At first the questions Stanton asked touched general problems. The Negroes told him that "slavery is receiving by irresistible power the work of another man, and not by consent." The Negroes said they "would prefer to live by ourselves, for there is a prejudice against us in the South that will take years to get over." If the Rebel leaders were to arm the slaves, Stanton heard, "they would fight as long as they were before the 'bayonet,' and just as soon as they could get away they would desert." Keep the state agents at home, they counseled, and let Negroes enlist "for the United States under the direction of General Sherman." Nichols reported that Stanton felt the Negroes understood the "principles" of a question "as well as any member of the Cabinet."

But now the interview took a surprising turn. Stanton looked at Sherman. Would the general leave the room? The intention was obvious. Stunned, Sherman could only feel it "a strange fact" that the Secretary "should have catechized Negroes concerning the character of a general who had commanded a hundred thousand men in battle, had captured cities, conducted sixty-five thousand men successfully across four hundred miles of hostile territory, and had just brought tens of thousands of freedmen to a place of security." Sherman withdrew from the room, but his heart seethed. Because he had "not loaded down [the] army by other hundreds of thousands of poor Negroes" he was being construed "as hostile to the black race"! Halleck had warned him about this! The fools in Washington were bending the President's ear, accusing him, Sherman, of having "manifested an almost *criminal* dislike to the Negro," saying he should "have brought . . . to Savannah fifty thousand more" slaves instead of driving them from his ranks, "cutting the bridges," and causing "the massacre of large numbers by Wheeler's cavalry"! So Stanton believed this? It would benefit the Secretary, then, to listen to the Negroes who "understood their own interests far better than did the men in Washington, who tried to make political capital out of this Negro question." God save Lincoln, surrounded by "the influences that poison a political capital," men who would "torture his life by suspicions of the officers who were toiling with the single purpose to bring the war to a successful end, and thereby to liberate *all* slaves." Sherman could state succinctly, for Mr. Stanton or Mr. Lincoln, what his aim was:

> . . . to whip the rebels, to humble their pride, to follow them to their innermost recesses, and make them fear and dread us. . . . [But] I did not want them to cast in our teeth what General Hood had once done in Atlanta, that we had called on their *slaves* to help us to subdue them. . . .

With General Sherman out of the room, the Secretary of War asked a single question:

> State what is the feeling of the colored people toward General Sherman, and how far do you regard his sentiments and actions as friendly to their rights and interests, or otherwise?

The Negro clergymen answered Stanton gravely:

> We looked upon General Sherman, prior to his arrival, as a man, in the providence of God, specially set aside to accomplish this work, and we unanimously felt inexpres-

sible gratitude to him, looking upon him as a man who should be honored for the faithful performance of his duty. Some of us called upon him immediately upon his arrival, and it is probable he did not meet the secretary with more courtesy than he did us. His conduct and deportment toward us characterized him as a friend and gentleman. We have confidence in General Sherman, and think what concerns us could not be in better hands. This is our opinion now, from the short acquaintance and intercourse we have had.

To Halleck on this day of humiliation Sherman would write: "The South deserves all she has got for her injustice to the Negro, but that is no reason why we should go to the other extreme." Sherman detested the State recruiting agents; he neither wanted his pioneer corps disrupted nor to play into the hands of the Radicals. "During Mr. Stanton's stay in Savannah we discussed this Negro question very fully," Sherman said, and the result of these conferences was the issuance of a mutually agreed-upon field order, providing areas "reserved and set apart for the settlement of the Negroes now made free by acts of war and the proclamation of the President of the United States," stating that "the Negro is free, and must be dealt with as such," and that "young and able-bodied Negroes must be encouraged to enlist as soldiers in the service of the United States, to contribute their share toward maintaining their own freedom," but Federal and not State officers would handle the bounties for such enlistments. A plan of homesteading was established, "whenever three respectable Negroes, heads of families, shall desire to settle on land" and "the islands from Charleston south, the abandoned rice-fields along the rivers for thirty miles back from the sea" in addition to the "country bordering the St. John's River, Florida" would be reserved for this purpose with the understanding that no family plot should exceed forty acres nor "more than eight hundred feet water-front."

Whereas Stanton appeared "robust and strong," Sherman said that the Secretary "complained a good deal of internal pains" threatening "his life" and compelling "him soon to quit public life." Sherman reported that Stanton

> . . . spoke unreservedly of the bickerings and jealousies at the national capital; of the interminable quarrels of the State Governors about their quotas, and more particularly of the financial troubles that threatened the very existence of the Government itself. He said that the price of everything had so risen in comparison with the depreciated money, that there was danger of national bankruptcy, and he appealed to me, as a soldier and patriot, to hurry up matters so as to bring the war to a close.

In the estimation of Secretary of Navy Gideon Welles, Sherman had become "the favored general . . . supposed to have eclipsed Grant." For thirty-two days the North, worried and fretful, had wondered where Sherman had gone, and Lincoln, addressing Congress on December 6, could say nothing concrete, for he had been as much in ignorance of Sherman's whereabouts as anyone else. Then Sherman had sent the President his Christmas gift: the news that Sherman had reached Savannah brought a joyous outburst, and soon even the song pluggers of the North were busy producing *Sherman's on the Track.* A popular verse ran:

> The railroads hab been torn to smash,
> De lockies cannot run,
> Old Hood has got his boiler bust,
> And dat hab stopt *his* fun,
> Poor Beauregard *lies* berry sick,
> Wid rupture and wid gout,
> While Bobby Lee begins to see,
> De game am most played out.

In the cafés and saloons singing waiters extolled Sherman as "de doctor man away from Tennessee" who would see that

277

"Massa's goin' to die" and who would "knock de breff from poor old Jeff." *Marching through Georgia* became part of the nation's folklore, and one Southern historian would observe with asperity that this poem "we learn by evidence, was a favorite canticle of Murray the kidnapper and butcher of captive Polynesians."

Outwardly Sherman might enjoy the quiet behavior of Savannah—"an old place, and usually accounted a handsome one"—and half a century hence Savannah Negroes might date events by the "time when Tecumpsey was here," but the journal of Fanny Cohen Taylor revealed the derisive scorn often underlying this beguiling composure. On the "saddest Christmas that I have ever spent," Fanny noted:

> . . . my only pleasure . . . has been in looking forward to spending my next Christmas in the Confederacy. This morning my uncle . . . told us of a party given the evening before by the Negroes of Genl. Geary's Hd Qrts when the Gen went into the kitchen and desired an introduction to the *ladies* and *gentlemen* there assembled. . . . he asked who were slaves and who were free. There was but one slave present, a servant girl of my Aunt's, who acknowledged the fact. This elegant gentleman enquired into her private history and finding that she was a married woman . . . presented [her husband], as a Christmas gift, with a *free wife*. The girl was so much amused, having always been a favorite servant and treated like one of the family, that she told it to her mistress as a good joke. In the afternoon we had a real *rebel* meeting. . . . We abused the Yankees to our hearts' content and congratulated ourselves on being once more together. Dr R—— told of a newspaper that had been issued, called *The Loyal Georgian** with this Motto: "Redeemed, re-

---

* Three issues of *The Loyal Georgian* were published. In addition to reporting the war news from a Northern bias the paper featured such items as the opening in Savannah of a Union barber shop. Obviously the editor felt that Yankee throats ran less chance of a slashing there.

generated and disenthralled—the Union must and shall
be preserved." This of course created great merriment,
the first time I had a hearty laugh since the Goths had
been among us.

Doubtless Sherman felt pleasure in reading *The Loyal
Georgian,* and with the problems the occupation of Savannah
brought him, perhaps he could be forgiven for finding such
respite as he could. Among the first of Sherman's headaches,
Nichols reported, were the Northern speculators, who, running the blockade, wanted to pick up a quick fortune. "You
have come to the wrong place, gentlemen," Nichols quoted the
general as saying—unless, of course, they wished to be "put
in the guard house." Nichols chuckled at the hustle of the
speculators in getting out of Savannah. As the roadside philosopher would have said, a man could have played dominoes
on their flying coat-tails.

One of the prizes of war in Savannah which had brought
Stanton on the run from Washington had been cotton worth
thirteen million dollars. Sherman's attitude toward cotton
would be stated on January 15, 1865, in response to "Resolutions of Chamber of Commerce" concerning the disposition of
this captured horde. The general said:

. . . The sooner all the cotton in the South is burned
up, the sooner will the people of the South come to their
senses. The outside world has nothing to do with it, for it
is reduced to a simple question of war, which was chosen
by the South, and the issues accepted by us. When war is
done we can soon bring order out of chaos and prosperity
out of misery and destruction. Let it be clearly understood
throughout the land that war means misery, ruin, starvation, and pestilence, and the sooner will the deluded
planters and people of the South realize how much better
it would have been for them to appeal to the tribunes of
Law and Justice instead of the armed tortures of war.

279

Part Five: "AND MAKE GEORGIA HOWL"

When Anthony Barclay of the British Consul claimed part of the cotton in Savannah, Sherman damned the English smuggling of cotton to the West Indies and told Barclay that "it would afford me great satisfaction to conduct an army to Nassau and wipe out that nest of pirates." To Halleck he wrote: "Neither cotton, the Negro, nor a single interest should govern us."

Sherman's temper was growing distinctly short. Savannah —or was it speculators, Stanton, Negroes, and cotton?—had begun to fray his nerves. Anyhow, he was ready to move on. To Halleck, on the day before Christmas, he confessed what was in his mind:

> . . . this war differs from European wars in this particular: we are not only fighting hostile armies, but a hostile people, and must make old and young, rich and poor, feel the hard hand of war. . . . I know that this recent movement of mine through Georgia has had a wonderful effect in this respect . . . and before we have done with her South Carolina will not be quite so tempestuous.

Flattering though Grant's suggestion might be, that he didn't feel so confident of whipping Lee as he would with Sherman in Virginia, to Halleck Sherman would admit:

> . . . The truth is, the whole army is burning with an insatiable desire to wreak vengeance upon South Carolina. I almost tremble at her fate, but feel that she deserves all that seems in store for her.
>
> Many and many a person in Georgia asked me why we did not go to South Carolina: and, when I answered that we were *en route* for that State, the invariable reply was, "Well, if you will make those people feel the utmost severities of war, we will pardon you for your desolation of Georgia."

Archly to "Old Brains," Sherman could remark: "I look upon Columbia as quite as bad as Charleston, and I doubt if we shall spare the public buildings there as we did at Milledgeville."

Ben Butler, supported by a fleet under Porter, had tried to take Fort Fisher at Wilmington, North Carolina, and failed, not to the surprise of Halleck, who said: "I had nothing to do with it, except to express the opinion that Butler's torpedo ship would have as much effect on the forts as if he should —— at them." Grant sent Butler back to Massachusetts, where Sherman believed he could accomplish more confining "his bellicose operations to the factory girls," and on the 15th of January Fort Fisher fell to Major General A. H. Terry. In Sherman's proposed march north, only Wilmington and Fort Fisher had threatened the delay of a siege by land and sea. Freed of this possible obstacle, already informed by Grant that

> . . . I did think the best thing to do was to bring the greater part of your army here, and wipe out Lee. . . . I doubt whether you may not accomplish more toward that result where you are than if brought here. . . .

Sherman now could go as he wished. On the 21st of January he left Savannah by steamer. He seemed worried by the fact that:

> . . . Somehow, our men had got the idea that South Carolina was the cause of all our trouble; her people was the first to fire on Fort Sumter, had been in a great hurry to precipitate the country into civil war; and therefore on them should fall the scourge of war in its worst form. Taunting messages had also come to us, when in Georgia, to the effect that, when we should reach South Carolina, we would find a people less passive, who would fight us to the bitter end, daring us to come over, etc.; so that I saw

and felt that we would not be able longer to restrain **our** men as we had done in Georgia.

If Sherman squirmed under these uneasy premonitions, history would justify his restlessness.

PART SIX

✳✳✳✳✳✳✳✳✳✳✳✳✳✳✳✳✳✳✳✳✳✳✳✳✳✳✳✳✳✳✳✳✳✳

The General Reaches Hell

— the sack and burning of Columbia

1. "THE STATE THEY HATE MOST"

Wⁱᵗʰ Sherman in Savannah, few heads rested easily throughout South Carolina. Cavalry General Kilpatrick—his own men now called him Kill-Cavalry—openly boasted to the troops of the 2nd Minnesota: "There'll be damn little for you infantrymen to destroy after I've passed through that hellhole of secession." From the Savannah River to the Peedee every home shrank from the stored-up fury that Sherman's swaggering, triumphant mood threatened; tight-lipped, nervous, and unhappy, South Carolinians believed that no family or no principle of decency would be secure under the reign of the redheaded, redbearded general who once had gloated that he would "bring every Southern woman to the washtub." In Columbia, South Carolina, a seventeen-year-old girl wrote in her journal as 1864 drew to a dreary, heartbreaking close:

> . . . They are planning to hurl destruction upon the State they hate most of all, and Sherman the brute avows his intention of converting South Carolina into a wilderness.

Throughout January the feeling of impending disaster changed from wild rumor into the acute physical constriction of personal dread. Everywhere in South Carolina the belief was rampant, as the same seventeen-year-old diarist would testify, that Sherman's "licentious troops—whites and Negroes—shall be turned loose to ravage and violate." Even the debonair Mary Boykin Chestnut felt her courage ebbing and on January 14th confessed: "Yesterday I broke down and gave way to abject terror under the news of Sherman's advance." Men, women, and children trembled before the doom hanging over them, and in the Executive Department at Charleston Judge A. G. Magrath, whom, Mrs. Chestnut said, had been painted five years earlier in the awesome act of "tearing off his robes of office in rage and disgust at Lincoln's election," now penned a blunt letter to Jefferson Davis. Charleston must be defended to the last extremity, the judge insisted, or all was lost—Augusta and Macon, Columbus and Columbia, even Richmond. Magrath asked:

> . . . How under this torrent of disaster can confidence be retained? How can hope be preserved? In every state the paralysis of fear will be felt. . . . A chill will attend every effort, with which in vain you will attempt to remove or dispel the gloom. . . .

With all of the calamities that had befallen the Confederacy, Magrath wrote, the South was not yet physically overcome, "but we are morally so in a greater degree."

In Columbia on the 17th of January the streets swarmed with "troopless generals"—Joe Johnston, Lovell, Governor Manning. Among the church-goers that Sabbath was Mrs. Chestnut, who remembered that during the service "a great railroad character was called out. He soon returned and whispered something to Joe Johnston, and they went out together. Somehow the whisper moved around to us. 'Sherman is at Branchville.'"

Nerves already tauntened were twisted anew. With Sherman at Branchville, straddling the Charleston and Savannah Railroad, the Union troops had reached a point sixty-five miles equidistant from Charleston, Augusta, and Columbia. The normal expectation, clearly revealed in Magrath's letter to Davis, was that Sherman's "Hellhounds" first would turn their wrath on noble old Charleston as the cradle of the Confederacy, for here in St. Andrews Hall amid the ringing of church bells on a crisp December evening in 1860 the state's new "sovereign" convention by a vote of 169 Yeas to 0 Nays had declared that "the union now subsisting between South Carolina and other states, under the name of 'The United States of America,' is hereby dissolved." In a strict sense, secession had been conceived three days earlier when the convention had met in the Baptist Church in Columbia, but the delegates had no more than appointed a committee to draft an Ordinance of Secession when a threatened outbreak of smallpox hastened their departure to Charleston—a perfect demonstration, Mrs. Chestnut observed, of how "men, who are all, like Governor Pickens, 'insensible to fear,' are very sensible in case of smallpox."

Among the cities of the South, many believed that next to Richmond and Charleston, Columbia must be defended. As Sherman thrust forward into South Carolina, Columbia had become a city of refugees with a population more than double its normal ten thousand and with less than one man for every forty women. To William Gilmore Simms, in whom the South took pride as a novelist and a poet second only to Edgar Allan Poe, these circumstances were entirely comprehensible: "Young women of family were sent in large numbers to a city where numbers seemed to promise a degree of security not to be hoped for in any obscure rural abode." The faith in Columbia's safety had grown so firm that all the banks of Charleston had been removed to there; and there also, Simms said, "was to be found an accumulation of wealth, in plate, jewels, pictures, books, manufacture of art and *virtu*, not to be estimated—not, perhaps to be paralleled—in any other town of the Confederacy."

But Sherman by now had learned not to ignore the obvious, and, pausing at Branchville, calculated other features that distinguished Columbia—its abundance of manufactures, the Confederate Treasury, the connecting rail lines on which

Lee's army and Richmond must depend. If there was any decision to make, Sherman quickly reached it. Columbia was a ripe plum dangling on a limb and begging to be plucked.

2. "I LOOK FORWARD WITH TERROR"

FOR Emma Florence LeConte the four long years of war that had begun when she was thirteen could be reduced to a single bitter sentence: "No pleasure, no enjoyment—nothing but rigid economy and hard work—nothing but the stern realities of life." For Emma this statement was only partly true, for early in the war she had known moments of gayety and lightheartedness. As long as the girl lived, each 13th of April would turn her mind back to 1861 and the first Fort Sumter Day:

> . . . The joy—the excitement—how well I remember it. For weeks we had been in a fever of excitement. On the day the news came of the fall of Sumter we were all sitting in the library at Uncle John's. The bell commenced to ring. At the first tap we knew the joyful tidings had come. Father and Uncle John made a dash for their hats—Jule and Johnny followed. We women ran trembling to the verandah—to the front gate, eagerly asking news of the passers-by. The whole town was in a joyful tumult. . . .

Now, just short of four years later, a dreadful change had come; Georgia had been desolated, boys of sixteen conscripted, and the South starved by its own speculators and extortioners. With Lee losing ground in Virginia, with Hood defeated in detail in Tennessee, any hope that remained was not for victory on the battlefield, but for an honorably negotiated peace.

Even that hope seemed woefully scant to Emma, since "a sea rolls between them and us—a sea of blood." With the march to the sea the Yankees had widened the breach between North and South by a thousand new atrocities, so that submission became unthinkable. Passionately, the girl confided to her journal: "Smoking houses, outraged women, murdered fathers, brothers and husbands forbid such a union!" The crimes charged against Sherman impressed Emma as crimes against human decency: "Poor Aunt Sallie suffered dreadfully, and her babe was born dead—the result of the fright she experienced when the enemy passed through Milledgeville."

Emma's decision to keep a journal had helped to ease days not only filled with apprehension and struggle, but also with loneliness. Her father, a professor of chemistry at the State College in Columbia, now worked as a consulting chemist for the Confederate States Nitre and Mining Bureau and often was forced to be away from home. With the outbreak of the war South Carolina College had volunteered almost to a boy, and the buildings on the campus, where Emma lived, had been converted into a Confederate hospital zone. No matter where the girl turned the suffering of the war surrounded her. Living out the diffiicult weeks of January and February in a household of women, there crossed Emma's mind many thoughts much better left unspoken. The pages of her neatly written journal became her refuge. Here she could speak as she pleased, sometimes angry with those who lost heart, sometimes agonized by the danger her father faced on his trips, but more often simply the honest, bewildered girl who had seen "so little of the exuberant joy that people talk about as the natural heritage of youth."

I am constantly thinking of the time when Columbia will be given up to the enemy [Emma confessed to her journal on the 4th of January]. The horrible picture is constantly before my mind. . . . Mother wants to send me off, but of course I would not leave her. I can only hope that their conduct in the city will not be so shocking as it has been through the country. Yet no doubt the college buildings will be burned, with other public buildings, and we will at least lose our home.

Later in the month Emma decided: "Now that everything is lost perhaps we will all have to work for a living before long," but Emma much preferred this alternative to buckling under to the Yankees! Hardship and privation were scarcely unique bedfellows in most Columbia households. Emma's underclothing was of even coarser unbleached homespun than she once had given to the Negroes, and she knitted her own stockings and wore shoes of heavy calfskin. With calico selling at sixteen dollars a yard, she could feel fortunate in possessing two calico dresses to piece out a wardrobe of "a homespun of black and white plaid, and an old delaine of prewar times that hangs on in a dilapidated condition, a reminiscence of better days." Happily, she still owned a couple of old silks, "carefully preserved for great occasions and which do not look too shabby for the simple reason that all the other silks that survive the war are in the same state of decay."

Mealtime, especially when Emma must plan the menu, tested the girl's fortitude. The family ate twice a day. Two plates of bread made a good breakfast; for dinner, a very small piece of meat, usually beef, a few potatoes, a dish of hominy, and a pone of corn bread was nourishing if monotonous. The only fire in the house burned in the dining room where the family gathered, but at a hundred dollars a load every stick of wood deserved its own blessing. "We have no reason to complain," Emma scolded herself. "So many families are so much worse off." And she thought of the homes where there hadn't been a taste of meat for months, or of the few families who, like her own, had a cow and could make butter.

Damp, dismal, and chilly, January crept through its apportioned days; some nights a haze hung over the moon, on others the creaking of the branches in the night winds gave a moaning uneasiness to the long hours. Then it was the 14th of February, St. Valentine's Day, a day for a seventeen-year-old girl to blush and to toss her head and to find hidden meaning in a shy masculine smile, but for Emma St. Valentine's Day in '65 stood apart:

What a panic the whole town is in! I have not been out of the house myself, but Father says the intensest excitement prevails on the street. The Yankees are reported a few miles off on the other side of the river. How strong no one seems to know. . . . It is thought Columbia can hardly be taken by raid as we have the whole of Butler's cavalry here—and if they do we have to take the consequences. It is true some think Sherman will burn the town, but we can hardly believe that. Besides these buildings [at the College], though they are State property, yet the fact that they are used as a hospital will, it is thought, protect them. I have been busily making large pockets to wear under my hoopskirt—they will hardly search our persons.

Emma did not feel so frightened as she thought she might. Were the Yankees really coming? "I hope still this is a false alarm," she said, giving away her secret fear. She reached out toward Maggie Adams and her husband, who had promised to stay with the LeContes. Since Maggie was a Yankee, Emma thought, she "may be some protection or help." The girl struggled against the disquieting apprehension that kept needling her mind like a persistent debt:

. . . Alas, what may we have gone through by the end of this week! I look forward with terror, and yet with a kind of callousness to their approach.

3. "THE ALARM BELL IS RINGING"

STEADILY Sherman and his armies drove through the most highly improved and cultivated region of South Carolina—through Hardeeville, Grahamville, Gillisonville, McPhersonville, Barnwell [which the Yankees renamed Burnwell], Blackwell, Midway, Orangeburg, and Lexington—a path of eighty miles wrought with flame. Like a god of vengeance, Sherman came on, relentlessly determined that the state that had bred secession should now get "a bellyful of war," and the black smoke and the gray ashes marking his way became the symbols of the gospel he had set out to preach: "Fear is the beginning of wisdom." As Connolly marched past the magnolias and cypress, those bleak February days, he would feel the men "had it in" for South Carolina.

So, too, would Alabama-born Henry Hitchcock, riding at Sherman's elbow, who would sneer: "Of all the mean humbugs, South Carolina Chivalry is the meanest." And Chaplain John J. Hight of the 58th Indiana would think: "Poor South Carolina must suffer now. None of the soldiers are storing up mercy for her. Her deluded people will . . . reap the full reward of all their folly and crimes." Kilpatrick, the chaplain said, "fitted all the boys' saddlebags with matches before leaving Savannah." As the army marched on, Chaplain Hight testified: "Sometimes the world seemed on fire. We were almost stifled by smoke and flames."

The portents of Sherman's ruthless advance mounted hourly in Columbia. To William Gilmore Simms the devil had crossed the Styx and marched with sixty thousand fallen angels. Old Simms raised his square jaw, his dark, deepset eyes snapped angrily, and he wrote as though every chigger in South Carolina had bored into his hide:

Day by day brought to the people of Columbia tidings of atrocities committed, and more extended progress.

Daily did long trains of fugitives line the roads, with wives and children, and horses and stock and cattle, seeking refuge from the pursuers. Long lines of wagons covered the highways. Half naked people cowered from the winter under bush tents in the thickets, under the eaves of the houses, under the railroad sheds, and in old cars left them along the route. All these repeated the same story of suffering, violence, poverty and nakedness. Habitation after habitation, village after village—one sending up its flames to the other, presaging for it the same fate—lighted the winter midnight sky with crimson horror.

Simms penned prose that somehow fitted his finely shaped head, his curly white hair, and his soft, graceful beard. The sights that Simms saw wrung his heart:

Granaries were emptied, and where the grain was not carried off, it was strewn to waste under the feet of the cavalry or consigned to the fire which consumed the dwelling. The Negroes were robbed equally with the whites of food and clothing. The roads were covered with butchered cattle, hogs, mules, and the costliest furniture. Valuable cabinets, rich pianos were not only hewn to pieces, but bottles of ink, turpentine, oil, whatever could efface or destroy, was employed to defile.

With every vault in Columbia almost bursting with treasure, the city trembled. Nothing appeared sacred to Sherman's crowd—that much Simms could tell his fellow townsmen with a rising rage:

The beautiful homesteads of the parish country, with their wonderful tropical gardens, were ruined; ancient dwellings of black cypress, one hundred years old, which had been reared by the fathers of the Republic— men whose names were famous in the Revolutionary history—were given to the torch as recklessly as were the rude hovels; choice pictures and works of art, from Europe, select and numerous libraries, objects of peace wholly, were all destroyed. The inhabitants, black no less than white, were left to starve, compelled to feed only on the garbage to be found in the abandoned camps of the soldiers.

Thus, plundering and burning, Simms saw the Yankees approach Columbia. The havoc Sherman wrought became complete: "Every implement of the worker, tools, plows, hoes, gins, looms, wagons, vehicles, was made to feel the flames." Everyone in Columbia knew and loved Simms; anything "Gilmer" wrote received wide circulation. But at that moment Columbia hardly needed Simms to explain that it had become a city gripped with panic. Fear touched the deepening lines in every face and haunted the darkening splotches under many pairs of eyes. Fear crept into every tale of atrocity that was told and retold, magnified and distorted until soon nothing—or anything—seemed believable. Fear shared the hollow of the pillow where Emma LeConte pressed her head on the morning of February 15.

That morning a terrific explosion shook the city. In every house, in every store and office and factory, in every street and alley, people stopped. For one terrible instant all of Columbia seemed to have lost its heartbeat. But the explosion, which wrecked the railroad depot, had been accidental. Negroes and whites alike scrambled into the smoldering wreckage to carry off bags of grain and meal, adding to the confusion of the crowds jamming the streets and roads in search of any avenue of escape. "How is it possible to write amid this excitement?" Emma asked her journal. With every conveyance the government could muster, warehouses, granaries, and ammunition depots were being emptied. "All day the trains have been running, whistles blowing and wagons rattling through the streets," Emma said. Although the LeConte home on the campus was too far off from the scene of this activity for the girl to see or to hear much, her journal reflected the mounting tension:

> . . . All day we have been listening to the booming of cannon—receiving conflicting reports of the fighting. All day wagons and ambulances have been bringing in the wounded over the muddy streets and through the drizzling rain, with the dark gloomy clouds overhead. . . .

With open trunks standing about and clothing strewn everywhere, the LeConte back parlor belonged to the "general feeling of misery" that "pervaded the atmosphere." "Everything is to go that can be sent," Emma said, running down the list in her own mind: house-linen, blankets, clothing, silver, jewelry, even the wine. The house was as cold as a barn, for the LeContes were without wood with no prospect of securing any since "the country people will not venture in town lest their horses should be impressed." Shivering, Emma tried to coax a handful of wet pine to burn.

Night closed in. Emma, back writing in her journal with a dogged resolution, realized how much nearer, how much more distinctly the cannon sounded. "It is heart-sickening to listen to it," she thought. For two or three hours after dinner the cannonade ceased, and hope stirred the pound of almost every heart. Abruptly, the hope ended, and with a bitter resignation Emma continued writing: ". . . the same sounds, with the roar of musketry, break upon us—frightfully near and sounding above the din of a tumultuous town and above the rattling carts. . . ." Then:

> . . . The alarm bell is ringing. Just now when I first heard it clang out my heart gave a leap, and I thought at once, "It's the Yankees!" So nervous have I grown that the slightest unusual sound startles me. Of course I knew it was a fire, yet it was with a beating heart I threw open the window to see the western horizon lit up with the glow of flames. Although we are composed, our souls are sick with anxiety.

If it were true that the approaching enemy was one of Sherman's corps, what resistance could the Confederates offer with a handful of troops under Wade Hampton? Emma sniffed. Wade Hampton! Everyone seemed to have forgotten now that the old general's wounds at Manassas and Chickahominy had made him a hero. Hampton called himself the special defender of South Carolina, but the brutal truth remained that Hampton wouldn't have been in Columbia if he hadn't come home in a huff after a row with Lee! Naturally no South Carolinian would agree with Sherman on anything, and least of all with his characterization of Wade Hampton as a worthless "braggart," but Emma, facing the situation honestly, could wish: "If Cheatham's corps could only come! Beauregard said he was expecting it in thirteen hours, and that was about 2 p.m. They therefore should be here early tomorrow morning—will they come?"

But Emma must have known that Cheatham's corps would never arrive. By coming to Branchville where the Federals could turn to Charleston or Augusta or Columbia, Sherman had executed a wily move. Hardee had dug in at Charleston on the assumption that he must bear the brunt of Sherman's assault, and now Hardee and the twelve thousand troops he could muster were of less interest than last month's headlines. Likewise the Rebel forces in Augusta had sat tight, believing that they were Sherman's objective, and there they could sit, as far as Sherman cared, throughout eternity. Sherman's grin was almost visible behind the lines he wrote in his *Memoirs:*

> . . . So they abandoned poor Columbia to the care of Hampton's cavalry, which was confused by the rumors that poured in on it, so that both Beauregard and Wade Hampton, who were in Columbia, seemed to have lost their heads.

However, in Columbia that night one realistic military mind existed. The Kentuckian was named Davis, and Emma's father had met him during his travels for the Confederate

States Nitre and Mining Bureau. To Joseph LeConte a puzzling air of mystery surrounded the Kentuckian:

> Mr. Davis (so he calls himself) is certainly a queer fellow. This companion whom we have picked up is quick, ready-witted, his senses all awake, and yet *apparently* open and frank. Though so young—only twenty, he says—he has evidently seen much of the world. . . . Sister thinks he is a Yankee spy. *He* says he is a Confederate spy—that he is a Kentuckian, a member of Lewis's Kentucky cavalry brigade—that he fought the Yankees all through Georgia with Wheeler. As we pass along from time to time he points out places of desperate conflict; yonder, under that tree, he killed a Yankee in self-defense; here he made a narrow escape.

Sleep had become impossible for Emma. When she came downstairs she "found in the back parlor with father a man calling himself Davis." The Kentuckian baffled Emma; she considered him both "coarse and uneducated, but wonderfully keen and penetrating." Davis liked to read characters; he was quite amusing at it. Anyone with a pair of eyes could see that the Kentuckian had taken "an unaccountable fancy" to Joseph LeConte; and although Davis tried to keep the evening light-hearted with his character-reading, he would break off "again and again" to assure Emma's father "that he will have us protected during the presence of the Yankees here." Suspicion rooted in the girl's mind. Why was he so uneasy because Joseph LeConte had not yet departed? Why did he continue to urge her father to go, even offering to lend him a horse? And how could he know "more than the generals"?

At last Davis won his point; Joseph LeConte embraced his wife and daughter and fled into the night. Emma could not sleep and she wanted to be sure her father "was safely off." Alone now with the Kentuckian, she tried to prod something tangible from him. How did she think Columbia would be treated? Davis looked down at the girl. A long moment passed between them. His eyes may have been tender or cautious; it was difficult to tell. Then he shook his head. Why should he alarm her unnecessarily? Irritated, Emma thought: "Does he really know, or is he only pretending?" Her journal said further:

> . . . It was three o'clock before I lay down and fell into a disturbed doze which lasted till seven. Davis stayed and slept on the ground floor, but he was gone before we awoke.

Where had he gone?

4. "WITH LOATHING AND DISGUST"

THE morning of the 16th brought to South Carolina one of those February days that can be clear, crisp, and brittle. The LeConte women huddled together on the piazza watching a brigade of cavalry passing to the front; they resembled the tableau of a compact family group united against the world. Inside in the dining room a sparse fire fluttered cheerlessly on the grate. As they adjourned to its pale warmth their spirits were low, and someone said: "Wouldn't it be dreadful if they should shell the city?"

Emma's mother answered reasonably: "They would not do that, for they have not demanded its surrender."

Jane, the nurse, rushed in crying that the city *was* being shelled. With Jane and Mrs. LeConte, Emma ran to the front door "just in time to hear a shell whirring past. It fell and exploded not far off." Emma remembered that

> . . . I leaned against the door, fairly shivering, partly with cold, but chiefly from nervous excitement. . . . They were shelling the town from the Lexington heights across the river, and from the campus their troops could

be seen drawn up on the hill-tops. . . . The shelling was discontinued for an hour or two and then renewed with so much fury that we unanimously resolved to adjourn to the basement and abandon the upper rooms. . . . I was standing at my bureau with my arms full when I heard a loud report. The shell whistled right over my head and exploded. I stood breathless, really expecting to see it fall in the room.

Across the Congaree River, Sherman wondered what his artillerymen expected to achieve. With long, impatient strides, his cigar lit on one puff and unlit on the next, he pounced upon Captain DeGres, who had a section of twenty-pound Parrott guns unlimbered. Why all this damn racket? The town spread before them, flat and unimpressive except for the unfinished edifice of the State Capitol. DeGres stood his ground. He could see Rebel cavalry at the intersections of the streets. The idea obsessed him that a large force of Confederate infantry were concealed on the opposite bank. Sherman sighed tolerantly. He had never heard more nonsense. Below him the Congaree foamed with the yellow mud that lined its banks and river bed. That yellow foam threatened to be more of a hazard than any of Wade Hampton's graybacks. Still, he permitted DeGres to pound a few more shells into the smoldering ruins of the railroad depot "to scare away the Negroes who were appropriating the bags of corn and meal which we wanted," and, as a kind of consolation prize, to burst three shells into the unoccupied State House.

Davis, who had left the LeConte house with the first streaks of dawn, now returned with the falling shells. "He stood talking to me in the dining room," Emma wrote in her journal, "giving me a picture of the confusion up town. Our soldiers had opened and plundered some of the stores. He brought me a present of a box of fancy feathers and one or two other little things he had picked up." The bridge would be burned and the town evacuated that night, the Kentuckian believed.

If Davis's knowledge of coming events seemed somewhat infuriating, since he really explained nothing, no one could deny that he possessed the same prescience for appearing when most needed. Night came on, and at ten o'clock Emma had returned to writing in her journal, making a special note of the time as though emphasizing the fact that while the rest of the family slept, or pretended to sleep, slumber was out of the question for her. Once more Davis called from downstairs. The girl ordered the servant to light the gas in the hall, while "through the open door came the shouts of the soldiery drawn up along the streets ready to march out." With Wade Hampton's boys quitting without a fight, would the Yankees be in tonight? But she could honestly tell Davis: "I do not feel as frightened as I thought I would."

That night Sherman slept across the river from Columbia near an old prison bivouac the Yankees had named "Camp Sorghum." Here the general who had come into South Carolina "to vindicate the just powers of a government which received terrible insults at the hands of the people of that state," could see the mud hovels and the holes in the ground which the Federal captives had fashioned as shelters against the penetrating cold of winter and the sweltering heat of summer. Sherman wrapped up against the chill darkness, his mind at ease. Just above the corporate limits of Columbia the Broad and Saluda rivers joined to form the Congaree, on which the city stood, and his troops covered every strategic point. The XVth Corps was then ahead, reaching to the Broad River four miles above Columbia; the XVIth Corps camped on the Congaree, opposite the city; and the left wing and the cavalry had swung north toward Alston.

Daylight filtered through the low-hung clouds. Sherman rode to the head of Howard's column, found that during the night Howard had ordered Stone's Brigade of Woods' division of the XVth Corps ferried across the river by rafts, and watched this brigade deployed on the opposite bank covering the construction of a pontoon bridge. Sherman recalled:

I sat with General Howard on a log, watching the men lay the bridge; and about 9 or 10 a.m. a messenger came from Colonel Stone on the other side, saying that the Mayor of Columbia had come out of the city to surrender the place, and asking for orders. I simply remarked to General Howard that he had his orders, to let Colonel Stone go into the city, and that we would follow as soon as the bridge was ready.

By this same messenger I received a note in pencil from the Lady Superioress of a convent or school in Columbia, in which she claimed to have been a teacher in a convent in Brown County, Ohio, at the time my daughter Minnie was a pupil there, and therefore asking special protection. My recollection is, that I gave the note to my brother-in-law, Colonel Ewing, then inspector-general on my staff, with instructions to see this lady, and assure her that we contemplated no destruction of private property in Columbia at all.

Mayor T. J. Goodwyn surrendered the city to Colonel Stone, and, according to Simm's account, Stone assured Goodwyn "of the safety of the citizens and of the protection of their property, while under his command." Simm's implication is obvious: even Stone would not assume responsibility for what might happen once Sherman crossed the river. Sherman detailed the precise circumstances under which he arrived soon afterwards, in Columbia:

As soon as the bridge was done, I led my horse over it, followed by my whole staff. General Howard accompanied me with his, and General Logan was next in order, followed by General C. R. Woods, and the whole of the Fifteenth Corps. Ascending the hill, we soon emerged into a broad road leading into Columbia, between old fields of corn and cotton, and, entering the city, we found seemingly all the population, white and black, in the streets. A high and boisterous wind was prevailing from the north, and flakes of cotton were flying about in the air and lodging in the limbs of the trees, reminding us of a Northern snowstorm.

Near the market-square we found Stone's brigade halted, with arms stacked, and a large detail of his men, along with some citizens, engaged with an old fire-engine, trying to put out the fire in a long pile of cotton-bales, which I was told had been fired by the Rebel cavalry on withdrawing from the city that morning. I know that, to avoid this row of burning cotton-bales, I had to ride my horse on the sidewalk. In the market-square had collected an immense crowd of whites and blacks, among whom was the mayor of the city, Dr. Goodwyn, quite a respectable old gentleman, who was extremely anxious to protect the interests of the citizens. He was on foot, and I on horseback, and it was probable I told him then not to be uneasy, that we did not intend to stay long, and had no purpose to injure the private citizens or private property.

About this time I noticed several men trying to get through the crowd to speak with me, and called to some black people to make room for them; when they reached me, they explained that they were officers of our army, who had been prisoners, had escaped from the Rebel prison and guard, and were of course overjoyed to find themselves safe with us. . . . One of them handed me a paper, asking me to read it at my leisure; I put it in my breast-pocket and rode on. General Howard was still with me, and, riding down the street which led by the right to the Charleston depot, we found it and a large storehouse burned to the ground, but there were, on the platform and the ground near by, piles of cotton bags filled with corn and corn-meal, partially burned. . . .

Thus Sherman described himself arriving in Columbia on the 17th of February, a day that would end in a terror and a destruction seldom equaled on the continent of North America. Each point Sherman stresses was a part of the picture he wished to create for history—the high wind, the fires left smoldering by Hampton's men, the flakes of cotton in the air. Later he would upbraid the inhabitants of Columbia for having their cellars filled with intoxicants, and his *Memoirs* would relate how he "noticed . . . several of the men were evidently in liquor" and "I called General Howard's attention to it." To Wade Hampton such statements simply would demonstrate that Sherman would go to his grave "a robber and incendiary" incapable of telling the truth.

But the bitter, endless quarrel over Sherman's responsibility for the torture Columbia would suffer that 17th of February still belonged to the mysteries of unfolding history. In the morning everyone in this city, where the women outnumbered the men by more than forty to one, clung to the hope that the Yankee occupation would be quickly ended and lightly felt. "Well, they are here," Emma LeConte could write, as though finding relief in the succinct statement of the fact.

> I was sitting in the back parlor when I heard the shouting of the troops [she recorded]. I was at the front door in a moment. Jane came running and crying, "O Miss Emma, they've come at last!" She said they were marching down Main Street, before them flying a panic-stricken crowd of women and children who seemed crazy. . . .

Emma ran upstairs to her bedroom window. Each step she took echoed some memory of the war. She remembered the boys from the college who had organized their own company under their professor of mathematics and marched off to war as though it were a frolic. She remembered all the talk (in Mrs. Chestnut's words) of South Carolina as "a poor little hot-blooded, headlong, rash and troublesome sister state," and then the wonderfully exhilarating news that Virginia and North Carolina were arming to come to her rescue. She remembered the succession of victories under the magnificent

Lee before Gettysburg and Vicksburg, and then the ominous tidings that Sherman was at Chattanooga, at Atlanta, at Milledgeville, at Savannah. Now Sherman had reached Columbia. . . . Emma fled to the window in time to see the United States flag run up over the State House. Passionately she closed her eyes:

> O what a horror! What a degradation! After four long bitter years of bloodshed and hatred, now to float there at last! That hateful symbol of despotism! I do not think I could possibly describe my feelings. I know I could not look at it. I left the window and went downstairs to mother.

Presently a guard arrived to protect the hospital. Against the wall near the gate to the campus a shelter of boards was hammered together, and when Emma glanced out she saw sentinels stationed by the gate and the men cooking their dinners. A high wind blew their hats around. Emma's mouth tightened as she thought:

> This is the first sight we have had of these fiends except as prisoners. The sight does not stir up very pleasant feelings in our hearts. We cannot look at them with anything but horror and hatred—loathing and disgust.

5. "THE DRUNKEN DEVILS ROAMED ABOUT"

Was it true, as Simms testified, that a Yankee soldier told a housewife: "You'll see us coming back after the war—every man of us—to get a Carolina wife. We hate your men like hell, but we love your women!"?

Was it true, as Mayor Goodwyn reported to the Committee

Appointed to Collect Testimony in Relation to the Destruction of Columbia, that Sherman, coming upon a Negro shot through the heart, asked his soldiers: "How came the Negro shot?" and when told that the colored man had been guilty of great insolence to them, responded mildly: "Stop this, boys. This is all wrong. Take away the body and bury it."?

Was it true, as Emma LeConte wrote in her journal, that:

. . . some soldiers were pillaging the house of a lady. One asked if they had not humbled her pride *now*.

"No, indeed," she said, "nor can you ever."

"You *fear* us, anyway?"

"No," she said.

"By God, but you *shall* fear me," and he cocked his pistol and put it to her head. "Are you afraid now?"

She folded her arms and looking him steadily in the eye said contemptuously, "No."

He dropped his pistol and with an exclamation of admiration, left her.

These stories sound apocryphal, the kind of folk legend that springs up in a land through which a conquering army has swept. But history *would* support Simms when he recalled that "in some instances, where the parties complained of the misrule and robbery, their guards said to them, with a chuckle: 'This is nothing. Wait till tonight and you'll see hell!' "

Throughout the day Emma LeConte heard the Yankees as "they surged down Main Street and through the State House." Here some of the invaders amused themselves by taking shots at a picture of Jefferson Davis; others threw bricks at a statue of George Washington and broke off half of Washington's cane. Two corps, Howard's and Logan's, encamped in the woods below the college campus. Emma's indignation grew. One corps—Logan's—was "the diabolical 15th which Sherman has hitherto never permitted to enter a city on account of their vile and desperate character." Emma watched the "devils" stroll by, "well clad in dark, dirty-looking blue";

305

their wagon trains seemed immense. Simms became more disturbed by the way "liquors were drunk with such avidity as to astonish the veteran Bacchanals of Columbia." One vault on Main Street yielded seventeen casks of wine, which, Simms declared, "barely sufficed, once broken into, for the draughts of a single hour." Rye, corn, claret and Madeira each helped to excite the palates of the Federals.

For Sherman the afternoon passed peacefully. The command of the city had been assigned to Howard, and Sherman settled himself leisurely in the home of Blanton Duncan, a Kentuckian from Louisville who held the contract for manufacturing Confederate money and who had fled the city with Wade Hampton's cavalry. Now Sherman remembered the paper that the prisoner had handed him on entering Columbia; taking the sheet from his breast-pocket he found to his delight that it contained a song entitled *Sherman's March to the Sea* written by Adjutant S. H. M. Byers of the 5th Iowa Infantry. Resting in Blanton Duncan's home, Sherman's tongue rolled with pleasure over the vigorous lines Byers had composed:

> Then Kenesaw frowned in its glory,
>   Frowned down on the flag of the free;
> But the East and the West bore our standard,
>   As Sherman marched down to the sea!

And:

> Still onward we pressed, till our banners
>   Swept out from Atlanta's grim walls,
> And the blood of the patriot dampened
>   The soil where the traitor-flag falls. . . .

Toward evening a note of invitation came from the daughter of the Poyas family, whom Sherman had known well in the years from 1842 to 1846, when he had been stationed at Fort Moultrie. A hundred memories of youth awakened. The plantation dances, the fox hunts over the rice ditches, the hours spent learning to paint—these and a myriad of other recollections came rushing back, reviving echoes of music long stilled, of the laughter of girls long forgotten. As the general brushed his red hair and recalled the image of the Poyas girl, was he for a fleeting instant young Cump once more—the boy who had loved the South, the rambles beneath the noble old oaks, the balls he had attended with sword polished and epaulettes shining? He had come out of West Point still so much the loose-jointed "untamed animal from the Far West" and the South had taken him into its best home, given him a polish, taught him its love for culture, softened the rough edges. Did he remember?

The Poyas girl greeted him warmly. Had he not saved her home from desolation? Here was the proof—and she showed him the book she had flaunted under the nose of the Federal guard. There on the flyleaf was his name—W. T. Sherman. Had he forgotten the inscription he had written when he had given her the book as a gift twenty years before? Sherman, clearly flattered, paid "her a long social visit, and, before leaving Columbia, gave her a half-tierce of rice and about one hundred pounds of ham from our own mess stores." His mellow mood lingered. Again, with a wish "to show . . . that, personally, I had no malice or desire to destroy the city or its inhabitants," he visited the wife of the brother of the Honorable James Simons of Charleston, whom he had known during his Fort Moultrie days as Miss Wragg.

When Sherman returned to Blanton Duncan's house he wanted nothing so much as a nap, but he had scarcely closed his eyes before he was awakened by "a bright light . . . shining on the walls." At this point Sherman's *Memoirs* become discreetly mute, but not so the reminiscences of William Gilmore Simms:

> Among the first fires of evening was one about dark, which broke out in a filthy purlieu of low houses, of wood, on Gervais Street, occupied mostly as brothels. Almost at the same time a body of soldiers scattered over the

Eastern outskirts of the city, fired severally the dwellings of Mr. Secretary Trenholm, General Wade Hampton, Dr. John Wallace, and many others. There were then some twenty fires in full blast, in as many different quarters, and while the alarm sounded from these quarters, a similar alarm went up almost simultaneously from Cotton Town, the northernmost limit of the city, and from Main Street in its very centre . . . thus enveloping in flames almost every section of the devoted city. At this period, thus early in the evening, there were few shows of that drunkenness which prevailed at a late hour in the night, and only after all the grocery shops on Main Street had been rifled. The men engaged in this were well prepared with all the appliances essential to their work. They did not need the torch. They carried with them, from house to house, pots and vessels containing combustible liquids, composed probably of phosphorous and other similar agents, turpentine, etc., and with balls of cotton saturated in this liquid, with which they also overspread the floors and walls; they conveyed the flames with wonderful rapidity from dwelling to dwelling. Each had his ready box of Lucifer matches, and, with a scrape upon the walls, the flames began to rage. Where houses were closely contiguous, a brand from one was the means of conveying destruction to the other. . . .

Throughout "the whole of this terrible scene," Simms said, the Yankees "continued their search after spoil," and:

. . . Hundreds of iron safes, warranted "Impenetrable to fire and the burglar," it was soon satisfactorily demonstrated, were not "Yankee proof." They were split open and robbed, yielding, in some cases, very largely of Confederate money and bonds, if not gold and silver. Jewelry and plate in abundance was found. Men could be seen staggering off with huge waiters, vases, candelabra, to say nothing of cups, goblets and smaller vessels, all of solid silver. Clothes and shoes, when new, were appropriated—the rest left to burn. . . .

"What a night of horror, misery and agony!" Emma Le-Conte cried. "It even makes one sick to think of writing down such scenes." Whereas Emma had not expected to sleep, she had been "actually idiotic enough" to believe that Sherman would keep his word and that she could look forward "to a tolerably tranquil night." About seven o'clock that evening Emma stood on the back piazza on the third floor of the LeConte home. Below her the whole southern horizon "was lit up by camp-fires which dotted the woods." The burning of Wade Hampton's home, a few miles off in the country, illuminated one half the sky; buildings blazing near the river the other half. Sick at heart, Emma came downstairs where Henry, the man servant, shouted excitedly that there were fires on Main Street. "Sumter Street," the girl remembered, "was brightly lighted by a burning house so near our piazza that we could feel the heat." In the red glare she

. . . could watch the wretches walking—generally staggering—back and forth from the camp to the town—shouting—hurrahing—cursing South Carolina—swearing—blaspheming—singing ribald songs and using such obscene language that we were forced to go indoors. The fire on Main Street was now raging, and we anxiously watched its progress from the upper front windows. In a little while, however, the flames broke forth in every direction.

Wherever Emma looked she saw "the drunken devils" as they "roamed about setting fire to every house the flames seemed likely to spare." While rumors ran through the town. Stories to chill the blood passed quickly from ear to ear. Cowering in the cold dining room, Emma heard the wicked tales of how:

. . . Guards were rarely of any assistance—most generally they assisted in the pillaging and the firing. The wretched people rushing from their burning homes were not allowed to keep even the few necessaries they gathered up in their flight—even blankets and food were taken from them and destroyed. The firemen attempted to use their engines, but the hose was cut to pieces and their lives threatened. . . .

The wind howled in a gale, "wafting the flames from house to house." By midnight Emma beheld all of Columbia, except for the outskirts, "wrapped in one huge blaze." Had it been luck, or the intervention of the mysterious Davis, that explained why the fire had not threatened her immediate safety and not a single Yankee soldier had entered the LeConte house? Now the flames seemed actually to recede and Henry swore that the danger was over. Sick "of the dreadful scene," exhausted "with fatigue and excitement," Emma went to her room and tried to rest.

The girl "fell into a heavy kind of stupor." But she could not sleep long, and when she arose presently, the whole household throbbed with the bustle. Mrs. Caldwell, a neighbor, accompanied by her two sisters, stood before the grate in the dining room, wrapped in blankets and weeping bitterly. The Caldwell home roared with fire, and, Emma learned, "the great sea of flame had again swept down our way to the very campus walls." Filled with "a kind of sickening despair," she did not even stir to go out and look. Then Jane burst into the room, wild-eyed; between gasps, the nurse shouted that Aunt Josie's house had caught fire. Emma rushed to the front door with the others. Leaning weakly against the wall, she thought: "My God! What a scene!" The time was now about four o'clock in the morning; the State House had become "one grand conflagration." In the girl's mind the picture of terror fixed itself:

. . . Imagine night turning into noonday, only with a blazing, scorching glare that was horrible—a copper colored sky across which swept columns of black rolling smoke glittering with sparks and flying embers, while all around us were falling thickly showers of burning flakes. Everywhere the palpitating blaze walled the streets as far as the eye could reach—filling the air with its terrible roar. On every side the crackling and devouring fire, while every instant came the crashing of timbers and the thunder of falling buildings. A quivering molten ocean seemed to fill the air and sky. The Library opposite us seemed framed by the gushing flames and smoke, while through the windows gleamed the liquid fire. . . .

All along the side by the library now the college buildings had caught. Physicians and nurses scurried over the rooftops trying to save the buildings, and "the poor wounded inmates left to themselves, such as could crawled out while those who could not move waited to be burned to death." Emma shrank back, aghast, her senses almost numb. The common across from the college gate

. . . was crowded with homeless women and children, a few wrapped in blankets and many shivering in the night air. Such a scene as this with the drunken fiendish soldiery in their dark uniforms, infuriated, cursing, screaming, exulting in their work, came nearer the material ideal of hell than anything I ever expect to see again.

6. "HELLHOUNDS . . . RUFFIANS . . . DEMONS"

IN TESTIFYING before the committee that gathered evidence on the destruction of Columbia, the Reverend A. Toomer Porter described how "in the bright light of the burning city, General Sherman recognized me," and said: "This is a horrible sight!"

"Yes," Porter replied, "when you reflect that women and children are the victims."

"Your governor is responsible for this," Sherman insisted angrily. "Whoever heard of an evacuated city to be left a depot of liquor for an army to occupy? I found one hundred and twenty casks in one cellar. Your governor, being a lawyer or a judge, refused to have it destroyed, because it was private property, and now my men have got drunk and have got beyond my control, and this is the result."

James G. Gibbes, who would succeed Dr. Goodwyn as mayor, found Sherman in a much different mood. The storm of fire, "sublime in its grand awfulness," revealed to Gibbes a succession of unforgettable images, among them the sight of "General Sherman riding leisurely through the streets smoking a cigar." Almost whimsically, Gibbes reported that:

> . . . Dr. Templeton, a prominent physician of the city, was walking in the street just after the destruction of his house, when he was accosted politely by a soldier and asked what time of night it was. Pulling out his watch to look, the soldier jerked it from him and walked off.
>
> Dr. Templeton coolly said: "Hold on, my good fellow, here is the key; it is not a bit of use to me without the watch."
>
> The soldier said: "All right, pass it along."
>
> The Doctor had not gone fifty yards before he was asked the time by another soldier. "Ah, my friend," he

said, "you are just a little too late. One of your comrades was ahead of you."

But to William Gilmore Simms no incident associated with the sack and burning of Columbia could ever seem amusing. Simms took himself seriously in all things, as a man who likes to read his own poetry aloud invariably will; and although Mrs. Chestnut quickly forgot the content of one of "Gilmer's" readings she hastened to add: "It was not tiresome, however, and that is a great thing when people will persist in reading their own rhymes." Living in books and in the history of the Old South, Simms stood outraged as entire libraries, every record of the Surgeon-General's office, were destroyed by Sherman's men. No tale of Yankee infamy became too incredible for Simms to repeat:

The venerable Mr. H—— stood ready, with his *conteau de chasse*, made bare in his bosom, hovering around the persons of his innocent daughters. Mr. O——, on beholding some familiar approach to one of his daughters, bade the man stand off at the peril of his life; saying that while he submitted to being robbed of his property, he would sacrifice life without reserve—his own and that of his assailant—before his child's honor should be abused.

Mr. James G. Gibbes, with difficulty, pistol in hand, only with the assistance of a Yankee officer, rescued two young women from the clutches of as many ruffians.

We have been told of successful outrages of this unmentionable character being practiced upon women dwelling in the suburbs. Many are understood to have taken place in remote country settlements, and two cases are described where young Negresses were brutally forced by the wretches and afterwards murdered—one of them thrust, when half dead, head down in a mud puddle, and there held until she was suffocated.

Simms, Gibbes, and Emma LeConte each recorded that the fire, beginning at a given signal, stopped as soon as the order was given. "With the bugle's sound, and the entrance of fresh troops," Simms testified, "there was an instantaneous arrest of incendiarism. You could see the rioters carried off in groups and squads, from the several precincts they had ravaged, and those which they still meditated to destroy." But to the end Sherman held aloof from any charge that he had been responsible for the destruction of Columbia. He would contend:

> This whole subject has since been thoroughly and judicially investigated, in some cotton cases, by the mixed commission on American and British claims, under the Treaty of Washington, which commission failed to award a verdict in favor of the English claimants, and thereby settled the fact that the destruction of property in Columbia, during that night, did not result from the acts of the General Government of the United States—that is to say, the army.

As though realizing this was an evasion couched in stuffy legal paraphrases, Sherman added archly: "In my official report of the conflagration, I distinctly charged it to General Wade Hampton, and I confess I did so pointedly, to shake the faith of his people in him, for he was in my opinion a braggart."

Wade Hampton saw no reason for accepting Sherman's slurs without a fight, and this veteran cavalryman, whom many acclaimed as equal in reputation to the dashing Jeb Stuart, could brandish words as recklessly as he ever had brandished a saber. Hampton seethed at the bland accusation in Sherman's official report: "I charge Gen. Wade Hampton with having burned his own city of Columbia; not with malicious intent, as the manifestation of silly Roman stoicism, but from folly and want of sense in filling it with lint and tinder." In a letter to the editor of the *New York Day Book* Hampton exploded angrily that Sherman was a liar. Thousands of witnesses could testify that "not one bale of cotton was on fire when he [Sherman] took possession of the city," and Beauregard had issued specific orders "that *no* cotton in the town should be fired." At Chickahominy Hampton had kept to his horse after being shot through the foot, so that when the battle ended it became necessary to cut the boot from his swollen flesh. Something of the same gleam of battle now flashed in Hampton's eyes as he repeated the tales of outrage that had come to him.

Who but Sherman and his "Hellhounds" would have watched indifferently while old men, women, and children, "the flames . . . rolling and raging around them," were "driven out headlong by pistols clapped to their heads, violent hands laid on their throats and collars"? Who but Sherman and his "ruffians" could watch "ladies bustled from their chambers under the strong arm or with menacing pistols at their hearts, their ornaments plucked from their person, their bundles from their hands"? Who but the dastardly Sherman and his "rascals" would have permitted "a lady undergoing the pains of labor to be borne out on a mattress into the open air" while "they beheld the situation of the sufferer and laughed to scorn the prayer of safety"? Who but Sherman and his mob of "demons" would have broken into the room of a woman recently confined and whose "life hung on a hair," snatching rings from her fingers, the watch from beneath her pillow, and so overwhelming "her with terror that she sank under the treatment, surviving but a day or two"?

Hampton's thundering denunciation of Sherman's conduct pictured the stricken inhabitants seeking refuge in the churches, but "thither the hellish perseverance of the fiends followed them, and the churches of God were set on fire." Driven "into the recesses of Sidney Park," the unfortunate citizens now "fancied to find security," but "the ingenuity of hate and malice" of Sherman's drunken soldiers "were not to be baffled, and firebrands [were] thrown." With the contempt of a proud old man who would not allow even Lee to transfer the command of one of his brigades, Hampton's rancor flared on:

> Wherever he has taken his army in this State, women have been insulted or outraged, old men have been hung to extort from them hidden treasure. The fruits of the earth have been destroyed, leaving starvation where plenty once reigned, and the dwellings of rich and poor alike have been laid in ashes. For these deeds history will brand him as a robber and incendiary and will deservedly "damn him to everlasting fame."

Sherman, it was said, never acknowledged an error or repeated one. Scurrilous and blistering though Wade Hampton's attack proved, when Sherman published his *Memoirs* a decade later he still saw himself as blameless as when he had written in his official report: "We saved what of Columbia remains unconsumed." What remained "unconsumed" seemed little enough. Gibbes estimated that three hundred and sixty-six acres had been destroyed, Simms that the number of residences and stores devastated totaled 1,386. Laconically, Sherman would report:

> The morning sun of February 18th rose bright and clear over a ruined city. About half of it was in ashes and in smouldering heaps. Many of the people were houseless, and gathered in groups in the suburbs, or in the open parks and spaces, around their scanty piles of furniture. General Howard, in concert with the mayor, did all that was possible to provide other houses for them; and by my authority he turned over to the Sisters of Charity, the Methodist College, and to the mayor five hundred beef-cattle, to help feed the people; I also gave the mayor one hundred muskets, with which to arm a guard to maintain order after we should leave the neighborhood. During the 18th and 19th we remained in Columbia, General Howard's troops engaged in tearing up and destroying the railroad, back toward the Wateree, while a strong

detail, under the immediate supervision of Colonel O. M. Poe, United States Engineers, destroyed the State Arsenal, which was found to be well supplied with shot, shell, and ammunition. These were hauled in wagons to the Saluda River . . . and emptied into deep water, causing a very serious accident by the bursting of a percussion-shell, as it struck another on the margin of the water. The flame followed back a train of powder which had sifted out, killing sixteen men and destroying several wagons and teams of mules. We also destroyed several valuable foundries and the factory of Confederate money. The dies had been carried away, but about sixty handpresses remained. There was also found an immense quantity of money, in various stages of manufacture, which our men spent and gambled with in the most lavish manner.

7. "A QUEER FISH!"

On the 20th of February the right wing of Sherman's army began its march northward toward Winnsboro. In Lincolnton, North Carolina, to which Mrs. Chestnut had fled, the sad news arrived that Columbia had been burned to the ground, that Charleston and Wilmington had surrendered. Mrs. Chestnut bowed her head and sobbed aloud. "Shame, disgrace, beggary, all at once," she wrote in her diary. "They are hard to bear." Too late, Mrs. Chestnut thought, Wade Hampton had been raised to Lieutenant General, for "if he had been . . . given the command in South Carolina six months ago, I believe he would have saved us. But Achilles was sulking in his tent—and at such a time!" On February 22, as Sherman marched north from Winnsboro, President Lincoln ordered lights turned on the dome of the Capitol in

Washington, and multitudes marched through the streets, singing and shouting, in celebration of the victories at Columbia, Wilmington, and Charleston which had brought back under the flag of the United States a land that in 1860, as Mrs. Chestnut had observed, had become "the torment of herself and of everybody else."

Columbia, rid of Sherman and his troops in their "dark, dirty-looking blue," could not disguise its feeling of relief. The five hundred beef-cattle left behind by the Federals proved at best to be overaged and underfed, and Simms, with an audible snort, reported that the animals were "dying of exhaustion at the rate of fifteen to twenty head per diem." For a time after the strain of "the fearful excitement," Emma LeConte "seemed to sink into a dull apathy." On the day Sherman and his troops departed, Emma wrote:

> . . . How desolated and dreary we feel—how completely cut off from the world. No longer the shrill whistles of the engine—no daily mail—the morning brings no paper with news from the outside—there are no lights—no going to and fro. It is as if a city in the midst of business and activity were suddenly smitten with some appalling curse. One feels awed if by chance the dreary stillness is broken by a laugh or too loud a voice.

Two days later Emma ventured into town:

> I have seen it all—I have seen the "Abomination of Desolation." It is even worse than I thought. The place is literally in ruins. The entire heart of the city is in ashes—only the outer edges remain. On the whole length of Sumter Street not one house beyond the first block after the campus is standing, except the brick house of Mr. Mordecai. Standing in the centre of town, as far as the eye can reach nothing is to be seen but heaps of rubbish, tall dreary chimneys and shattered brick walls, while "In the hollow windows, dreary horror's sitting." Poor old

Columbia—where is all her beauty—so admired by strangers, so loved by her children! . . .

Blanding Street, the finest in town, crossing Main and Sumter at right angles, also presented "a sad picture." The beautiful Preston house, which General Logan had used as his headquarters, escaped, but other homes were less fortunate. Emma saw the Crawford house now "a heap of brick with most of its tall columns standing, blackened by smoke"; Bedell's "lovely little house" stood "in ruins while as if in mockery the shrubbery is not even scorched." Then entering Main Street, where "since the war in crowd and bustle it has rivalled a city thoroughfare," the girl felt the full shock of the desolation:

> . . . Everything has vanished as if by enchantment—stores, merchants, customers—all the eager faces gone—only three or four dismal looking people to be seen picking their way over heaps of rubbish, brick and timbers. The market is a ruined shell supported by crumbling arches—its spire fallen in and with it the old town clock whose familiar stroke we miss so much. After trying to distinguish localities and hunting for familiar buildings we turned to Arsenal Hill. Here things looked more natural. The Arsenal was destroyed but comparatively few dwellings. Also the Park and its surroundings looked familiar. As we passed the old State House going back I paused to gaze on the ruins—only the foundations and chimneys—and to recall the brilliant scene enacted there one short month ago. And I compared that scene with its beauty, gayety and festivity, the halls so elaborately decorated, the surging throng, to this. I reached home sad at heart and full of all I had seen.

On the 23rd of February, while the celebrations continued in Washington, Joseph LeConte was captured. Emma, still the unreconstructed Rebel, stoically wrote in her journal:

> . . . Somehow I feel we cannot be conquered. I would
> rather far have France or any other country for a mistress
> —anything but live as one nation with the *Yankees*—that
> word in my mind is a synonym for *all* that is *mean,* des-
> picable and abhorrent.

Meanwhile Sherman's army drove steadily northward, and
one of President Lincoln's favorite quips, as reported by
John H. Kennaway, a British observer, would be that "the
general had been flirting with Augusta, embracing Columbia, and, now that he was making approaches to Charlotte,
it was time that he should be giving some account of himself
to Mrs. Sherman." By March 12 Sherman could say: "I was
again in full communication with the outside world," and six
days later his army had advanced within twenty-seven miles
of Goldsboro, North Carolina, and five miles of Bentonville.

But the Confederate army opposing Sherman stirred with
new life. On March 16 the campaign diary of an aide to
General A. P. Stewart would record that "General J. E.
Johnston took command yesterday of the Army of the South,"
and the restoration of "Old Joe" to the command brought
"joy" among soldiers who felt that Johnston "endeavors to
conceal his greatness rather than to impress you with it."
Even Sherman admitted that "Old Joe" was to be feared, for
"he would not be misled by feints and false reports and would
compel me to exercise more caution than I hitherto had
done." On March 19 at Bentonville Sherman and Johnston
clashed.

The battle proved savage. Illinoisan Alexander C. McClurg
would tell how that morning General Jefferson C. Davis felt
that the sound of the skirmish line indicated "more than the
usual cavalry opposition."

"No, Jeff," Sherman replied in "his usual brisk, nervous,
and positive way," there was nothing ahead but cavalry and
Sherman wished Jeff to "brush them out of the way."

The Confederate "cavalry" refused to be brushed aside. As the men said: "They won't drive worth a damn."

McClurg would tell why this fact was so when at ten o'clock that morning the order came to advance, for "to the surprise of everyone," the Federals "dashed, all unprepared, against a line of earthworks manned with infantry and artillery." "Old Joe" began to make the Yankees dance under a destructive fire, and at half past one they were still dancing. A "galvanized Yankee"—a soldier, McClurg explained, "who had been captured and who, rather than endure prison life, had taken service in the Rebel army"—fell into Federal hands and related "a startling story." Johnston's army, the "galvanized Yankee" said, had "by night marches been concentrated in our immediate front and was strongly entrenched."

The Yankees were in a fix. There was no chance to withdraw, and "the men all were working like beavers, throwing up hasty field works, when the attack came on us like a whirlwind." McClurg said:

> The Rebel regiments in front were in full view, stretching through the fields as far as one could see, advancing rapidly and firing as they came. It was a gallant sight and contrasted signally with our center and left, where our thin line seemed to have been nearly wiped out of existence. The onward sweep of the Rebel lines was like the waves of the ocean, resistless.

Jeff C. Davis, who had been stung by the affair at "Ebenezar Causeway," plunged through a swamp on "his fiery white mare toward the reserve." James D. Morgan's brigade had not been engaged, and Jeff roared: "Where is that brigade?"

"Here it is, sir, ready to march."

Jeff shouted, ordering the brigade swung to the left: "Advance upon their flank; strike them wherever you find them!"

If these words "seem cold in print," McClurg declared:

. . . when uttered by a man born to command, they were electric. The men struck the unsuspecting enemy with impetuosity and were quickly engaged in a desperate conflict. On this movement, in all probability, turned the fortunes of the day. It was the right thing, done at the right time.

Colonel William Cogswell appeared with another brigade, fell upon the same flank, and his troops soon "were enveloped in fire and smoke." The Confederates "fell back in confusion and re-entered their works." A lull, lasting about an hour, spread across the whole front, and then toward five o'clock the graybacks swooped down over the open fields. Yankee artillery blazed. In waves Johnston's boys kept coming, shaking off the case shot and canister, and ignoring the whining nick of the musketry. But men can stand such punishment just so long. There was another lull. McClurg had gone back a few rods "when I caught a glimpse of a Confederate column moving directly in rear of our line. Hardee's corps, or a considerable part of it, had passed through an opening in our line."

Morgan saw the peril. Here was the showdown. He rallied his men to sustain the drive from the rear. When Hardee struck, Morgan was ready. "The struggle," McClurg said, "was sharp and bloody, but it was brief." Daylight faded. Exhausted men embraced the darkness, for with morning other troops from the right would swing the balance to the Yankees. But McClurg reflected soberly:

Never before had fortune and circumstances so united to favor Johnston, and never before had hope shone so brightly for him and his Confederate troops. If Sherman's army had been destroyed in the Battle of Bentonville, the Confederacy might yet have been inspired with new spirit. . . . But as the sun went down that night, it carried with it the last hopes of the Southern Confederacy.

On the 23rd of March Sherman rode into Goldsboro. Be
hind him lay five great rivers—the Edisto, Broad, Catawba,
Peedee, and Cape Fear. Columbia, Cheraw, and Fayetteville
had been captured, and Charleston evacuated. In fifty days,
since leaving Savannah, he had covered four hundred and
twenty-five miles. Understandably his mood was pleasant
when two days later he left to meet with Lincoln and Grant on
board the *River Queen* at City Point.

The President's curiosity about the march extended to "the
more ludicrous parts," which, Sherman explained, concerned
"the 'bummers' and their devices to collect food and forage
when the outside world supposed us to be starving." Grant inquired if Sherman had asked for "*Mrs.* Lincoln," and when
Sherman admitted that he did not know she was on board,
and that the President had not mentioned that fact, Grant
shook his head and said: "Well, you are a pretty pair!" Next
morning Grant accompanied Sherman to the President's
cabin, and pointedly inquired for Mrs. Lincoln, but "when the
President went to her state-room," he returned "and begged
us to excuse her, as she was not well."

Both Grant and Sherman supposed "that one or the other
of us would have to fight one more bloody battle"—Sherman
felt the battle would fall on him, somewhere near Raleigh—
"and that would be the *last*." Lincoln looked sad; blood
enough had been shed, he said. Questions of far-reaching impact filled the meeting. What was to be done with the Rebel
armies when defeated? What should be done with the political leaders? Should they be allowed to escape? The President
replied that "all he wanted of us was to defeat the opposing
armies, and to get the men composing the Confederate armies
back to their homes, at work on their farms and in their
shops." But what about Jeff Davis, Sherman insisted. Mr.
Lincoln told a story:

> . . . A man once had taken the total-abstinence
> pledge. When visiting a friend, he was invited to take a

drink, but declined, on the score of the pledge; when his friend suggested lemonade, which was accepted. In preparing the lemonade, the friend pointed to the brandy-bottle, and said the lemonade would be more palatable if he were to pour in a little brandy; when his guest said, if he could do so "unbeknown" to him, he would not object. . . .

Sherman got the point: "I inferred that Mr. Lincoln wanted Davis to escape, 'unbeknown' to him."

The "one more bloody battle" followed quickly in Virginia, at Five Forks, where Lee's long, thin lines broke so that Petersburg and Richmond became untenable. With the news of the fall of Petersburg on April 2, Jefferson Davis "quietly rose and left the church." Within hours he "started for Danville, whither I supposed Lee would proceed with his army." But Lee's supplies failed to reach Amelia Court House in time for him to press on to Danville, and "Little Phil" Sheridan struck a crushing blow at Sayler's Creek. The end was near. At Appomattox the surrender would come, and General Fitzhugh Lee would remember how:

> Slowly and painfully [General Robert E. Lee] turned to his soldiers and, with voice quivering with emotion, said, "Men, we have fought through the war together. I have done my best for you. My heart is too full to say more." . . .

It was, Fitzhugh Lee said, "a simple but most affecting scene." The pink dogwood of Virginia was all in bloom.

A few days later Sherman would be traveling from Raleigh to meet Joe Johnston and arrange surrender terms. As he departed, a message would reach him from Stanton that he dared not share with his men—then. In a small farmhouse on the Hillsboro Road the two generals sat down. Sherman showed Johnston the message from Stanton. Lincoln had been assassinated. "The perspiration came out in large drops on his forehead," Sherman recalled, "and he did not attempt to conceal his distress."

And so it was beside another President, Andrew Johnson, that on a late May day Sherman stood with Grant in a stand on the White House grounds and watched pass in review *his* army:

> . . . the most magnificent army in existence—sixty-five thousand men, in splendid *physique*, who had just completed a march of nearly two thousand miles in a hostile country, in good drill, and who realized that they were being closely scrutinized by thousands of their fellow country-men and by foreigners. . . . The steadiness of their tread, the careful dress on the guides, the uniform intervals between the companies, all eyes directly to the front, and the tattered and bullet-riven flags, festooned with flowers, all attracted universal notice. Many . . . up to that time, had looked upon our Western army as a sort of mob; but the world then saw, and recognized the fact, that it was an army in the proper sense, well organized, well commanded and disciplined; and there was no wonder that it had swept through the South like a tornado. For six and a half hours the strong tread of the Army of the West resounded along Pennsylvania Avenue; not a soul of that vast crowd of spectators left his place; and, when the rear of the column had passed by, thousands still lingered to express their sense of confidence in the strength of a Government which could claim such an army.

For Cump Sherman, the boy who had once watched his red hair turn green, who had loved the South, who almost had been washed out of the army as "crazy" and who had stood by Grant after Shiloh, who had distrusted Lincoln and then learned to love him, who had "been a damned sight smarter than Grant but more nervous," who had outwitted Johnston and Hood, Beauregard and Hardee, Jefferson Davis and the devil, and marched two thousand miles to fame and infamy, fighting because he was afraid and afraid because he fought, it was a great day. Cump Sherman, the general who had marched to the hell of Columbia, now stood beside Andy Johnson and watched his army march by! Sure it was a great day! Great as Johnston had been great reviving the shattered Army of Tennessee, great as French and Cheatham had been great at Kennesaw and Johnny Corse at Allatoona, great as little Carrie Berry had been great hoping she could have a birthday cake next year and Dolly Sumner Lunt had been great sobbing for "My boys! My boys!", great as Lincoln saying enough blood had been shed and Jefferson Davis speaking at Macon because he was fighting mad, great as William Gilmore Simms loving the South of his ancestors and Emma Florence LeConte loving the South of her disrupted youth, great as the last soldiers of the gray singing *Lorena* as they left Atlanta . . . yes, it had been a great day. Sherman would remember:

> Some little scenes enlivened the day, and called for the laughter and cheers of the crowd. Each division was followed by six ambulances, as a representative of its baggage-train. Some of the division commanders had added, by way of variety, goats, milch-cows, and pack-mules, whose loads consisted of game-cocks, poultry, hams, etc., and some of them had the families of freed slaves along, with the women leading their children. Each division was preceded by its corps of black pioneers, armed with picks and spades. These marched abreast in double ranks, keeping perfect dress and step, and added much to the interest of the occasion. On the whole, the grand review was a splendid success, and was a fitting conclusion to the campaign and the war.

To Emma Florence LeConte the war had yet to reveal one last mystery. Earlier in her journal the girl had written: "I can hardly help feeling that our total exemption from insult and plunder was due in some way to the influence of the strange man who called himself Davis and promised us protection." Now, with the Palm Sunday only a few days away when Grant would invite Lee to meet him and end the war, Emma made her final discovery:

> I mentioned in my account of the shelling of the town on Thursday that the man Davis brought me a box of feathers. I had laid them away and did not think of them till today, when I came across them and we were looking them over selecting some I thought would make a pretty fan. Near the bottom of the box Sallie [Emma's sister] spied a folded paper—a leaf from some notebook. She opened it. At the top of the page was a rude drawing of two hearts—this, the note said, "portrayed two hearts surrounded by rosebuds" (the rosebuds were imaginary). "May they," continued the note, "prove an emblem of our hearts, may they be joined by the golden links of friendship and may the rosebuds of life entwine them and though many hundred miles separate us may we be always firm friends." . . .

Emma put away the box of feathers. "Well," she thought, "if that individual is not a queer fish, I never met one!"

Bibliography

I. MANUSCRIPTS

BERRY, CARRIE M.: Diary, August 1, 1864 through January 26, 1865; ms. in possession of the Atlanta Historical Society, Atlanta, Ga.

CLAYTON, SALLIE: Miscellaneous reminiscences; ms. in possession of the Rev. Clayton Torrence, Richmond, Va.

DITZLER, L.: Letter to Jefferson Davis, September 15, 1864; ms. in possession of the Duke University Library, Durham, N.C.

HARDEE, W. J.: Letter to Jefferson Davis, June 22, 1864; ms. in possession of the Duke University Library, Durham, N.C.

HOOD, JOHN B.: Letter to Braxton Bragg, September 4, 1864, endorsed by Jefferson Davis, September 8, 1864; ms. in possession of the Duke University Library, Durham, N.C.

——: Letter to Jefferson Davis, March 31, 1865; ms. in possession of the Emory University Library, Atlanta, Ga.

LeCONTE, EMMA FLORENCE: Journal, December 31, 1864 through August 6, 1865; ms. in possession of the Southern Historical Collection, University of North Carolina, Chapel Hill, N.C.

MAGRATH, A. C.: Letter to Jefferson Davis, January 22, 1865; ms. in possession of the Emory University Library, Atlanta, Ga.

MALONE, JAMES: Letter to Jefferson Davis, October 25, 1864; ms. in possession of the Duke University Library, Durham, N.C.

RAY, MARY RAWSON: Diary; ms. in possession of the Atlanta Historical Society, Atlanta, Ga.

SHERMAN, WILLIAM T.: Letter in response to "Resolutions of Chamber of Commerce," January 15, 1865; ms. in possession of Missouri Historical Society, St. Louis, Mo.

——: Letter to Captain Inman [?], May 16, 1861; ms. in possession of George F. Scheer, Chapel Hill, N.C.

——: Letter to R. L. Johnson, December 22, 1886; ms. in possession of Alfred Whital Stern, Chicago, Ill.

Sherman Papers, The, Manuscripts Division, Library of Congress, Washington, D.C.

TAYLOR, FANNY COHEN: Diary; ms. in possession of the Southern Historical Collection, University of North Carolina, Chapel Hill, N.C.

II. SHEET MUSIC

AUGUSTIN, JOHN ALCÉE ("Ye Tragic"): "Short Rations." Augusta, Ga., c. 1864.

GAY, JAMES D.: "How Sherman's Veterans Took Atlanta." Philadelphia, 1864.

WARDEN, D. A.: "Sherman's on the Track." Philadelphia, 1865.

WEBSTER, H. D. L.: "Lorena." Macon and Savannah, Ga., 1863.

III. NEWSPAPERS AND MAGAZINES

American Historical Review.
Emory University Quarterly, The.
Georgia Historical Review, The.
Harper's New Monthly Magazine.
Harper's Weekly.
Index, The (London).
Journal of Southern History, The.
Kennesaw Gazette, The.
Leslie's Weekly.
Loyal Georgian, The.
New York Tribune, The.
Philadelphia Weekly Times, The.

IV. PUBLISHED SOURCES

ALEXANDER, E. PORTER. See Johnson and Buel: *Battles and Leaders of the Civil War.*

BADEAU, ADAM: *Grant in Peace.* Hartford, Conn., 1887.

BROOKS, NOAH: *Washington in Lincoln's Time.* New York, 1895.

BROWN, JOSEPH M.: "Battle of Kennesaw Mountain." *The Kennesaw Gazette,* n.d.

BUCK, IRVING A.: *Cleburne and His Command.* New York, 1908.

CATE, WIRT ARMISTEAD (ed.): *Two Soldiers. The Campaign Diaries of Thomas J. Key, C.S.A., December 7, 1863–May 17, 1865 and Robert J. Campbell, U.S.A., January 1, 1864–July 21, 1864.* Chapel Hill, N.C., 1938.

CHESTNUT, MARY BOYKIN: *A Diary from Dixie.* New York, 1905; re-edited by Ben Ames Williams, Boston, 1949.

CHURCH, W. C.: *Ulysses S. Grant.* Garden City, N.Y., 1926.

CONNOLLY, JAMES AUSTIN: See *Transactions of the Illinois State Historical Society for the Year 1928.*

CONYNGHAM, J. B.: *Sherman's March through the South.* New York, 1865.

CULLUM, G. W. (ed.): *Biographical Register of the Officers and Graduates of the United States Military Academy.* Washington, D.C., 1891. 2 volumes.

DANA, CHARLES A.: *Recollections of the Civil War.* New York, 1913.

DANIEL, FREDERICK S. (ed.): *The Richmond Examiner During the War, or the Writings of John M. Daniel.* New York, 1868.

DAVIS, JEFFERSON: *The Rise and Fall of the Confederate Government.* New York, 1881. 2 volumes.

DODSON, W. C. (ed.): *Campaigns of Wheeler and His Cavalry 1862–1865 from Material Furnished by Gen. Joseph Wheeler.* Atlanta, Ga., 1899.

DUBOSE, J. W.: *General Joseph Wheeler and the Army of Tennessee.* New York, 1912.

DWIGHT, HENRY O.: "How We Fight at Atlanta," *Harper's New Monthly Magazine* (Volume XXIX).

DYER, JOHN P.: *The Gallant Hood.* Indianapolis, 1950.

EISENCHIML, OTTO: *The Story of Shiloh.* Chicago, 1946.

—— and NEWMAN, RALPH (eds.): *The American Iliad.* Indianapolis, 1947.

FRENCH, SAMUEL G.: "Kennesaw Mountain," *The Kennesaw Gazette,* n.d.

Georgia, A Guide to its Towns and Countryside. Athens, Ga., 1946.

GIBBES, JAMES G.: On the sack and burning of Columbia, S.C., in *Who Burnt Columbia?* Also in *The Philadelphia Weekly Times,* September 20, 1880.

GRANT, ULYSSES S.: *Personal Memoirs.* Hartford, Conn., 1885.

HAMPTON, WADE: *Letter to The New York Day Book,* Saturday, July 15, 1865, in *Who Burnt Columbia?*

HARWELL, RICHARD B.: *Confederate Music.* Chapel Hill, N.C., 1950.

——: "Confederate Carrousel: Southern Songs of the Sixties," *Emory University Quarterly* (Volume VI).

HAY, JOHN: *Lincoln and the Civil War in the Diaries and Letters of John Hay.* New York, 1939.

HAY, THOMAS ROBSON: *Hood's Tennessee Campaign.* New York, 1929.

——: "Joseph Emerson Brown, Governor of Georgia, 1857–1865," reprinted from the *Georgia Historical Quarterly* (Volume XIII). Savannah, Ga., 1929. Pamphlet.

HENRY, RALPH SELPH: *The Story of the Confederacy.* Indianapolis, 1931.

HILL, LOUISE BILES: *Joseph E. Brown and the Confederacy.* Chapel Hill, N.C., 1939.

HOOD, JOHN B.: *Advance and Retreat.* New Orleans, La., 1880.

HORN, STANLEY F.: *The Army of Tennessee.* Indianapolis, 1941.

HOWARD, OLIVER OTIS: *Autobiography.* New York, 1908. 2 volumes. See also Johnson and Buel: *Battles and Leaders of the Civil War.*

HOWARD, W. P.: "Official Report to Governor Joseph E. Brown on the Destruction of Atlanta," *The Macon Telegraph,* December 10, 1864.

Howe, Mark A. DeWolfe (ed.): *Home Letters*. New York, 1894.

———: *Marching with Sherman, Passages from the Letters and Campaign Diaries of Henry Hitchcock, Major and Assistant Adjutant General of Volunteers, November, 1864–May, 1865*. New Haven, Conn., 1927.

Johnson, Robert Underwood and Buel, Clarence Clough (eds.): *Battles and Leaders of the Civil War*. New York, 1884–8. 4 volumes.

Johnston, Joseph E.: *Narrative of Military Operations*. New York, 1874.

Jones, J. B.: *A Rebel War Clerk's Diary*. Philadelphia, 1866.

Kennaway, John H.: *On Sherman's Track*. London, 1867.

Key, Thomas J.: See Cate, Wirt Armistead.

LeConte, Joseph: *'Ware Sherman. A Journal of Three Months' Personal Experience in the Last Days of the Confederacy*. Berkeley, Calif., 1937.

Lee, Fitz Hugh: *General Lee*. New York, 1894.

Leech, Margaret: *Reveille in Washington, 1860–1865*. New York, 1941.

Lewis, Lloyd: *Sherman, Fighting Prophet*. New York, 1932.

Lunt, Dolly Sumner: *A Woman's Wartime Journal*. New York, 1918.

McCook, Daniel: "Second Division at Shiloh," *Harper's New Monthly Magazine* (Volume XXVIII).

McClurg, Alexander C.: *The Last Chance of the Confederacy*. See Military Order of the Loyal Legion of the United States, Illinois Commandery, *Military Essays and Recollections*, Volume 1.

Milchrist, Thomas E.: *Reflections of a Subaltern on the Hood-Thomas Campaign in Tennessee*. See Military Order of the Loyal Legion of the United States, Illinois Commandery, *Military Essays and Recollections*, Volume IV.

Military Order of the Loyal Legion of the United States, Illinois Commandery: *Military Essays and Recollections*, Volume I. Chicago, 1891.

———: *Military Essays and Recollections*, Volume IV. Chicago, 1907.

Miller, Francis Trevelyan (ed.): *The Photographic History of the Civil War*. New York, 1911. 10 volumes.

Nichols, George Ward: *The Story of the Great March, from the Diary of a Staff Officer*. New York, 1865.

Nichols, Roy Franklin: *The Disruption of American Democracy*. New York, 1948.

Nicolay, John G.: *A Short Life of Abraham Lincoln, Condensed from Nicolay & Hay's Abraham Lincoln: A History*. New York, 1902.

O'Connor, Richard: *Hood: Cavalier General*. New York, 1949.

Pollard, Edward A.: *The Lost Cause*. New York, 1866.

———: *Southern History of the War*. New York, 1866. 2 volumes.

———: *Rebellion Record*. New York, 1863. 5 volumes.

Polley, J. B.: *Hood's Texas Brigade*. New York, 1910.

POLK, WILLIAM M.: *Leonidas Polk, Bishop and General.* New York, 1893. 2 volumes.

PRATT, FLETCHER: *Eleven Generals. Studies in American Command.* New York, 1949.

Report of the Committee Appointed to Collect Testimony in Relation to the Destruction of Columbia, S.C. on the 17th of February, 1865.

RHODES, JAMES FORD: "Who Burned Columbia?", *American Historical Review* (Volume VII).

———: *Historical Essays.* New York, 1909.

ROWLAND, DUNBAR (ed.): *Jefferson Davis, Constitutionalist: His Letters, Papers and Speeches.* Jackson, Miss., 1923. 10 volumes.

SANDBURG, CARL: *Abraham Lincoln, The Prairie Years.* New York, 1926. 2 volumes.

———: *Abraham Lincoln, The War Years.* New York, 1939. 4 volumes.

SHANKS, W. F. G.: "Recollections of Sherman," and "Recollections of General Thomas," *Harper's New Monthly Magazine* (Volume XXX).

SHERLOCK, E. J.: *Memorabilia of the Marches and Battles in Which the One Hundredth Regiment of Indiana Infantry Volunteers Took an Active Part.* Kansas City, Mo., 1897.

SHERMAN, JOHN: *Recollections of Forty Years in the House, Senate and Cabinet.* Chicago, 1895. 2 volumes.

SHERMAN, WILLIAM TECUMSEH: *Memoirs of General William T. Sherman Written by Himself.* New York, 1875. 2 volumes.

SIMMS, WILLIAM GILMORE: On the sack and burning of Columbia, S.C., in *Who Burnt Columbia?*

SNOWDEN, YATES: *Marching with Sherman.* Columbia, S.C., 1929. Pamphlet.

THORNDIKE, RACHEL SHERMAN (ed.): *The Sherman Letters, Correspondence between General and Senator Sherman from 1837 to 1891.* New York, 1894.

Transactions of the Illinois State Historical Society for the Year 1928. Springfield, Ill., 1928.

UPSON, THEODORE F.: See Winther, Oscar Osburn.

WALTERS, JOHN BENNETT: "General William T. Sherman and Total War," reprinted from *The Journal of Southern History* (Volume XIV). Baton Rouge, La., 1948. Pamphlet.

The War of the Rebellion: A Compilation of the Union and Confederate Armies. Washington, 1880–1901. 130 volumes.

WATKINS, SAM R.: *"Co. Aytch," Maury Grays, First Tennessee Regiment, or a Side Show of the Big Show.* Nashville, Tenn., 1882; Chattanooga, Tenn., 1900.

Who Burnt Columbia? Charleston, S.C., 1873. See also Gibbes, James G.; Hampton, Wade; and Simms, William Gilmore.

BIBLIOGRAPHY

WILLIAMS, BEN AMES (ed.): *A Diary from Dixie.* Boston, 1949. See Chestnut, Mary Boykin.

WILSON, JAMES HARRISON: *Under the Old Flag.* New York, 1912. 2 volumes.

WINTHER, OSCAR OSBURN (ed.): *With Sherman to the Sea, the Civil War Letters, Diaries and Reminiscences of Theodore F. Upson.* Baton Rouge, La., 1943.

WRIGHT, MRS. D. GIRAUD (Louly Wigfall): *A Southern Girl in '61.* New York, 1904.

YOUNG, L. D.: *Reminiscences of a Soldier of the Orphan Brigade.* Louisville, Ky., n.d.

Comments on Specific Sources

Part One:
"Men are Blind and Crazy"

1. "THE UNION ESTO PERPETUA."

THE letter from Sherman to the Governor of Louisiana will be found in *The Sherman Letters*, edited by Rachel Sherman Thorndike (New York, 1894), pages 105-6. These letters from General Sherman to his brother John cover the years from 1837 to 1891, and reveal as much as any source the development of Sherman's mind in the critical years before the Atlanta campaign. His growing affection for the South, his deep distrust for politicians, his conviction that the hot-headed misunderstandings arising out of the slavery issue had brought on an unnecessary war are facets of his mind clearly illustrated by this correspondence between the two brothers. Lloyd Lewis's *Sherman, Fighting Prophet* (New York, 1932) is a sensitive, reliable, interpretive biography, and is especially effective for these early years. I remember as one does the rare moments of experience the long, gay luncheon in Chicago when Lewis, Paul M. Angle, and I first discussed the plan for *The General Who Marched to Hell*. Huyler's restaurant that day belonged to another age; with an affectionate sense of intimacy the personalities involved in the incidents recorded in this book came alive during that luncheon; and it is my hope that some small part of that spirit has been retained.

2. "IN A HELL OF A FIX."

IN 1875 the two volumes of *Memoirs of General William T. Sherman Written by Himself* appeared. "You will be surprised and maybe alarmed," the General wrote John on January 23, 1875, that his memoirs now had been prepared "at great cost of labor and care." Historian Bancroft, "though he never saw the manuscript," was among those who urged publication "in the interest of history," and to allay any fear John might have as to the prudence with which this literary effort had been approached, the General added archly: "I have carefully eliminated everything calculated to raise controversy, except where sustained by documents embraced in the work itself, and then only with minor parties." When in late 1886 R. L. Johnson, associate editor of *Century Magazine*, asked General Sherman for further reminiscences the response was an eleven-page letter supporting

Sherman's reasons as to why he must "adhere to my former conclusion not to attempt a magazine article on any war event." This letter is in the collection of Alfred Whital Stern of Chicago, and is quoted with permission.

Sherman's visit to Washington in March of 1861 and the subsequent events in St. Louis are found in the *Memoirs*, Volume I, pages 167–75; his correspondence with John concerning enlistment as a volunteer or appointment with the War Department is drawn from *The Sherman Letters*, pages 110–19.

3. "A NERVOUS-SANGUINE TEMPERAMENT."

VOLUME I of the *Memoirs*, pages 176–217, gives Sherman's own account of Bull Run and the ill-fated command in Kentucky. A supporting source, especially for Sherman's attitude, his interview with Cameron and Thomas, and his controversy with Wilkerson, is "Recollections of General Sherman," W. F. G. Shanks, *Harper's*, Volume XXX, pages 640–6. Professor Roy F. Nichols of the University of Pennsylvania, who has been working for many years on a biography of John Sherman, is authority for the belief that there is well-substantiated evidence of insanity on the maternal side of the Sherman family.

4. "SHERMAN, YOU KNOW THAT I AM IN THE WAY."

SHERMAN'S *Memoirs*, Volume I, pages 223–55, describe the battle of Shiloh and the interview with Grant. The account of the battle by Daniel McCook appeared in *Harper's*, Volume XXVIII, pages 829–33. The bullets in the tree trunk and the son who almost shot his father are cited in Carl Sandburg's *Abraham Lincoln, The War Years* (New York, 1936), Volume I, pages 476–7. The death of Albert Sidney Johnston is described, and the mistakes of the battle evaluated, in Otto Eisenchiml's *The Story of Shiloh* (Chicago, 1946), pages 18–43. Ed Russell's last twenty minutes is drawn from Lewis's *Sherman, Fighting Prophet*, pages 225–6. Supporting references on Grant at Paducah, Donelson, and Shiloh include Grant's *Personal Memoirs* (Hartford, Conn., 1881) and Adam Badeau's *Grant in Peace* (Hartford, Conn., 1887). The first meeting in St. Louis between Grant and Sherman is told by W. C. Church in *Ulysses S. Grant* (Garden City, N.Y., 1926).

5. "VOX POPULI, VOX HUMBUG!"

SHERMAN'S reconstruction of his personal experiences at Vicksburg will be found in the *Memoirs*, Volume I, pages 304–43. The General's letters to John concerning the McClernand affair and renewed difficulties with the press are in *The Sherman Letters*, pages 181–2, 189–91.

The quotation attributed to Sandburg is in *Abraham Lincoln, The War Years*, Volume 2, page 113. Charles A. Dana's *Recollections of the Civil War* (New York, 1913) was a valuable source, and for an insight into the mood and temper of wartime Washington, Margaret Leech's *Reveille in Washington* (New York, 1941) remains unsurpassed. The statements by Edward S. Gregory and Osborn Oldroyd also are quoted in Ralph G. Newman's and Otto Eisenchiml's *The American Iliad* (Indianapolis, 1947), pages 448–9.

PART TWO:
A Night in May, 1864

1. "A GHASTLY, GHOSTLY SIGHT."

THE Civil War letters, diaries, and reminiscences of Theodore F. Upson cover the years from September 28, 1858 through June 8, 1865. Capably edited by Professor Oscar Osborn Winther, these memoirs have been separately published under the title of *With Sherman to the Sea* (Baton Rouge, La., 1943). The material from which Upson's attitudes and experiences have been reconstructed in this section appears on pages 2–3, 7–8, 9, 16–7, 86, and 107. A natural supporting reference is Captain E. J. Sherlock's *Memorabilia of the Marches and Battles in Which the One Hundredth Regiment of Indiana Infantry Volunteers Took an Active Part . . .* (Kansas City, Mo., 1896).

2. THE LITTLE TRAGEDIES OF WAR.

PROFESSOR E. Merton Coulter of the University of Georgia first drew my attention to the letters and diaries of Major James Austin Connolly published as part of the *Transactions of the Illinois State Historical Society for the Year 1928* (Springfield, Ill., 1928). Connolly's letters to his wife cover the period from February 24, 1862, through March 21, 1865; his diary relates his experiences during the march to the sea, when posting a letter became impossible. Connolly's writing has an immediacy of feeling difficult to equal; his own description of his account of the campaign with Sherman reveals why these reminiscences are so rich in this respect:

> It is not a record made after the events, but a record made day by day, in tent, in bivouac, by the roadside, in the saddle, just as the opportunity offered and the spirit moved. . . . Like the old army ambrotype, it may not be a delight, but it is a true picture just as it was taken in the stirring days of *Then*.

COMMENTS ON SPECIFIC SOURCES

The material quoted in this section is taken from the *1928 Illinois Transactions*, pages 320–9. The humor of the war years is well reflected month by month in "The Editor's Drawer" in *Harper's*.

3. "TO KNOCK JOS. JOHNSTON."

SHERMAN'S *Memoirs*, Volume 2, pages 5–31, supply the General's own account of his preparations for the Atlanta Campaign. W. F. G. Shanks's "Recollections of General Thomas" appeared in Volume XXX of *Harper's*, pages 754–9.

4. "UNFIT FOR ACTIVE SERVICE."

MANY sources were called upon for the background of the plight that beset the Army of Tennessee after Bragg's failure at Missionary Ridge. Stanley F. Horn's *The Army of Tennessee* (Indianapolis, 1941) deserves commendation, and Ralph Selph Henry's *The Story of the Confederacy* (Indianapolis, 1931) has come to be regarded as a standard reference. W. M. Polk's *Life of Leonidas Polk* (New York, 1915) and Jefferson Davis's *Rise and Fall of the Confederate Government* (New York, 1881), together with Dunbar Rowland's editing of the ten volumes of *Jefferson Davis, Constitutionalist: His Letters, Papers and Speeches* (Jackson, Miss., 1923), likewise were of helpfulness. But the major source used, of course, is *Narrative of Military Operations, Directed, During the Late War Between the States, by Joseph E. Johnston* (New York, 1874). Sherman and Johnston were to be solicited for their memoirs by the same publisher, and when the *Narrative* appeared what should seem more to the point than to elicit from Sherman a blurb in behalf of his old antagonist's recollections? Sherman responded handsomely, declaring that

> General Johnston is most favorably known to the military world, and is regarded by many as the most skillful general on the Southern side. He is also ready with his pen, and whatever he records will receive the closest attention by students of the art of war on this continent, and will enter largely into the future Military History of the Civil War.

Johnston's account of his correspondence with Seddon and Davis and of the depressed condition in which he found the Army of Tennessee at Dalton appears in the *Narrative* on pages 262–303. The authority for Lee's behavior at Gettysburg is E. Porter Alexander, in *Battles and Leaders of the Civil War* (New York, 1884–8), Volume 3, pages 366–7.

5. "THE PALADIN OF THE FIGHT."

THE continuing fascination with John Bell Hood is not easily explained. Perhaps, as Mary Boykin Chestnut explained in the selection from *A Diary from Dixie* (Boston, 1949), page 297, Hood captivated everyone as "that type of beau ideal of wild Texans," even though a Texan by adoption. A sober and competent evaluation of Hood as a soldier will be found in *Hood's Tennessee Campaign*, by Thomas Robson Hay (New York, 1929), and more recent studies include *Hood: Cavalier General* by Richard O'Connor (New York, 1949) and *The Gallant Hood* by John P. Dyer (Indianapolis, 1950). However, Hood's own narrative, *Advance and Retreat* (New Orleans, La., 1880), still reveals most intimately the essential character of this tormented man. Even the imprint on the title page carries a note of sad unfulfillment:

Published for the
HOOD ORPHAN MEMORIAL FUND.
G. T. Beauregard,
New Orleans, La.

Pages 64–8 of *Advance and Retreat* provide the main source for the introduction to Hood's mental attitudes as here reconstructed.

6. "A FACE LESS PLUTONIAN."

Short Rations was published by Blackmar & Bro. (Augusta, Ga., *c.* 1864), and a copy exists in the Emory University Library. "Ye Tragic" is identified as John Alcée Augustin in Richard B. Harwell's *Confederate Music* (Chapel Hill, 1950), page 84.

The campaign diaries of Thomas J. Key, covering the period from December 7, 1863 through May 17, 1865, are included in Wirt Armistead Cate's excellently edited volume, *Two Soldiers* (Chapel Hill, 1938). The material from which this first portrait of Key has been drawn will be found on pages 3–83. An understandable supporting source is Irving A. Buck's *Cleburne and His Command* (New York, 1908).

PART THREE:
Sherman Runs the Ends

7. "FIGHT ANYTHING THAT COMES."

For statements of the various participating officers for the action from Resaca through Atlanta (May 1 through September 8, 1864) the first source is the *Official Records*. The reports all are grouped in Series I, Volume XXXVIII, Parts I, II, and III; the correspondence in Parts IV and V. L.D. Young's statements will be found in *Reminiscences of a Soldier of the Orphan Brigade* (Louisville, n.d.), and the incomparable Sam R. Watkins lives on in his own classic *"Co. Aytch," Maury Grays, First Tennessee Regiment, or a Side Show of the Big Show* (Nashville, 1882). I thought of the buoyant Sam the day I visited Resaca. The battlefield is well marked by a map along the highway, but half a mile down a little dirt road the weedy, overgrown cemetery once kept by the Daughters of the Confederacy could not disguise its years of accumulating neglect. A small girl in a gingham dress told me: "Don't nobody come now—never!" Nobody, I daresay, but the ghost of Sam Watkins! Howard's reminiscences will be found in his *Autobiography* (New York, 1908) and in *Battles and Leaders*.

2. THE "PRIDE, POMP AND CIRCUMSTANCE OF GLORIOUS WAR."

THE story of Oliver and his peculiar injury is recounted in *Campaigns of Wheeler and His Cavalry 1862–1865* . . . (Atlanta, 1899), pages 183–4. Johnston's mental attitude is reconstructed from statements in his *Narrative*, pages 317–18; that of Hood from statements in *Advance and Retreat*, pages 131–2. In the *Memoirs*, Volume II, pages 39–41, Sherman relates post-bellum conversations with both Johnston and Hood relative to the indecision at Cassville. The testimony by Captain Morris is quoted in *Advance and Retreat*, pages 110–16.

3. "GOOD LUCK, YANK!"

HOWARD'S "The Struggle for Atlanta," *Battles and Leaders*, Volume IV, pages 306–7, gives his comment on the battle of New Hope Church; Sherman's own account of the fighting is taken from the *Memoirs*, Volume II, pages 43–6; Upson's description of the fighting at Dallas is in *With Sherman to the Sea*, pages 108–14; the statements attributed to Cleburne and Hardee are in the *Official Records*, those attributed to Connolly in the *1928 Illinois Transactions*, page 336.

4. THE BLOODLESS BATTLE AT BALTIMORE.

A CONTEMPORARY account of the convention of the Radical Democracy appeared in the August, 1864 issue of *Harper's*, the cartoon in the June 18, 1864 issue of *Harper's Weekly*. The account of the Baltimore convention is drawn from the *New York Tribune* for June 9, 1864, and natural supporting sources for background material on both these meetings were Noah Brooks's *Washington in Lincoln's Time* (New York, 1896), John Hay's *Lincoln and the Civil War in the Diaries and Letters of John Hay* (New York, 1939), and John G. Nicolay's *A Short Life of Abraham Lincoln* (New York, 1902). A commendable study of the tension that arose between Jefferson

Davis and Governor Brown is Louise Biles Hill's *Joseph E. Brown and the Confederacy* (Chapel Hill, 1939); the statement of Lieutenant Markall concerning Hood is in the *Official Records*.

5. "THE BURROWING YANKEES."

SHERMAN's *Memoirs*, Volume II, pages 50–64, tell the General's own story of Kenesaw Mountain; Connolly's comments are in the *1928 Illinois Transactions*, pages 339–41; Hardee's letter to Davis on the death of Leonidas Polk has been hitherto unpublished and is used with the permission of the Duke University Library; Johnston's personal reminiscences are in the *Narrative*, pages 338–43; the reports of Smith, Lightburn, Fulton, *et al.* are in the *Official Records:* Upson tells his story of Kenesaw Mountain on pages 115–17 of *With Sherman to the Sea.*

That the memory of Kenesaw should not soon fade became the dogged resolution of the W. & A. Railroad, and in addition to issuing pamphlets on "The Mountain Campaigns in Georgia, or War Scenes of the W. & A.," the railroad regularly published *The Kennesaw Gazette*. The few scattered files of this journal that now exist are an invaluable source to the historian, and it was in the pages of the *Gazette* that the account of Kenesaw Mountain as seen through the eyes of General French appeared, extracted from a paper read before the Louisville branch of the Southern Historical Society.

6. NO. 1 VERSUS NO. 44.

JOHNSTON's version of his removal as commander of the Army of Tennessee appears in the *Narrative*, pages 348–50; Hood's in *Advance and Retreat*, pages 126–8. Upson relates the hazards of guarding the Rossville factory girls in *With Sherman to the Sea*, page 119.

PART FOUR:
"And Fairly Won"

1. ATLANTA HONORS A GENERAL.

IN A work such as this an author incurs obligations both tangible and intangible. I drove to Richmond, Virginia, with George Scheer, now of Chapel Hill, North Carolina, who had grown up in the Confederate capital. Mr. Scheer's attitude said simply that if a damn Yankee must write a book about Sherman, at least he was going to be exposed to the *facts*, and in this spirit of patriotic enterprise Miss India Thomas graciously opened the doors of the Confederate Museum on a day when it normally was closed to the public. I examined old uniforms, sheet music, weapons, and took copious notes seated at the rosewood table where Jefferson Davis so often worked. Then Mr. Scheer led me to the Virginia Historical Society and the Rev. Clayton Torrence, its executive secretary. Here, appropriately, I was seated at a desk Robert E. Lee once had used and given the Sallie Clayton papers to read. Long years had passed since Sallie set down her memories of Atlanta during the war; Sallie had died, the papers were crisp, the ink faded; but the sentences were still alive, brimming with the ardor and the sadness of vanished dreams, and with Mr. Torrence's gracious permission I have extracted from these unpublished papers this portrait of the Atlanta that Sallie remembered.

2. "THE LEE AND JACKSON SCHOOL" *and*
3. "BLEEDING, WOUNDED AND RIDERLESS."

PAGES 161–72 of *Advance and Retreat* supply the background from which Hood's personal attitudes are drawn during the siege of Atlanta, pages 65–95 of Volume II of the *Memoirs* serve the same purpose for Sherman's attitudes, and both, of course, supplement the *Official Records*. Key's recollections of the engagements appear in *Two Soldiers*, pages 89–106; the quotation of Ingersoll is cited in Buck's *Cleburne and His Command*, pages 284–5.

4. "IT WILL BE A USED UP COMMUNITY."

HENRY O. DWIGHT's excellent article, "How We Fight at Atlanta," appeared in *Harper's* (Volume XXIX), pages 663–6. The diary of ten-year-old Carrie M. Berry, covering the period from August 1, 1864 through January 26, 1866, is owned by the Atlanta Historical Society, hitherto has been unpublished, and is used with permission. Sherman's *Memoirs*, Volume II, pages 96–105, detail the events of August, 1864.

5. "IT ALL MEANS PEACE."

A REPRODUCTION of the inscription appearing on the windowpane in Meadville, Pennsylvania, will be found in Sandburg's *Abraham Lincoln, The War Years*, Volume IV, page 325. The account in *Harper's* of the failure of the mission between Mr. Greeley and the Confederate emissaries at Niagara Falls appears in its issue for September, 1864, page 542. The speeches of Messrs. Belmont, Bigler, and Seymour are extracted from *Harper's* for October, 1864, page 671; the editorial on the nomination of

McClellan appeared in the *New York Tribune* for August 29, 1864; the letter from L. Ditzler to Jefferson Davis has been used with permission of the Duke University Library; and the account of Frémont's withdrawal from the 1864 Presidential contest will be found in *Harper's* for November, 1864, page 805.

6. "THE SALUTE WILL BE FIRED AMID GREAT REJOICING!"

THE *Official Records*, Sherman's *Memoirs* (Volume II, pages 105–11), and Hood's *Advance and Retreat* (pages 193–210) give the main facts of the fall of Atlanta. Upson's description of destroying the railroad is in *With Sherman to the Sea*, page 122, his account of the death of Billy on page 125. Connolly recounts the final moment of victory at Jonesboro in *1928 Illinois Transactions*, pages 360–1.

7. "THOUGH MINE BEAT FASTER FAR THAN THINE"

MISS RUTH M. BLAIR, secretary of the Atlanta Historical Society, is authority for the information that the last Confederate soldiers were singing *Lorena* as they left Atlanta. The unpublished diary of Mary Rawson Ray is owned by the Atlanta Historical Society, and its use has been sanctioned. The troubles that beset Sherman in his correspondence with Hood, and in enforcing his evacuation order, will be found in the *Memoirs*, Volume II, pages 112–36. *The Index* for August 4, 1864, page 489, carried its editorial predicting Sherman would fail; *The Index* for September 22, 1864, page 600, faced coolly the fact that Atlanta had fallen.

PART FIVE:
"And Make Georgia Howl"

1. "AM ABLE TO WHIP ALL HELL."

CONNOLLY's letter to his wife describing the quiet Sabbath evening appears in the *1928 Illinois Transactions*, pages 362–3. At about this time, as Sherman began shifting around after Hood and mail became irregular, Connolly began keeping a diary, which begins on page 384 of the *Transactions*. Connolly's account of the night march to Marietta is from this second source and appears on page 386.

I am indebted to Richard B. Harwell of the Emory University Library for the words of *How Sherman's Veterans Took Atlanta.* Sherman's *Memoirs,* Volume II, pages 137–47, offer a picture of the action up to the battle at Allatoona. Mrs. Chestnut's observations on Davis's Macon speech are in *A Diary from Dixie,* pages 437–40.

2. "THE WILD ADVENTURE OF A CRAZY FOOL."

HOOD's report to the Adjutant General can be found in many sources, including the appendix to *Advance and Retreat.* The letter to Bragg, which Davis so sadly endorsed, is in the Duke University Library, who kindly released its publication. Corse's rousing report on the fighting at Allatoona will be found in the *Official Records.* Connolly's comments as quoted in this section appear on pages 386–9, and 366 of the *1928 Illinois Transactions;* Sherman's report on his activities through the end of the chase of Hood at Gaylesville is in the *Memoirs,* Volume II, pages 152–70. James H. Wilson recounts his conversation with Sherman in *Under the Old Flag* (New York: 1912), Volume II, page 17.

3. "BEHIND US LAY ATLANTA."

FROM the moment Sherman turns back to Atlanta, and the march to the sea becomes inevitable, four sources are used as a continuing part of the narrative to give the greatest sense of immediacy. The Carrie Berry diary is one, and the others are George Ward Nichols's *The Story of the Great March, from the Diary of a Staff Officer* (New York, 1865), pages 38–41, 58–9, 74–7, 90–1; Connolly's diary in the *1928 Illinois Transactions,* pages 394–498; and the *Memoirs,* Volume II, pages 171–267. The background from these sources has been supplemented by other authorities, as will be presently noted.

Both Lloyd Lewis and Carl Sandburg cite the figures—happily identical —for the geographical distribution of the regiments that followed Sherman to the sea. A good picture of Lincoln and the tension in Washington on election day, 1864, will be found in John Hay's *Diaries and Letters,* pages 232–6.

The Atlanta Historical Society graciously provided a photostatic copy of a press clipping of the report of General Howard to Governor Brown. Howard's report appeared originally in the *Macon Telegraph* for December 10, 1864. Howard obviously arrived after Sherman's troops had departed; he was scandalized by the pillaging that had been carried on by "bushwhackers, robbers, deserters, and citizens from the surrounding country, for a distance of fifty miles"; and he would tell Brown: "Could I have arrived ten days earlier, with a guard of one hundred men, I could have saved the state and city a million of dollars." Some Atlantans were not unmindful of the economic salvage—others of the economic gain—that might follow Sherman's appearance and departure. A typical tax exemption claim for the year 1864, filed by Thomas Magiane, totaled $35,481.70, and listed among his losses as the result of the Union invasion such items as four pounds of salt worth $3.20, twelve packs of envelopes worth $18, one bar of solder worth $5, six mules worth $5,000, and four Negroes worth $13,000. This handwritten claim is in the Emory University Library. Even Howard's report contained a dark note: "Many of the finest houses mysteriously left unburned were filled with the finest furniture, carpets, pianos, mirrors, etc., and occupied by parties, who six months ago lived in humble style." It was no secret that Atlanta quickly recovered during Reconstruction; how soon after—or with—Sherman's presence her recovery began seemed a provocative question; and it was for this reason that so earnest an effort was made to secure access to the amnesty papers filed with the War Department. The quest proved tantalizing, the result disappointing. Still, the papers surely exist and for strategic reasons remain stubbornly guarded. Some future researcher may be more fortunate than I, and should be able to add interesting background to the story of those stirring days now almost ninety years behind us.

4. "ALL SHADES AND SIZES."

IN MILLEDGEVILLE Henry Hitchcock wrote in his diary (*Marching with Sherman*, M. A. DeW. Howe, ed., New Haven, Conn., 1927):

> . . . I think Sherman lacking in discipline. Brilliant and daring, fertile, rapid and terrible, he does not seem to me to carry out things in this respect.

Obviously Connolly held the same opinion—at least in Milledgeville—but both Hitchcock and Connolly would grow indifferent to this "lack of discipline" as the march progressed. Yates Snowden of the University of South Carolina, commenting in *Marching With Sherman* (Columbia, S.C., 1929) on Hitchcock's growing callousness, could simply say that

> . . . however lonesome Major Hitchcock may have felt among the carpetbaggers in his native Alabama, he would have found congenial spirits in Boston, during the sad, mad, bad days of Reconstruction.

For the essence of Yankeeism, Dr. Snowden quotes Elinor Wylie:

> Down in the Puritan marrow of my bones,
> There's something in this richness that I hate.

5. "LET EVERY MAN FLY TO ARMS."

FOR the recollections of Sallie Clayton, as here drawn from her manuscripts, the author once more is indebted to the Rev. Clayton

Torrence. The letter from James Malone to Jefferson Davis is drawn with permission from the manuscript collections of the Duke University Library. No reminiscences of what it must have been like to watch Sherman's army approach quite surpass Dolly Sumner Lunt's *A Woman's Wartime Journal* (New York, 1918; Macon, Ga., 1926). The portions here extracted are drawn from the Macon edition, pages 25 and 29–42. The copyright is held by Mrs. L. D. Bolton.

6. "THE BEST MOVE IN MY CAREER AS A SOLDIER."

HOOD's recounting of the Tennessee campaign in *Advance and Retreat* occupies pages 292–304. The Emory University Library supplied from its manuscript collection the letter from Hood to Jefferson Davis from which I have quoted. The comment by Thomas E. Milchrist is drawn from Volume IV of the *Military Essays and Recollections* of the Illinois Commandery of the Loyal Legion.

7. "A SOLDIER'S LIFE IS ALWAYS GAY."

WILLIAM CAREY DODSON was editor of the *Campaigns of Wheeler and His Cavalry* "from material furnished by Gen. Joseph Wheeler," and the Wheeler material here used is taken from pages 284–9 of that volume. J. B. Conyngham wrote *Sherman's March through the South* (New York, 1865); the "officer of the 70th Indiana" is cited in Lloyd Lewis's *Sherman, Fighting Prophet*, page 440.

8. "THIS NIGGER WILL HAVE NO SLEEP THIS NIGHT."

DESPITE Connolly's fear that his frank criticism of the treatment of the Negroes at Ebenezar Causeway would cost him any chance of promotion, on January 18, 1865, he would write his wife that for "a second time" his commander had "recommended me for promotion to Brevet Lieut. Col."

9. "I BEG TO PRESENT AS A CHRISTMAS GIFT."

CONNOLLY, writing his wife on March 21, 1865, remarked: "We have a report, I don't know how it came, that General Baird's promotion to Brevet Major General was confirmed by the Senate and that General Davis' was not confirmed." Davis, however, received his promotion.

Mr. Harwell and the Emory University Library again incur the author's indebtedness for the words of *Sherman's on the Track*. Yates Snowden is responsible for the comment on the piratical attraction of *Marching Through Georgia*. The Southern Historical Collection of the University of North

Carolina owns the manuscript of the journal of Fanny Cohen Taylor and has kindly permitted its use in this volume. To the Georgia Historical Society in Savannah special thanks is due for making available its file of *The Loyal Georgian*.

PART SIX:
The General Reaches Hell

1. "THE STATE THEY HATE MOST" *and*

2. "I LOOK FORWARD WITH TERROR."

THE, seventeen-year-old girl quoted is Emma Florence LeConte, whose journal, covering the period from December 31, 1864, through August 6, 1865, is preserved in manuscript in the Southern Historical Collection of the University of North Carolina. The letter from Judge Magrath to President Davis belongs to the Emory University Library. Permission for the use of both documents was graciously granted. The quotations from Mrs. Chestnut's *A Diary from Dixie* occur on pages 3 and 473. The reminiscences of William Gilmore Simms on the sack and burning of Columbia originally were published on paper intended for Confederate banknotes.

3. "THE ALARM BELL IS RINGING."

YATES SNOWDEN cites the testimony of Chaplain John J. Hight. The journal of Joseph LeConte, Emma's father, has been separately published under the title of '*Ware Sherman* (Berkeley, 1937), and the description of the Kentuckian Davis appears on page 75.

4. "WITH LOATHING AND DISGUST."

SHERMAN's own recollections of his arrival and experiences in Columbia are in the *Memoirs*, Volume II, pages 278–88. On the side of the State House three stars have been embedded to show where the shots fired by Captain DeGres hit their mark.

5. "THE DRUNKEN DEVILS ROAMED ABOUT."

Who Burnt Columbia? (Charleston, S.C., 1875) contains the evidence on the sack and burning of Columbia given by William Gilmore Simms, James G. Gibbes, and Wade Hampton, and also extracts from the

Report of the Committee Appointed to Collect Testimony in Relation to the Destruction of Columbia, S.C. on the 17th of February, 1865 and from the testimony given in the case of J. J. Browne vs. the United States.

The statue of George Washington with half a cane still stands before the State House in Columbia. On the pedestal of the statue a bronze tablet reads:

DURING THE OCCUPATION OF
COLUMBIA BY SHERMAN'S ARMY
FEBRUARY 17–19, 1865,
SOLDIERS BRICKBATTED THIS
STATUE AND BROKE OFF THE
LOWER PART OF THE
WALKING CANE

6. "HELLHOUNDS . . . RUFFIANS . . . DEMONS."

THE dispute over who burned Columbia resolves itself down to two simple points. Did Sherman give specific orders for the burning of the city? No. Judging from the attitude of his troops, were they ready to wreak their vengeance on Columbia? Yes. Testifying in the case of J. J. Browne vs. the United States—the cotton cases to which Sherman refers—the General revealed the temper with which his soldiers entered South Carolina:

Q: Were you at any time before crossing the Savannah River, or before reaching Columbia, aware of a spirit of vengeance—a desire of vengeance—animating your troops to be wreaked upon South Carolina?

A [Sherman's]: I was; the feeling was universal; and pervaded all ranks.

Q: Officers and all?

A: Officers and all; we looked upon South Carolina as the cause of our woes.

Q: And thought that she thoroughly deserved severe treatment?

A: Yes, sir; that she thoroughly deserved extirpation.

James Ford Rhodes read before the Massachusetts Historical Society at its November meeting in 1901 a scholarly dissertation on "Who Burned Columbia?" The serious reader will find the opinions of Rhodes in the *American Historical Review* (Volume VII) and in his *Historical Essays* (New York, 1909).

7. "A QUEER FISH."

Mrs. Chestnut's sad reactions on the fall of Columbia will be found in *A Diary from Dixie*, pages 484–5. The *Official Records* and the reminiscences of Alexander C. McClurg in Volume I of the *Military Essays and Recollections* of the Illinois Commandery of the Loyal Legion supply the main background for the brief reconstruction of the action at Betonville, North Carolina. The remarks of John Kennaway appear in *On Sherman's Track* (London, 1867), page 13. The account of Lee at Appomattox appears in Fitz Hugh Lee's *General Lee* (New York, 1894), page 396. For the story of Sherman's part in these closing moments of the war see the *Memoirs*, Volume II, pages 348–78.

Index

i

INDEX

Lucas, Turner & Co., x, xi
Lumpkin, Martha, vii
Lumpkin's Station, Ga., 256
Lunt, Dolly Sumner, describes coming of Yankees and devastation of her plantation, 236–9; 326
Lunt, Sadai, 237, 238

McAllister, Fort, 264; taking of, 265–7; fall of announced, 268; 269
McClellan, Gen. George B. (U.S.A.), 12, 28, 55, 62, 171, 178, 189, 190, 193, 217
PRESIDENTIAL CANDIDACY, 166–8
McClernand, Gen. John A. (U.S.A.), 27–8
McClurg, Alexander C., 320–2
McCook, Gen. Daniel (U.S.A.), 22
McDonough Road, 145, 178, 223
McDowell, Gen. Irvin (U.S.A.), 28
McLaws, Gen. Lafayette (C.S.A.), 257, 259
McNair, Gen. Evander (C.S.A.), 58
McPherson, Gen. James B. (U.S.A.), 48, 50, 94, 95, 97, 98, 112, 114, 115, 116, 118, 124, 127, 223, 224
AS HEAD OF THE ARMY OF THE TENNESSEE, 45; moves on Snake Creek, 78–9; before Resaca, 79–80; position unknown to Hood, 137–8; fighting at Peachtree Creek, 139; left flank exposed, 143; West Point memories, 143–5; position on July 22nd, 146; killed, 146, 148; command given to Logan, then Howard, 149
McPhersonville, S.C., 292
Macon, Ga., 92, 128, 135, 137, 138, 159, 161, 187, 188, 197, 206, 249, 255, 257, 286, 326
Macon Railroad, 138, 158, 160, 172, 177
Macon Road, 196
Macon Telegraph, 222 n, 229 n
Magrath, Judge A. G., letter to Davis, 286
Makall, Lt. T. B. (U.S.A.), 110
Malone, James, 236
Manassas Junction, Va., ix, 11, 28, 55, 296
Manning, Gov. John, 286
Mansfield, O., ix, 39
Marching through Georgia, 278
Marietta, Ga., vii, 92, 93, 94, 111, 113, 115, 119, 124, 125, 200, 219
Marietta Road, 117, 119, 125
Marthasville (Atlanta), Ga., vii

Massachusetts, regiments: (2nd) 182; (23rd) 182
Maury, Gen. Dabney H. (C.S.A.), 172
Meadville, Pa., 128, 162
Memphis and Charleston Railroad, 20, 37
Memphis Appeal, 70
Memphis, Tenn., 37, 65, 113, 182
Meridian, Miss., 60, 61
Mexican War, x, 25
Midway, S.C., 292
Milchrist, Capt. Thomas E. (U.S.A.), 241
Mill Creek, 78, 261
Mill Creek Gap, 59; Johnston repulses Thomas, 60
Milledgeville, Ga., 92, 109, 188, 195, 197, 198, 209, 230, 240, 246, 250, 289, 304
OCCUPIED BY YANKEES, 231–3
Millen, Ga., 198, 209, 251
SHERMAN'S ARRIVAL, 256; depot burned, 257–8; prison pen, 258–9
Minnesota, 2nd regiment, 285
Missionary Ridge, Tenn., Battle of, 37, 40, 46, 57–8, 59, 65, 66, 68, 69, 70, 113, 126, 140, 141, 201
BATTLE DESCRIBED, 50–2; Sallie Clayton's visit, 134
Mississippi River, 3, 18, 26, 27, 28, 29, 30, 41, 56, 188
Missouri, regiments: (13th) 22; (23rd) 230
Mobile, Ala., 48, 60, 72, 92, 187, 199, 236
Mobile Bay, 159
Monroe Doctrine, 101, 106
Montgomery, Ala., 6, 199, 234, 235
Moon Lake, 25, 26
Moore, Gov. T. O., 3, 5
Morgan, Gen. James D. (U.S.A.), 210, 321–2
Morgan, Gen. John H. (U.S.A.), 43, 109, 132–3
Morris, Bishop, 69, 70
Morris, Capt. Walter J. (C.S.A.), 90
Morrow's Mill, Ga., 171
Moultrie, Fort, ix, x, 7, 306, 307
Mount Gilead Church, Ga., 171
Mount Gilead, O., 39
Mower, Gen. Joseph A. (U.S.A.), 211, 265
Muddy Bayou, 25
Murfreesboro, Tenn., 56, 70
Murray's Battery (U.S.A.), 148

Napoleon, Emperor, 122
Nasby, Petroleum V., 217

x

A NOTE ON THE TYPE
IN WHICH THIS BOOK IS SET

This book is set in Monotype BASKERVILLE, *a facsimile cutting from type cast from the original matrices of a face designed by John Baskerville. The original face was the forerunner of the "modern" group of type faces.*

John Baskerville (1706–75), of Birmingham, England, a writing-master, with a special renown for cutting inscriptions in stone, began experimenting about 1750 with punch-cutting and making typographical material. It was not until 1757 that he published his first work, a Virgil in royal quarto, with great-primer letters. This was followed by his famous editions of Milton, the Bible, the Book of Common Prayer, and several Latin classic authors. His types, at first criticized as unnecessarily slender, delicate, and feminine, in time were recognized as both distinct and elegant, and his types as well as his printing were greatly admired. Four years after his death Baskerville's widow sold all his punches and matrices to the Société Littéraire-typographique, which used some of the types for the sumptuous Kehl edition of Voltaire's works in seventy volumes.